Schopenhauer on the
Character of the World

Schopenhauer on the Character of the World

The Metaphysics of Will

John E. Atwell

UNIVERSITY OF CALIFORNIA PRESS
Berkeley   Los Angeles   London

193
S37 zatw

University of California Press
Berkeley and Los Angeles, California

University of California Press
London, England

Copyright © 1995 by

The Regents of the University of California

Library of Congress Cataloging-in-Publication Data
Atwell, John E.
    Schopenhauer on the character of the world: the metaphysics of will /
John E. Atwell.
        p.   cm.
    Includes bibliographical references and index.
    ISBN 0–520–08770–4 (alk. paper)
    1. Schopenhauer, Arthur, 1788–1860.   2. Will.   I. Title.
B3148.A892   1995
193—dc20   94–18811
                                                                              CIP

Printed in the United States of America

1   2   3   4   5   6   7   8   9

To Tom and Sandra,
masters in the art of xenia

Ihr folget falscher Spur,
Denkt nicht, wir scherzen!
Ist nicht der Kern der Natur
Menschen im Herzen?
GOETHE

CONTENTS

PREFACE

Arthur Schopenhauer (1788–1860) occupies a curious, even anomalous, position in the history of Western thought: Living through the Age of Napoleon on past the liberal revolution of 1848, he put forth a philosophical system totally free from the political turmoil of his time; writing during a period in which "historical philosophizing" reached its apex, he expelled history from his conception of philosophy; growing up during and maturing just after the Age of Reason (the Enlightenment), he demoted reason from its erstwhile predominance in human life and placed will in its stead (volition, passion, emotion, conation); belonging to the Classical Age of German Letters, he cast no nostalgic eye toward the Golden Age of ancient Greece (except for the thought of "the divine Plato"); implanted in the heyday of German speculative idealism, with its highly abstract, seemingly optimistic turn of mind, he advanced a "realistic," experience-based, and seemingly pessimistic portrait of the world and its inhabitants. If it can be said of anyone that he was *not* a child of his time, it can be said of Arthur Schopenhauer.

Although Schopenhauer believed himself to be the one true follower of "the marvelous Kant"—who, at the time, was reckoned not only the "all-pulverizer" (*Alleszermalmer*) of the so-called objective world, but also the implacable foe of any metaphysics designed to portray "ultimate reality"—Schopenhauer put forth a brand of metaphysics that has to be called traditional and even anti-Kantian. Schopenhauer's metaphysics commences with the supposition, reaching back to the birth of Western philosophy, that every individual thing discernible in the world of experience is at bottom one and the same; that is, that despite the apparent multiplicity and diversity of individual things they all share and express the same inner essence. In a phrase, "all is one." But what is this one—this one that gets expressed so variously and differently in the many? It is, Schopenhauer proposes, will, and the many is representation. And how is this conclusion—the solution to the fundamental problem of metaphysics—reached? By what strategy or mode of inquiry can the essence of things be uncovered? There is one and only one procedure by which the philosophical inquirer can gain access to the essence of things (to the one in the many, to the inner nature of the world), and that is by attending first of all to his or her own essence, which, Schopenhauer believes, each of us knows immediately as will; subsequently, given that the essence of anything is the essence of everything, the philosophical inquirer may, or indeed must, denominate will as the essence of the world, which is otherwise known only indirectly through the medium of perception or intuition. This complicated (and no doubt unclear) procedure may be clarified somewhat by citing what Schopenhauer calls "my revolutionary principle," namely, "From yourself you are to understand nature, not yourself from nature." Or, to state Schopenhauer's procedure in still other terms: From a comprehension of oneself (the microcosm) one is to gain a comprehension of the world (the macrocosm), and indeed on the model of self-comprehension such that the world facing oneself is properly designatable as the great human being (the macranthropos). In short, the key to understanding the world is self-understanding—a proposition that would justify calling this work "the world as macranthropos." My chief aim is to relate the story of Schopenhauer's venture into a metaphysics of the grand style, taking fully into account the ineradicable paradox of such a venture for an alleged champion of the Kantian philosophy with its unrelenting opposition to classical metaphysics. Schopenhauer believed, no doubt, that this paradox could be resolved, or at least abated, by tracing out the implications of Kant's emphasis on the will and then—through "continued reflection"—by recognizing the character of the world as parallel to the character of the human individual. Consequently, I suggest, whenever the reader finds Schopenhauer's conception of the world puzzling or even unintelligible, he or she is most likely to achieve clarity by considering Schopenhauer's conception of the human self or human character—for which reason I recommend to the reader of this book my companion work, *Schopenhauer: The Human Character* (Philadelphia: Temple University Press, 1990).

In the course of preparing this work I have benefited from a study of three important commentaries and expositions: *Willing and Unwilling: A Study in the Philosophy of Arthur Schopenhauer*, by Julian Young; *Self and World in Schopenhauer's Philosophy*, by Christopher Janaway; and *Der eine Gedanke: Hinführung zur Philosophie Arthur Schopenhauers*, by Rudolf Malter.

(Full references to these works, as well as to the somewhat older works by Arthur Hübscher, Frederick Copleston, Patrick Gardiner, D. W. Hamlyn, and Bryan Magee, are given as needed in the appropriate places.) I have also benefited greatly from numerous articles on Schopenhauer by David E. Cartwright, whose essays—if I assiduously cited them—would be referred to on dozens of pages. A pleasant and very helpful correspondence with Moira Nicholls must also be mentioned, along with published and unpublished papers by several of my students, above all, Terri Graves Taylor, Mark Cyzyk, Honi Haber, James Snow, Harold Weiss, Michael Sullens, and Mark Conard. And, for a third time, I must extend my gratitude to Nadia Kravchenko for typing and retyping, with cordiality and alacrity, a long manuscript. Ed Dimendberg of the University of California Press provided encouragement and helpful suggestions during the final stages of preparing this work for publication, so my thanks go also to him, as well as to two readers for that Press, David E. Cartwright and Dale Jacquette. In addition, thanks go to Wendy Belcher, copy editor, who saved me from several errors, and to Caroline Meline, who aided me at the end of the production.

INTRODUCTION

On 28 March 1818 Dr. Arthur Schopenhauer wrote to the publisher F. A. Brockhaus of Leipzig about a manuscript that he had been working on for four years. "My work," he said, "is a new philosophical system, but new in the complete sense of the word—not a new presentation of what is already on hand, but a series of thoughts hanging together in the highest degree that up to now has never come into any human head." He went on to express his "firm conviction" that the book would later "become the source and occasion of a hundred other books."[1] This conviction, seemingly unwarranted for decades, has probably been borne out: *The World as Will and Representation* (*Die Welt als Wille und Vorstellung*) has spawned scores of books, dozens of dissertations, and countless shorter discussions.[2]

In almost every case, however, critics of Schopenhauer's "main work" argue that the "series of thoughts" contained therein do not "hang together" at all. They contend, in other words, that Schopenhauer's "philosophical system" cannot be regarded as a genuine system, for it is riddled with inconsistencies, contradictions, and irresolvable paradoxes. This judgment has not persuaded all critics to dismiss Schopenhauer's philosophy entirely—for many individual aspects have been lauded and appreciated—but it has convinced most of them that as a whole his philosophy cannot withstand critical scrutiny. Many critics claim that there is not even a modicum of unity in Schopenhauer's main work, the judgment being that Schopenhauer (as he admits) takes up one idea, then another, and subsequently others simply as they occur to him, without any consideration for how these ideas might fit together. Perhaps this procedure attests to Schopenhauer's honesty, but, the critics continue, it hardly conduces to a consistent, coherent philosophy.

The chief aim of this book is not to enumerate, examine, and possibly resolve, one by one, the alleged inconsistencies in Schopenhauer's main work (although certain central ones will be dealt with in some detail); it is rather to discover "the single thought" that unifies the several aspects of *The World as Will and Representation* and then to indicate how that "thought" applies to the various topics and issues that Schopenhauer addresses. I refer to "the single thought" because in the preface to the first edition of *The World as Will and Representation* (appearing in late 1818, but dated 1819) Schopenhauer informs the reader that the whole of his book "imparts" no "system of thoughts" but only "a single thought."[3] A system of thoughts (*System von Gedanken*), he suggests, resembles a huge building whose parts are connected such that one part supports a higher part but is not supported by it, and the foundation stone bears all higher parts up to the pinnacle that upholds no part at all. As a consequence, the soundness of the whole architectonically connected structure depends on the soundness of every supporting part and ultimately on the soundness of the foundation stone. And in like fashion such a philosophical system will be sound only if every supporting thought truly bears the one above it and the foundational thought bears them all. If any part proves unsound, everything above it will crumble; and if the foundational thought is faulty, the entire edifice will collapse. Hence, the mere fact that a system of thoughts consists of many "thought-parts," arranged architectonically, threatens the unity or coherence of the system.

> On the other hand, a single thought [*ein einziger Gedanke*], however comprehensive, must preserve the most perfect unity. If, all the same, it can be split up into parts for the purpose of being communicated, then the connection of these parts must once more be organic, i.e., of such a kind that every part supports the whole just as much as it is supported by the whole; a connection in which no part is first and no part last, in which the whole gains in clearness from every part, and even the smallest part cannot be fully understood until the whole has been first understood.[4]

A single thought resembles, then, not a huge building but a living organism, every part of which supports and is supported by every other part, and no specific part can be called foundational. So, in the case of such a philosophical system, the soundness of the whole does not depend on the soundness of a foundational part: Either all parts of it are sound or none is.

Schopenhauer frequently likens his philosophy to an organic body, indeed, to a human body whose overall soundness (health and vitality) rests with the satisfactory interrelationships of its several parts. As early as 1813 he compared his quickening philosophical work to the development of a child in the mother's womb.[5] Probably because he was so certain of the appropriateness of this comparison, he was confident that "his child" would remain free from contradiction and, like any healthy organism, long endure. He described himself thus: "I become aware of *one* member, *one* blood vessel, *one* part after another, i.e., I write them down unconcerned how each will fit the whole; for I know that it is all sprung from one basis. Thus originates an organic whole and only such a thing can live."[6] If in fact *The World as Will and Representation* does contain only "a single thought," then it cannot contradict itself: A self-contradiction requires at least a double thought. Whether there is a single thought uniting the contents of Schopenhauer's main work, and if so what that thought is, will be explicitly discussed in chapter 1, and alluded to throughout the entire book.

Given Schopenhauer's conception of his philosophical system as an organic whole or simply a single thought, it is not surprising that the first demand made on the reader of *The World as Will and Representation* is to read the book twice, and, he adds, "to do so the first time with much patience."[7] Later parts will clarify earlier parts, he notes, and earlier parts will clarify later parts; hence full understanding of the book requires (at least) two readings. Schopenhauer admits, however, that the beginning does not presuppose the ending as much as the ending presupposes the beginning, so where the system commences is not entirely arbitrary; and indeed, he adds, he has made an effort to place early on what can be fairly easily grasped upon initial reading. Chapter 2 of this book, called "From Perceptual Knowledge to Metaphysical Inquiry," examines the first aspect of Schopenhauer's system.

Observed further is the fact that Schopenhauer's book will occasionally be repetitious: "The structure of the whole, which is organic and not like a chain, in itself makes it necessary sometimes to touch twice on the same points."[8] The book's organic structure and its interconnected parts make unnecessary and indeed inappropriate a division of the contents into chapters and sections, for that would suggest (what is not the case) that one unit leads logically into the next, which leads logically into a subsequent unit, and so on. (And we may note that the contents were not divided in this manner in the first edition.)[9] The book does consist, however, of "four principal divisions, four aspects [*Gesichtspunkten*], as it were, of the one thought."[10] When Schopenhauer comes to these divisions, he calls them Books, hence *The World as Will and Representation* consists of four Books. In just a moment I shall provide a sketch, or general picture, of these four Books, and then discuss the important facets thereof in separate chapters later on. By means of the initial sketch, I am trying to accommodate, as best as I can, Schopenhauer's admonition to the reader to read his work twice.

The second demand that Schopenhauer makes on the reader is that "the introduction be read before the book itself,"[11] by which he means his doctoral dissertation of 1813: *Ueber die vierfache Wurzel des Satzes vom zureichenden Grunde—Eine philosophische Abhandlung (On the Fourfold Root of the*

Principle of Sufficient Reason: A Philosophical Essay).[12] "Without an acquaintance with this introduction and propaedeutic," Schopenhauer writes, "it is quite impossible to understand the present work properly, and the subject-matter of that essay is always presupposed here as if it were included in the book."[13] The dissertation, which will be outlined briefly in this introduction, contains two highly significant theses: The subject of knowing is (somehow) identical with the subject of willing; and the principle of sufficient reason, expressed in four forms and rooted in four kinds of representations, is the law of objects that the subject of knowing knows.[14]

The third, and final, demand that Schopenhauer makes on the reader is "an acquaintance with the most important phenomenon which has appeared in philosophy for two thousand years," namely, "the principal works of Kant." He remarks further that "the effect those works produce in the mind to which they really speak is very like that of an operation for cataract on a blind man."[15] Schopenhauer devotes a long appendix to a "critique of the Kantian philosophy," and he says that "it would be advisable to read the appendix first." What then does Schopenhauer find so significant in Kant's works? He certainly does not agree with everything that Kant espoused, as he makes abundantly clear, but he never fails to acknowledge his considerable debt to Kant; indeed, he writes, "my work presupposes an acquaintance with the Kantian philosophy," and in many letters he claims to be a Kantian.[16] Just how valid this self-assessment is will be discussed several times in this book, with special attention focused on, how Schopenhauer can purport to advance a metaphysics of will when, apparently, Kant had closed the door on such a project?

"Kant's greatest merit," Schopenhauer asserts in the appendix, "is the distinction of the phenomenon [*Erscheinung*, appearance] from the thing in itself."[17] And although Kant did not come to recognize that "the phenomenon is the world as representation and the thing in itself is the will,"[18] he did show that "the phenomenal world [*die erscheinende Welt*] is conditioned by subject and object," so that "the most universal forms" of the phenomenal world can be recognized by examining the subject as well as the object. Kant concludes, however, that recognizing the forms connecting subject and object precludes our recognition of the "inner nature" of either the subject or the object, hence he makes "the essence of the world, the thing in itself," unknowable. Kant did not come to see that the thing in itself, either on the side of the object or on the side of the subject, is will, but he made a great step in this direction by calling attention to "the undeniable ethical significance of human conduct," which he showed to be completely different from and not dependent on "the laws of the phenomenon [*Erscheinung*]."[19] So, although Kant left the essence of the world, or the thing in itself, shrouded in darkness, he actually pointed to its very nature by locating the ethical significance of human conduct not in the external world of normal phenomena but in the internal world of the willing human agent. It is this clue that Schopenhauer exploits in arriving at the conclusion that the essence of the world, or the thing in itself, is will. Kant's emphasis on the ethical significance of human conduct constitutes, Schopenhauer holds, "the second great point of view for assessing his merit."[20]

The third point is that Kant completely overthrew scholastic philosophy, which extends, according to Schopenhauer, from Augustine up to Kant's time, and not merely up to, say, 1500.[21] Specifically, Kant demonstrated the impossibility of proving the existence of God (speculative theology) or the immortality of the soul (rational psychology).[22] From now on, then, philosophy must abandon all alleged knowledge of God and of an immortal soul; indeed, philosophy must become wholly secular, free from every trace of theology or religion. By much the same token, philosophy must reject realism (that is, the theory that objects of normal perception have an existence apart from being perceived) and accept idealism (that is, the theory that objects are "conditioned by" the knowing subject). Schopenhauer suggests that Kant's destruction of scholastic philosophy amounts to a destruction of realism, and, indirectly, to an advocacy of idealism.[23]

With the rejection of realism, Kant also redefined the province of ethics. No more is ethics tied to the phenomenon, where it consisted of a doctrine of happiness (eudaimonism, a set of rules for achieving personal happiness), or of obedience to the will of God, or of conformity to the concept of human perfection—all of which ideas presuppose that ethical conduct remains situated in the alleged real world of phenomena, hence in the world of space, time, and causality. What Kant showed is that "the undeniable, great ethical significance of actions" belongs to the nonphenomenal world, that is, to the thing in itself or the innermost nature of the world.[24] In short, the moral worth of human actions—their genuine ethical significance—is "not of this world"; it does not pertain to the world of nature, that is, the world investigated by the natural sciences. This, too, Kant has demonstrated.

Of the demands made on the reader—and formidable ones they are!—the third, namely, to study Kant's principal works, has been touched on, but hardly more than touched on. Perhaps, however, enough has been said to proceed. The second demand, to examine Schopenhauer's dissertation of 1813, will now be treated briefly, with emphasis placed on those points that figure importantly in the main work. And then, to accommodate the demand that the reader read *The World as Will and Representation* twice, I shall provide an overall sketch of the book. This introduction will then prepare us for a close examination of the salient features of Schopenhauer's main work.

The Fourfold Root is a relatively short monograph on philosophical (or any cognitive) inquiry.[25] It is meant to be a propaedeutic, or set of procedural instructions, whose several tenets must be observed if confusion and obscurity are to be avoided and lucidity and precision are to be attained. As a general formulation, the principle of sufficient reason may be stated thus: Nothing is without a reason for being rather than not being. This principle, Schopenhauer holds, is the basis of all science (*Wissenschaft*); it is the ultimate principle of explanation and demonstration or proof; it is further that principle that allows us to ask of anything "why (is it so and not otherwise)?"

Everyone, Schopenhauer notes, appeals to the principle of sufficient reason in the course of presenting a line of argument, but almost no one makes clear what sort of sufficient reason or ground (*Grund*) is actually meant at specific times. Especially unfortunate, Schopenhauer believes, is the widespread tendency of philosophers to conflate the notion of ground as *cause* (*Ursache*) and the notion of ground as *reason* (*Grund*). Quite clearly, he believes, a cause is very different from a reason, and indeed the two notions operate in very different areas of philosophical and cognitive inquiry. For example, when we ask for the ground of an object's suddenly igniting, we have in mind ground as cause; and when we ask for the ground of a conclusion in a syllogism, we have in mind ground as reason. Schopenhauer proposes to establish that the general notion of sufficient reason or ground must be broken down into four subnotions, or four roots; further, he wants to show that the four roots correspond to four distinct faculties of the human mind and *a fortiori* they apply to four distinct classes of possible objects of knowledge.

The first class consists of intuitive representations, that is, of natural objects in time and space, whose changes (such as a match's igniting) are governed by the law of causality. This law is also called the principle of sufficient reason of *becoming*, no doubt because it operates in the realm of change. Whenever a change in a natural (spatio-temporal) object occurs, that faculty of our mind known as the understanding assigns, albeit preconsciously, to this change a cause—whether known or not—whereby the change itself is deemed an effect. And the necessity of the effect from the cause—which necessity derives from the principle of sufficient reason in general—goes by the name of physical necessity. In short, every change in the natural or physical world has a cause, which cause is in turn the effect of a preceding cause, and so on and so on, implying that there can be for the human mind at least no such thing as a "first cause." It follows, for Schopenhauer, that God cannot be conceived as the first cause of all subsequent natural causes, and that it makes no sense to speak of "the cause" of the entire series of natural causes; in his judgment, the series of natural causes goes on endlessly, and this series cannot have a cause because it is not itself a change or effect at all. On these grounds Schopenhauer rejects the so-called cosmological (or first cause) "proof" of the existence of God.

The second class of possible objects of knowledge consists of abstract representations or concepts (*Begriffe*), which, when joined to each other in various ways, make up judgments. Pursuant to the principle of sufficient reason of *knowing*, which operates in this area, a judgment qualifies as genuine knowledge only if it is justified by (or grounded on) something other than itself, such as another judgment, an empirical experience, a condition for any experience (e.g., an arithmetical or geometrical truth, or the law of causality), or a law of logic. The faculty of mind that forms concepts and draws inferences from a ground to a consequent is reason—which only human beings possess—and the sort of necessity holding between the ground and consequent is "logical." Nothing, at least for our purposes, turns on all of this except that a ground as reason for a conclusion (say, in a syllogism) is not to be identified with a ground as cause of an effect. It might be added, however, that in this section of the dissertation Schopenhauer says a good deal about language, the use of concepts in science, rational action, and abstract thinking.

The third class of possible objects has only two members, the pure or a priori intuitions of space and time. Or they might be called mathematical objects whose properties of space and time mutually entail each other. For, according to Schopenhauer, space provides the basis of geometry and time serves as the basis of arithmetic. Every division in space determines and is determined by every other one, and every instant of time is conditioned by the preceding one and conditions the succeeding one. The principle of sufficient reason operative in this class is called the principle of *being*, presumably because geometrical and arithmetical relations are not subject to becoming or change: The sides of a triangle determine and are determined by the angles, and the number ten determines and is determined by the sum of, say, six and four. The sort of necessity pertinent here is called mathematical, and the faculty of mind operative here is called pure sensibility.

The fourth class of objects has only one member, the will. In the dissertation Schopenhauer claims that it is subject to a form of the principle of sufficient reason, namely, to the law of motivation, though in the main work five years later this claim will be denied. Here, however, the principle of sufficient reason is said to be that of *willing or acting*, and the law it yields is the law of motivation. This means that for any action one performs there has to have been a sufficient reason in the form of a motive, such that nothing but that action could have been performed at the time. Hence we may speak of moral necessity, where "moral" refers directly to the notion of will or conduct and not specifically to ethics or virtue. This form of the general principle of sufficient reason is supposed to derive from self-consciousness.

A sketch:

Principle of Sufficient Reason

Roots:	Becoming	Knowing	Being	Willing or acting
Ground:	Cause	Reason	Mutual implication	Motive
Faculty:	Understanding	Reason	Pure Sensibility	Self-consciousness
Objects:	Natural; intuitive representations	Concepts; abstract representations	A priori intuitions; time and space	Will

In § 16, called "The Root of the Principle of Sufficient Reason," Schopenhauer provides this full statement:

> *Our consciousness, so far as it appears in sensibility, understanding, and reason, is divisible into subject and object, and contains, until then, nothing else. To be object for the subject and to be our representation are the same. All our representations are objects of the subject, and all objects of the subject are our representations. But nothing obtaining for itself and independent, also nothing single and detached, can become object for us; rather, all our representations stand [to each other] in a lawful connection that according to form are determinable a priori.* This connection is that kind of relation that the principle of sufficient reason expresses, taken in general. That law ruling over all our representations is the root of the principle of sufficient reason. It is fact and the principle of sufficient reason is its expression.

Schopenhauer has therefore an explanation for the old Latin saying, *natura non facit saltum* (nature makes no leap): The human mind or subject of consciousness allows no leap in nature, which is to say that its very constitution precludes any natural object's arising spontaneously, unconditionally, detachedly, independently, or nonrelationally. Quite to the contrary: Every object of the knowing subject, hence every natural object or intuitive representation, is encountered only in connection with other objects (whether known or not), and none can "leap" into the world of objects all by itself. The truth expressed in the principle of sufficient reason cannot be proved, that is, derived from any higher or preceding principle, because it is the ultimate principle of all proof or derivation. Since that principle has its source in the knowing subject, since it is, as it were, imposed by the knowing subject on every possible object of knowledge, it is not learned by observing what occurs in the world of objects; and this is to say that the principle of sufficient reason is knowable a priori. Without it there would be no knowledge or observation of the world of objects at all; it is, in other words, a condition of all such knowledge, hence not something gained by such knowledge. The most significant entailment of this argument is that the principle of causality, which governs changes in natural objects, is not empirical and its linguistic formulation is not a synthetic proposition a posteriori, but rather a priori and its formulation is a synthetic proposition a priori. (Later, Schopenhauer will claim that the statement "subject and object mutually entail each other"—the principle of knowing—is an analytic proposition knowable a priori, and the principle of sufficient reason per se is a synthetic proposition knowable a priori.)

To acknowledge both the unity of the principle of sufficient reason and the variety of its applications (its four roots) is to conform to the procedural laws of all cognitive inquiry recommended by "the divine Plato" and "the marvelous Kant," namely, the law of homogeneity and the law of specification. The law of homogeneity instructs us to unite kinds of things into species, then into wider genera, and finally into the highest unity that embraces everything; and the law of specification instructs us to distinguish from each other the species comprehended under a wider genus, and then to distinguish from each other the kinds of things falling within a species. In short, it may be said, the first law tells us to seek the one in the many, and the second tells us to seek each of the many and keep them separate from each other; or, as Schopenhauer puts it, "the number of entities must not be increased unnecessarily" and "the varieties of entities must not be diminished unnecessarily." With the principle of sufficient reason, Schopenhauer has observed the law of homogeneity, for it is the one principle of all knowledge; and with the four varieties or "roots" of this principle, he has observed the law of specification, for they are the four specific versions of the one principle.

What Schopenhauer's dissertation aims to accomplish is truly remarkable: To condense into one ultimate principle, while never forgetting its four "roots," the vast, complicated, many-sided cognitive apparatus that Kant had attributed to the human faculty of knowledge. With Kant, there are two forms of sensibility (time and space), twelve categories of the understanding (substance, causality, etc.), the so-called transcendental unity of apperception (the "I think" that must accompany all of one's experiences), and more; but for Schopenhauer, all of the human being's cognitive functions can be comprehended in one fundamental principle, the principle of sufficient reason, albeit with its four "roots" corresponding to the four possible classes of objects of knowledge. All of our knowledge presupposes the correlativity of subject and object, and all types of knowledge—empirical, logical, mathematical, and motivational—have one and only one basis, consequent of a ground. Everything knowable is conditioned by or dependent on something else, hence occasionally the principle of sufficient reason is called the "principle of dependence."

In the dissertation of 1813 Schopenhauer says practically nothing about two issues that figure prominently in his subsequent thought: the Platonic Ideas and the Kantian thing in itself. He does not even mention the Ideas, and he speaks only once of the thing in itself, and then in a derogatory manner (§ 59). Castigating his predecessors with conflating cause and reason, Schopenhauer remarks that "Kant himself speaks of the infamous thing in itself as the *Grund* of appearance," then of the *Grund* of the possibility of all appearance, then of the intelligible *Grund* of appearances, of the intelligible cause, and so on. Not even the marvelous Kant is free from the error that Schopenhauer exposes. In later discussions Schopenhauer will insist that the thing in itself and appearance or representation are not connected by any version of the principle of sufficient reason, for that principle has application only within the world of appearance or representation, hence not between that world and something outside or other than it.

All the same, in § 46 of the dissertation Schopenhauer is quite willing to acknowledge the empirical and the intelligible character, where the former belongs to appearance or representation and the latter belongs to the thing in itself. This paragraph, which does not appear in the revised version of 1847, has this title: "Motive, Decision, Empirical and Intelligible Character." Schopenhauer's concern in this paragraph is to explain how a wish differs from a decision, or specifically, how competing wishes eventuate in one decision: One wishes to do A and one wishes to do B (both of which pertain, often strongly, to one's will), but one cannot do both A and B; then one decides to do one rather than the other. What accounts for that? One can be motivated or at least volitionally "inclined" to do something that one does not actually decide to do. So does this mean that the decision (and the deed) is completely unconditioned, subject to no rule at all, or does it mean that the decision presupposes a condition of the subject of willing which cannot be perceived? The latter alternative is the correct one. It points to an enduring condition of the subject of willing, from which its decisions follow with necessity, and according to which one and the same person under exactly the same conditions acts always in the same way. And the person has the liveliest consciousness that he could act in a completely different way if only he had wanted to, that is, that his will is not determined by anything foreign; and here there is no talk of capacity but only of a willing that by its very nature is free in the highest degree, and indeed is itself the innermost essence of the person independent of everything else. The inner nature of the person, which accounts for actual decisions in contrast to mere wishes, is a permanent condition outside of time, and as such there is for it no expression. Figuratively, it might be called a universal act of will outside of time, of which all acts occurring in time are its manifestation or appearance. "Kant," Schopenhauer adds, "called this the intelligible character (perhaps more correctly the unintelligible)."

Another crucial topic for what Schopenhauer called his "main work," *The World as Will and Representation,* is the relation between the subject of knowing and the subject of willing. In § 47 of the dissertation Schopenhauer suggests that "the will has causality not only on the immediate object [i.e., the body] and thus on the external world, but also on the knowing subject; it necessitates knowing to repeat representations that at one time were present to knowing, mainly by directing attention to this or that and to call back at pleasure a series of thoughts." Later, in the "main work," Schopenhauer will deny that the will causally acts on the body, and in the later edition of *The Fourfold Root* he will claim that the will exercises influence, not causality, through the "identity" of the two. In § 43 this "identity" is said to be "absolutely inconceivable," but nevertheless "*immediately given*"; as a consequence it may be called "the miracle *par excellence* [*das Wunder kat' exochen*]." This curious discussion has to be noted because in *The World as Will and Representation* Schopenhauer remarks that that entire work "to a certain extent" is an explanation of the "coincidence" of the subject of knowing and the subject of willing.[26]

What follows now is an overview or general picture of Schopenhauer's "main work," a work that he divides into four Books, each of which allegedly portrays a distinctive aspect of "the single thought."[27] Book 1 considers the world as intuitive or perceptual representation (*anschauliche Vorstellung*), which, because its topic is "the representation subject to the principle of sufficient reason," repeats material dealt with in the earlier dissertation. From this first aspect the world is simply a world of knowledge or cognition, hence it is a one-sided world in that it disregards any explicit reference to the world as will. The world as representation has two components: the knowing subject and the known object. Being mutually implicatory, there is no object without a subject and no subject without an object, that is, no representation without a representer and no representer without a representation. Schopenhauer therefore denies that objects exist apart from being known (by the subject) and he denies that the subject exists apart from knowing (objects). He contends that normal perceptual objects have only a relative or conditioned existence, for they are relative to or conditioned by the knowing subject: They have, as objects, no existence absolutely or unconditionally, that is, in themselves. Normal perceptual objects are objects only relative to the knowing subject, and they are qualified in three ways—temporally, spatially, and causally—in virtue of the knowing subject's modes of knowing objects. This final provision entails that normal perceptual objects are, as it were, tied to each other in a gigantic network of time, space, and causality, such that no object can be known (intuited, perceived) or even conceived independently of its relations to other objects.

Although very little is said about will in Book 1, it becomes evident later on that the knowing subject of normal perceptual objects (or "intuitive representations") is governed by will: In fact it is because of this that these objects are necessarily related to each other temporally, spatially, and causally. In Book 1 Schopenhauer also discusses abstract representations or concepts (*Begriffe*), which are said to be "representations of (intuitive) representations" built up by the human faculty of reason (*Vernunft*). Only human beings possess the faculty of reason, while they share with animals the faculty of understanding (*Verstand*) whereby normal perception or intuition (*Anschauung*) comes about on the basis of sensation (*Empfindung*). Reason has several functions: It accounts for the creation of "general objects" or concepts (such as traveling, the human race, animate being, etc.); it is that by means of which inferring or drawing conclusions in thought occurs, hence it makes possible doubt and error; it allows human beings to survey the past and anticipate the future, thereby occasioning the unpleasant experiences of repentance or regret (*Reue*) and concern (*Sorge*) along with knowledge of an oncoming death; and it permits human beings to formulate in language their conceptual thoughts. So, in a way, reason is both a blessing and a curse. What reason cannot do, Schopenhauer suggests here, is create concepts that have no basis in percepts, that is, concepts that are not mere generalizations of intuitive representations. "The first cause," for example, is a pseudo concept, for it has no basis in intuition or perception.

Having learned that perceptual objects are nothing but intuitive representations according to their general form—in virtue of which they have temporal, spatial, and causal properties—we now, in Book 2, want to inquire into their content or meaning. We ask whether the perceptual world is mere representation of the knowing subject, which accounts for its being object with its three formal dimensions (time, space, causality), or whether it is "something more," something that would provide it with content, meaning, or, as it were, "substance." In short, do intuitive representations have an essence, or foundation, or reality, in addition to being perceived and thus conditioned by the knowing subject? Many past philosophers (so-called realists) have held that some object existing independently of the intuitive representation is the foundation or basis of the intuitive representation. But, says Schopenhauer, we have no way of distinguishing object from representation; indeed, as shown in Book 1, object and representation are one and the same. So this sort of philosophy cannot help us locate what we are inquiring into; nor can mathematics or the physical sciences.

Fortunately, we who are asking about the content of intuitive representations are not simply knowing subjects (if we were, we could never find an answer); we are also bodies, hence not just knowers of the world of representation but also members of that world. It is the body then that serves as the entrance point into the inner nature of the world as representation. Each of us is aware of his or her body in a twofold manner: as an object like all other objects, hence as a representation of the knowing subject, and as will, hence as a willing or conative subject that undergoes pleasant or unpleasant feelings and that "acts." From the recognition that in us will is the essence or underlying nature of the body, we may conclude that will is the real nature of the perceptual "bodies" that otherwise are mere representations of the knowing subject. Hence these representations are not mere representations; their "formal" dimensions, namely, time, space, and causality, all of which derive from the knowing subject, do not exhaust them; they have (or "point to") a genuine reality—and it is that which we find in ourselves as will. Not only is the world representation; it is also will.

In effect, then, about halfway through Book 2 Schopenhauer has completed his presentation of "the world as will and representation." And one might expect that there would be nothing further to say. What is called the essence of the world and nature has been discovered (alternatively, what Kant called the thing in itself has been identified), and it is will; all representations are therefore merely manifestations of will; and the story is completed. But Schopenhauer continues. What prompts him to continue is the recognition that will is manifested not so clearly in individual representations (such as this chair, that dog, etc.) as in different kinds of things, which he calls "grades" (or levels) of the will's objectification (or "objectity" or visibility). The grades range from the lowest and most pervasive things of nature (such as gravity) to the highest and most rare (such as the human genius), with countless examples between (from crystallization to the sunflower to the dog to the common human being). These grades, and not their innumerable instances, are the proper or genuine manifestations of will: It is in them that, above all, will objectifies and reveals itself. (These grades, Schopenhauer contends, are what Plato called Ideas.) A close examination of nature shows us that the various grades, *through their individual instances*, are in constant conflict. This is particularly obvious on the animal level, at which a beast of prey (such as the lion) pursues and feeds on another animal (such as the gazelle). It is pretty obvious on the human level too; typically, individuals struggle against one another for whatever they happen to want. For the most part human life is, as Thomas Hobbes said, a war of all against all. Indeed, life in general is a gigantic arena in which one grade of the will preys on another grade, and in which individuals by the millions perish: Life is suffering, and the source of this suffering is the will's conflict with itself.

In Book 3 Schopenhauer turns to that release from enslavement to will that comes to some people, now and again, in aesthetic contemplation (after which he discusses in great detail various types of art). It is here that the second aspect of representation—what I shall call the "pure" aspect—comes to the fore. That which is represented here is a grade of the will's objectification, that is, a Platonic Idea. It is an object for a knowing subject, as every representation is, but it is a special object—an object that is not subject to the specific forms of the principle of sufficient reason, and therefore not subject to temporal, spatial, and causal dimensions. In other words, the Idea retains only the universal form of representation, namely, that of being a certain kind of object, but it gets free from the three aforementioned specific forms of representation, namely, time, space, and causality.

If the knowing subject were always and necessarily subordinate to the willing subject (if all knowing were enslaved to willing), then the knowing subject would always and necessarily be "individual" and its objects would always and necessarily be "individual" too. For a knowing subject to be individual is for it to be governed by will, the consequence of which makes the subject's objects individual, that is, caught up in the network of time, space, and causality, and regardable solely as potential motives for action. In such a case the knowing subject could not discern those grades of the will's objectification called Platonic Ideas. But the power of will over knowing is not absolute, and this fact makes possible knowledge of the Ideas. It is the subject's mode of knowing that determines the kind of object known; hence if that mode of knowing is individual (i.e., dominated by willful interest) then the known object is individual (i.e., viewed as to its utility); hence, further, the Ideas can become objects of knowledge only if individuality in the knowing subject is suppressed. The knowing subject must become "pure," free from will and therefore objective or disinterested, which means that it must not be concerned with any motivation the object might offer; then, and only then, the object becomes "pure" too, free from the subordinate forms of the principle of sufficient reason, and therefore Idea. Such knowledge occurs when one, so to speak, "loses" oneself in a natural object or work of art, whereby the Idea of the natural object or the Idea expressed in the work of art "fills one's consciousness." Knowing exists, but willing disappears; pure delight obtains, and suffering vanishes. But not very often, not for very long, and not for very many.

The chief concern of Book 4 is ethics, understood not as a prescriptive discipline that lays down moral rules but as a descriptive study that interprets and explains human conduct. The secondary, and perhaps ultimately more important, concern is an analysis of the denial of the will to live exemplified most poignantly in the mystic, whereby the entire world, both as representation and as will, sinks into "relative" nothingness and salvation ensues.

The life of an individual human being caught up in affirmation of will consists of a perpetual struggle to live and to propagate, but the individual encounters frustrations at every turn and inevitable death at the end. Momentary experiences of happiness give way to new pursuits or boredom: Lasting contentment is not the human being's lot. The world of the individual human being, whose motivations are almost exclusively egoistic, is a "vale of tears" (*Jammerthal*), not unlike a penal colony to which the individual is condemned upon birth and from which he or she is released only upon death. This conception of human life reflects the Idea of humanity insofar as affirmation of will (egoism, hedonism, sexuality) holds the upper hand. It is this conception of human life that lies at the basis of Schopenhauer's pessimism.

Now and again, however, nature produces a moral saint, whose behavior can be understood as a sort of identification with other suffering creatures: Such an individual, as rare in ethics as is the genius in art, pierces through the forms of time and space, and thereby overcomes the separation and antagonism that typically characterizes human relationships. To the moral saint one must attribute the knowledge that all "individual wills" are really one, that others' suffering is the saint's own suffering, that individuation is at bottom illusion. The moral saint's "knowledge" is not theoretical; it does not consist of conceptual and theoretical assent to the deep philosophical truth contained in the Sanskrit formula, *Tat tvam asi* (this art thou), that is, the inner nature of others is identical with your inner nature; indeed, it has nothing to do with intellect or philosophical insight. The moral saint's "knowledge" is practical; it is exhibited in behavior that seeks to relieve others' suffering and that, if necessary, forfeits personal life for the benefit of others. Although it is not explicable by means of our typical forms of explication—those forms dictating that human behavior is subject to egoistic motivation—the conduct of the compassionate moral saint can be seen (though hardly fully understood) as release from the world of separate, differentiated existence and as entry into the world of will wherein only the one will reigns supreme.

Beyond even the moral saint is the ascetic, in whom—to take the extreme case—the will has been denied altogether. Consequently, this person, also rare, becomes indifferent to all suffering, which is to say that he or she makes no effort to avoid personal suffering or to relieve the suffering of others. In some sense the extreme ascetic "identifies" with all of reality, such that in him or her the divisions and distinctions obtaining in the world disappear, along with the world itself. At this point, Schopenhauer fully realizes, all human cognition, and thus all philosophy, ceases. For this reason, the "state" of the extreme ascetic (or perhaps better of the mystic) cannot be conceptually described or communicated; and if a being were to depict this "state," we human beings occupying the world would understand nothing of it. Nevertheless, Schopenhauer believes, the "state" of the extreme ascetic (or of the mystic) must be acknowledged—even though no legitimate metaphysics can characterize it positively; at most it may be said that this "state" is *not* that of the world. (The issues sketched here are taken up in some detail in chapter 7.)

I hope that the three demands that Schopenhauer makes on the reader of *The World as Will and Representation* have now been satisfied. But there should be a fourth demand, without which Schopenhauer's inquiry into "the essence of the world"—that is, his asking "What is the world besides representation?"—cannot be comprehended. No one asks about the "essence" of the world, no one poses the question, "What is the world ultimately or at bottom?" without a special reason. Something must be regarded as troubling, disturbing, mysterious, or puzzling about "the world" if one is to seek that which would resolve "the riddle of the world." In short, if the core of philosophy (let it be called metaphysics) is to resolve the riddle of the world, then this pursuit presupposes that there is from the start a genuine riddle. So Schopenhauer might have explicitly urged his reader to reflect upon life and the world, convinced that if the reader does so, he or she will realize that suffering permeates the whole of conscious existence, upon which he or she will then very likely wonder what can possibly explain this fact, this "riddle of the world." It is this very wonder that, for Schopenhauer, constitutes the metaphysical thrust. Anyone lacking this wonder will be wholly unreceptive to Schopenhauer's philosophy as a whole. And any critic who fails to recognize the fourth demand that Schopenhauer makes on his reader will never understand what the metaphysician of will is all about.

In his youth Schopenhauer accompanied his father and mother on a long trip throughout much of Europe. The long journey had a powerful, lasting effect: the teeming masses in London appalled him, the plight of 6,000 galley prisoners in Toulon horrified him, and the general misery of human life in all of Europe stamped itself on his mind. In later years he was to note:

> In my 17th year, without any learned school education, I was gripped by the *misery of life*, as was Buddha in his youth when he looked upon sickness, old age, pain, and death . . . and my conclusion was that this world could not be the work of an all-good being, but rather that of a devil who had brought creatures into existence in order to take delight in their suffering; to this the data pointed, and the belief that it is so won the upperhand."[28]

A few years later, when Schopenhauer was developing his philosophical scheme, he ascribes the source of the world and life not to the devil, but to something just as evil—the will manifested in the world. Schopenhauer provides us, therefore, with a wholly nonreligious account of the misery of life, probably the only one in the history of Western thought. But he also offers a "way out" of this world of suffering: denial of the will to live.

One could well divide Schopenhauer's philosophy into three main parts: (1) an observation—the world and life is essentially suffering; (2) a diagnosis—the world and life of suffering is the manifestation of the blind, irrational will to live; and (3) a cure—by ceasing to will, suffering abates and, in the extreme case, totally disappears. Metaphysics figures primarily as the diagnosis of the world and life of suffering: It aims at an account of the world and life whereby the existence of suffering will be rendered intelligible, and possibly even recognized as justified. For the world is as it is because the will—as the essence of every being—is as it is. On the individual and personal level, my world and life is essentially suffering because, and solely because, my will is as it is; hence in not too strange a sense, I am fully responsible for the suffering I experience, and indeed I deserve it. On this note—Schopenhauer's effort to advance a sort of "theodicy," a justification of suffering and misery—I close the introduction.[29]

ONE

The Single Thought

After the emphasis that Schopenhauer places on the single thought—the one thought to be delineated in *The World as Will and Representation*—one would expect him to inform the reader of exactly what that thought is. Remarkably, however, he does not do so; in fact, nowhere in the entire book does Schopenhauer explicitly refer to the single thought and then state it succinctly.[1] Perhaps it cannot be stated concisely, perhaps no single proposition can express the full content of the single thought (which would not be surprising given the wide range of topics discussed in *The World as Will and Representation*). Indeed, Schopenhauer suggests as much when he writes that "in spite of all my efforts, I have not been able to find a shorter way of imparting that thought than the whole of this book"[2]—a book numbering, in the original edition, 590 pages plus a 135-page appendix, *Kritik der Kantischen Philosophie*. But Schopenhauer does reveal that he considers "this thought to be that which has been sought for a very long time under the name of philosophy," and he remarks that under one aspect it appears as metaphysics, under another aspect as ethics, and under yet another as aesthetics.[3] Consequently, Schopenhauer sometimes speaks of three aspects under which the single thought appears, but he at other times (even in the same short preface) speaks of the four aspects of the one thought, meaning no doubt the four principal divisions (or Books) of the very long work.[4] These two ways of speaking generate no self-contradiction, but they may occasion some confusion or at least unclarity in the mind of the reader.

Understanding Schopenhauer's philosophy, as presented in his main work, would surely be facilitated if we could discover a single proposition that, clearly expressing the single thought, holds the wide-ranging work together and manifests its underlying unity. On the other hand, should such an effort prove futile—say, because only the aspects of the single thought but not the single thought itself can be expressed in propositional form, or more radically because there simply is no underlying unity—then this too should yield enlightenment. The task before us is not intellectual skullduggery. For what, if anything, one takes the single thought to be reveals one's overall conception of Schopenhauer's philosophical endeavor. If one concludes that no single thought can be discovered, then one will be inclined to join the ranks of those critics who charge Schopenhauer with serious internal inconsistencies. Or, if one determines the single thought to be, for example, "The world is will," then one will classify Schopenhauer's philosophy as monistic: The world is one thing alone, and it is will. Another possible answer, namely, "The world is will and representation," will lead one to dub Schopenhauer a dualist (there are two worlds, one of will and one of representation) or a double-aspect theorist (there is one world viewable in two ways, as will and as representation). And so on. How Schopenhauer is to be understood is the chief concern of this entire study, hence it quite properly starts with the search for a linguistic expression of the (alleged) single thought.

Judging from the title of Schopenhauer's main work, the fundamental question of philosophy is "What is the world?" and the answer, hence presumably the single thought, is "The world is will and representation." Before examining this answer, we have to discover the meaning of the question: What does Schopenhauer mean by "the world"? Does the world encompass everything that can be said to exist? Or is the world only that which, as it were, stands over against the human being or the self? Some philosophers speak of "the world," or "the universe," in the all-encompassing sense, meaning all of existence, including oneself. Other philosophers mean by "the world" only that which the self faces, perceives or knows, and interacts with, as indicated, for example, by the expression, "the self *and* the world." Which conception of the world does Schopenhauer have in mind when he speaks of "the world as will and representation"? As a provisional answer—and it is only provisional—we may respond that by "the world" he has in mind that which stands over against the self (just as some people think of nature as something over against the human being). Another way of putting this provisional answer is this: By "the world" Schopenhauer means the entire set of objects that the knowing subject perceives, hence, in a sense, the world will consist of everything that can be an object for the subject, including one's own body.

To assert that "the world is will and representation" is to assert, in popular language, that the world on the surface is representation (or appearance) and the world in its depth is will (or thing in itself). The tree I see outside this window is both an appearance and, underlying that appearance, will. As an appearance, it is a representation of the knowing subject (which, in this case, is in me); but "in itself" or in reality, hence apart from its being a representation of the knowing subject, it is will. Since ancient times philosophers have distinguished between appearance (how things seem) and reality (how things really are), and Schopenhauer can be placed in this long tradition in that he takes "the world" to be, on the one hand, appearance (that is, representation of the knowing subject) and, on the other hand, reality (which he judges to be will). For Schopenhauer, then, will is the underlying reality of everything that appears to, or is represented by, the knowing subject. To reaffirm Schopenhauer's idealism (of a sort), it may be noted that normal perceptual objects (such as the tree outside the window) do not exist *as objects* independently of being perceived by the knowing subject. What the knowing subject does is "objectify" things, that is, make objects out of something very different from objects, namely, out of sensations. And in making objects out of sensations, the knowing subject—through its ways of knowing—transforms sensations into the "objective" world of time, space, and causality. These perceptual objects then appear to us as temporally, spatially, and causally related, but their underlying reality or essence—that is, will—is not temporal, or spatial, or causal.

It is perfectly reasonable to express Schopenhauer's single thought as "the world is will and representation," for as he himself says (*ipse dixit*), "this world in which we live and exist is, according to its whole nature [*Wesen*], through and through *will* and at the same time through and through *representation*."[5] In fact, in the paragraph from which this quotation is taken, Schopenhauer seems to indicate that this very proposition expresses the single thought. Occurring in the first sentence of the final section of Book 2, section 29, it is prefaced by: "Here I conclude the second main part of my discussion in the hope that, as far as is possible in the case of the very first communication of a thought [*Gedanke*] that has never previously existed . . . I have succeeded in conveying the clear certainty that."[6]

In the immediate sequel Schopenhauer asks what would remain in "this world in which we live and exist" if we eliminated from it representation—that is, the knowing relation of subject and object along with time, space, and causality—and, he says, "the answer is that, as something *toto genere* different from the representation, this cannot be anything but *will*, which is therefore the *thing in itself* proper." Schopenhauer then continues with this most significant passage:

> Everyone finds himself to be this will, in which the inner nature of the world consists, and he also finds himself to be the knowing subject, whose representation is the whole world; and this world has an existence only in reference to the knowing subject's consciousness as its necessary supporter. Thus

everyone in this twofold regard is the whole world itself, the microcosm; he finds its two sides whole and complete within himself. And what he thus recognizes as his own inner being also exhausts the inner being of the whole world, of the macrocosm. Thus the whole world, like man himself, is through and through will and through and through representation, and beyond this there is nothing.[7]

Yet there is present in "man himself" something that is lacking in "the whole world," and that is the knowing subject. In other words, the world is representation only as object, but the human being is representation both as object (as a body that can be perceived and that causally interacts with "outer" bodies) and as subject (as the knower of perceptual objects). Hence, although the world and the human being may be both will and representation, they are at least representation in different ways: The world does not include the knowing subject, but the human being does. Other than this, perhaps, it may be said that both the world (the macrocosm) and the human being (the microcosm) are both representation and will. And possibly this very proposition does best express the sought-for single thought. To accept this conclusion would be to assent to Arthur Hübscher's contention that the title of the main work, *The World as Will and Representation*, "brings into a short formula" the "one thought."[8]

Whether the statement that "the world is will and representation" expresses the single thought remains in question, but it is without doubt a central claim of Schopenhauer's philosophy. It is, however, an ambiguous claim in any case: Does it mean that there is one world with two aspects or does it mean that there are two worlds? Should we, in Schopenhauer's judgment, speak of the world *as* will and the (same) world *as* representation, or should we speak of the world *of* will and the world *of* representation? If he maintains that there is one world with two aspects, or one world viewable from two standpoints, then he may be called a "double-aspect theorist." Accordingly, we might then compare the world to the coin now in front of me: There is only one coin, but from one aspect (*Betrachtung*) it is this coin-as-heads, and from another aspect it is this coin-as-tails. Schopenhauer often suggests this very doctrine, not only about "the whole world" but also about every individual thing in the world, including (as we have seen) the human being or oneself. And there seems to be no particular problem with talking about one thing, whether the most general (the whole world) or the most specific (any individual object), viewable from two (or even more) aspects: The moon, for example, has an apparent side (comparable to it as representation), and it has a hidden side (comparable to it as will), yet the moon is one thing.[9] Nothing could be less controversial, one might conclude.

Yet the double-aspect theory seems to allow a curious question, and a surprising thesis, about the world. If the world from one aspect is will and from another aspect representation or appearance, then what is it in itself? What is the world apart from being will from one aspect and apart from being representation from another aspect? That we cannot answer this question, hence that the world in itself remains forever concealed from human comprehension, is a thesis Julian Young puts forth in his effort to show that Schopenhauer subscribes to Kant's insistence on the unknowability of the thing in itself. Young writes:

> Following this thread, I argue that he [Schopenhauer] does not, in fact, claim the world in itself to be will at all. Rather, he agrees with Kant that it is, to the rational mind at least, unknowable. As I read him, while the world may appear "as Representation" and, on a deeper level, "as Will," it remains, like an actor who appears as Macbeth and as Hamlet but never as himself, in itself, inscrutable.[10]

Applied to the double-aspect theory, this interpretation can be stated thus: The world appears as and is knowable as representation, and the world appears as and is knowable as will, but the world does not appear as and is not knowable as it is in itself. Similarly, still following Young, an actor appears as Macbeth and then as Hamlet, but never as himself, for instance, never as Sir Laurence Olivier. Presumably, this thesis may be extended to anything: For any x, x is knowable as R (as representation) and x is knowable or at least inferable as W (as will), but x is not knowable as x. (Some problems raised by this thesis will be discussed in chapter 5.)

A further difficulty generated by the double-aspect theory, at least with regard to Schopenhauer, is this: How can the world from one aspect be representation and from another will, when the properties of representation are (as Schopenhauer always insists) *toto genere* different from the properties of will?[11] To say that the properties of the former are "*toto genere* different" from the properties of the latter is to say that the two have no properties in common, or indeed that the properties of the one are, as it were, the antiproperties of the other. Time, space, and causality are properties of the representation, but not one of them is a property of will, in fact, will is characterized precisely as nontemporal, nonspatial, and noncausal. How then can it be said that representation and will are the two "sides" or aspects of one and the same world? If we have no way of identifying this "one and the same world" directly, if from one perspective we encounter the world of representation and from another perspective we encounter the world of will, what possible justification do we have for even talking about one and the same world at all? Why not simply give up the doctrine of one world viewable from two aspects and openly acknowledge a dualism—the world *of* representation and the very different world *of* will? (Notice that the problem cannot be solved by taking into account the commonplace example of blood, which is red to the naked, unaided eye and which is nearly colorless under a microscope.[12] With this case we have different color properties of one and the same thing, but with Schopenhauer's "world" we have two entirely different *kinds* of properties.) In short, if "the world is representation and will," in accord with the double-aspect theory, it is a very difficult thought to understand—perhaps even incoherent.

We are apparently left, therefore, with an extremely sharp dualism: There are two worlds, one of representation and one of will. Somehow, it will be claimed, these two worlds parallel or relate to each other, but then the standard difficulty of all sharp dualisms arises: What sort of parallel or relation could there be between two types of entities, or (in this case) two worlds, when their properties are "*toto genere* different" or indeed antithetical?[13] And what sense could be made of Schopenhauer's fundamental tenet that the world as representation is the manifestation or objectivation of the world as will? Schopenhauer wants representation to be completely different from, yet closely tied to, will. But has he not made the working out of such a theory impossible? The answer seems to be yes, if he subscribes to either the double-aspect theory or dualism, at least as these doctrines have been described so far. It seems evident then that neither of these doctrines can be the expression of "the single thought."

What is basically mistaken about those two doctrines, as far as Schopenhauer is concerned, is that they assign no priority to will over representation. He certainly holds that, in some fashion or another, the world is will and representation, but he does not hold that the world is just will on the one hand and just representation on the other—as if will and representation stood ("ontologically") on a par with each other. According to Schopenhauer, at least usually, will is not dependent on representation (or appearance), but representation (or appearance) is dependent on will, hence in terms of dependence will has a definite priority over representation. In referring to "the aseity of the will"[14] Schopenhauer means to point out that the will is self-existent, that is, that it is not dependent on anything for its existence; and he flatly denies that representation has "aseity." He urges much the same point in claiming that the human being is basically will and only secondarily intellect or mind[15]—the latter being the faculty by which there is knowledge and thus representation. And sometimes he asserts that nature before the emergence of animate beings (with brains and thus with intellect) has to be assigned will, but nature did not yet "appear"; in short, there was will but no representation prior to animate beings.[16]

A second general candidate for expressing the single thought—and, I shall continue to assume, for answering "What is the world?"—is this: The world is will.[17] How one might settle on this answer can be rather easily explained, namely, by taking Schopenhauer at his word when, first, he declares the whole world of perceptual objects to be "mere" appearance or "merely" our representation, and when, second, he denies reality to all things that originate and perish. The former position Schopenhauer would assign to the ancient sages of India, who, on his interpretation, believed that all individual, discrete things of ordinary sense-perception have no more reality than the objects of our dreams, and that only the deceptive "web of Maya" leads us to attribute reality to perceptual objects. Moreover, the very words "appearance" (*Erscheinung*) and "representation" (*Vorstellung*) sometimes lead Schopenhauer to regard perceptual objects as unreal: "Appearance" points to what appears, not to what truly is; and "representation" pertains to what is imagined or supposed, not to what truly exists. In denying reality to all things that originate and perish Schopenhauer believes himself aligned to "the divine Plato," who, in his judgment, believed ordinary perceptual objects to be, in effect, shadows cast on a wall, hence mere pictures constantly changing, without genuine substance.[18] And sometimes Schopenhauer takes Kant to have shown that what we typically regard as perceptual objects "outside" us are actually mental fabrications "inside" us, and accordingly have no real being in themselves. All of these considerations might lead one to express Schopenhauer's single thought in terms of his fundamental belief that, despite appearances and hence in reality, "the world is will."

In many passages Schopenhauer does assert that the world is will, indeed, occasionally he suggests that there exists nothing but will.[19] Accordingly, he commits himself to a form of ontological monism: The world is simply will and "everything else" is "mere" appearance, hence ultimately illusion or nonbeing. I take Schopenhauer to hold, however, that the world is will in appearance, that will is that which appears in appearance, or equally that will is the essence or inner nature of the world of appearance. Although this judgment cannot yet be established, it has the advantage of saving both appearance and will (which simple monism fails to do) while assigning priority to will over appearance (which both the double-aspect theory and dualism fail to do). And these two provisions must be accommodated.

Now if Schopenhauer does in fact hold that the world is will in appearance, if he advocates a sort of essentialism (the essence of appearance is will) and rejects simple monism (nothing but will exists), then the proposition, "the world is will," cannot express the single thought to be "imparted" in *The World as Will and Representation*. (Or at least that proposition is not the apt expression of the single thought.) On the other hand, if "the world is will" is meant to say that the world of appearance is in essence will or that will is what the world of appearance manifests, then the proposition may very well express the single thought. For it assuredly approaches the heart of Schopenhauer's metaphysics. But there is good reason to entertain a further candidate for the single thought.

I refer to a note from the *Nachlaß* that Schopenhauer jotted down in 1817: "My entire philosophy can be summarized in the one expression: the world is the self-knowledge of the will."[20] To the best of my knowledge, no English-writing critic refers to this note except Christopher Janaway, who calls it "an enigmatic statement which in a way rephrases the title of his [Schopenhauer's] main work, *The World as Will and Representation*."[21] But he makes little of it except for this brief observation:

> Intellect and will must be clearly distinguished, Schopenhauer argues, and the "I" seen as a kind of composite of the two, but with the will in many respects the dominant partner. In fact, since it is conditional on the growth of an organism complete with brain and nervous system, the intellect is as much a natural manifestation of the will as anything else in organic nature. This is how Schopenhauer can claim that in us the will becomes conscious of itself.[22]

This line of reasoning seems to be that since the intellect is "a natural manifestation of the will," it can be said that "in us the will becomes conscious of itself." This, I fear, is even more "enigmatic" than Schopenhauer's original statement. To begin with, "the world is the self-knowledge of the will" does not seem to be equivalent with "in us the will becomes conscious of itself"; and, in any case, Schopenhauer does not here actually make the latter claim—even if, on some construal, he believes it to be true. Furthermore, that the intellect is "a natural manifestation of the will"—being "conditional on the growth of an organism complete with brain and nervous system"—does not seem to be a reason for claiming *either* "in us the will becomes conscious of itself" *or* "the world is the self-knowledge of the will." It may turn out, however, that these two assertions do amount to much the same thing, especially if we take very seriously and understand properly Schopenhauer's supposition that, in effect, what is true of the human being (the microcosm) is equally true of the world (the macrocosm). Accordingly, if I am somehow the self-knowledge of the will, then the world is somehow self-knowledge of the will. Or possibly it may be said that the world "in us," or even "our world," is the self-knowledge of the will. And just conceivably Janaway has something like this in mind when he speaks, quite rightly, of the "I" as a kind of composite of intellect and will. It is hard to tell.[23]

"The world is the self-knowledge of the will" is precisely what Rudolf Malter's book *Der eine Gedanke* (*The One Thought*) alludes to, and it is the thought that underlies Malter's account of *The World as Will and Representation*. According to Malter, this thought, or rather the proposition expressing it, is Schopenhauer's answer to the question "what this world, and in particular the questioner himself, is."[24] The questioner, proceeding from "a negative world-experience," finds himself driven to reflect on the essence of the world, life, and himself; and the single thought stated above is the answer arrived at. In the remainder of this chapter, and beyond, I shall be guided to a considerable extent by Malter's account.

Among the several puzzles attending Schopenhauer's "single thought" as just expressed, the principal one is that it makes no sense to speak of "the self-knowledge of the will." For, in Schopenhauer's scheme of things, the will has no knowledge, neither of itself nor of anything else. What the will does is will, and nothing more, indeed it does so blindly (that is, it does not know that or what it wills); only the intellect, which does not will, knows anything (and that which it knows are objects, never itself).[25] From his earliest philosophical notes to his latest essays, Schopenhauer sharply distinguishes the will from the intellect, arguing again and again that the will is not cognitive or rational or intellectual, that there is no such thing as a "rational will" (contrary to Kant), that the will is not guided by reason or intellect—all of which gets summed up, perhaps, in the pronouncement that the will is "all-powerful."[26] Consequently, apart from some very special provision, no proposition about the self-knowledge of the will, including the proposition that "the world is the self-knowledge of the will," can be made intelligible.

The special provision, following Malter,[27] derives from the "*immediately given*," but "absolutely inconceivable," identity of the subject of knowing and the subject of willing, which, as noted in my introduction, Schopenhauer briefly discusses in the dissertation of 1813. "Whoever rightly grasps the inconceivability of this identity," he says, "will with me call it the miracle *par excellence* [*das Wunder kat' exochen*]."[28] Why inconceivable? Why a miracle? The first, most general reason is that this "identity" defies the sharp distinction usually drawn between knowing and willing, between the intellect and the will; second, it amounts to a relation of "identity" of two subjects, although—according to the whole thrust of the dissertation— only objects can be related in any way, including identically related; and third, as "*immediately given*," whereby the subject of willing somehow becomes object for the subject of knowing, there is instanced an "identity" of a subject with its object, which is clearly inconceivable. So, indeed, the identity of the subject of knowing and the subject of willing, though "*immediately given*," is "absolutely inconceivable."

If we grant this mysterious identity, as perhaps we must,[29] we are agreeing that the "I" (or self, or "soul") is a whole with two parts or a unity with two aspects, namely, the subject of knowing and the subject of willing, and that these two subjects are identical or coincide precisely because they are two parts of one and the same whole or two aspects of one and the same unity. In *The World as Will and Representation* Schopenhauer makes this significant statement:

> In the essay on the Principle of Sufficient Reason the will, or rather the subject of willing, is treated as a special class of representations or objects [which is now denied]. But even there we saw this object coinciding with the subject, i.e., ceasing to be object. We there called this coincidence [*Zusammenfallen*] the miracle *par excellence* [*das Wunder kat' exochen*]; to a certain extent the whole present work is a clarification of this.[30]

In self-consciousness I as knowing subject coincide or become one with myself as willing subject: The two subjects, as it were, melt together. (When I know myself really as object, hence other than in self-consciousness, I know myself as body.) Now the question is how the identity or coincidence of the subject of knowing and the subject of willing helps clarify the proposition, "The world is the self-knowledge of the will."

The first thing to keep firmly in mind is this: The will *as such* has no knowledge (consciousness, awareness) of anything, hence it has no knowledge of itself. Dozens of passages reveal this to be Schopenhauer's unwavering position. As early as 1814 he writes: "*The world as thing in itself* is a great will, which does not know what it wills; for it knows not [at all] but merely *wills*, precisely because it is a will and nothing else."[31] And in the first edition of the main work he writes: "The will, considered purely in itself, is devoid of knowledge and is only a blind, irresistible urge, as we see it appear in inorganic and vegetable nature and in their laws, and also in the vegetative part of our own life."[32] In the second volume of *The World as Will and Representation* (1844) Schopenhauer repeats the claim that "the will-in-itself is without knowledge," that it "merely wills and does not know."[33] In *On the Will in Nature* (1836) he remarks that the will becomes conscious of itself only when knowledge is added to it (hence not by itself alone).[34] In his last original work, *Parerga and Paralipomena* (1851) Schopenhauer states that "the will is incapable of any self-knowledge because, in and by itself, it is something that merely wills, not something that *knows*."[35] These passages make it absolutely clear that the will, or the subject of willing, cannot "in and by itself" have knowledge of itself; they also show that self-consciousness cannot be found in any being lacking a brain and nervous system, hence lacking intellect. Only in that peculiar creature called "the human being," and not even in higher animals such as dogs and monkeys, can self-consciousness occur.[36]

A second fundamental point to keep in mind is this: The fact that self-consciousness does occur in the human being—whereby the subject of knowing is both "identical" with and yet conscious of the subject of willing—does not make clear how "the world" can be "the self-knowledge of the will." We can perhaps understand the proposition (mentioned by

Janaway) that "in us the will becomes conscious of itself," provided it means
that I, as a composite of knower and willer, am conscious of being a willer,
so that in me the willer, conjoined to the knower, is conscious of itself as
willer. But this says at most that there is "in me" self-knowledge of the will,
that is, that I am conscious of being will; it does not show that, or how,
"the world is the self-knowledge of the will." And, after all, it is supposed
to be the world, and not (or not just) myself, that is the self-knowledge of
the will.

As a matter of fact, the statement that "the will becomes conscious of itself" is ambiguous: It can mean that the will (or actually, the union of will
and intellect) becomes conscious of being will, that is, that it wills; or it
can mean that the will (or, again, the union of will and intellect) becomes
conscious of what it wills, what its nature is, or what sort of will it is.[37]
Schopenhauer probably holds that consciousness of being will cannot occur apart from consciousness of the world, but he most assuredly holds
that consciousness of the nature of the will requires consciousness of the
world. What "the world" signifies in the present context is the world of appearance; in it and only in it can it be said of the will that "it knows what it
wills."[38] In other words, the will-intellect union knows, in virtue of the intellect component, what it as will wills, that is, what its nature is, only by
knowing the world of appearance. Or, to reverse the matter, the world of
appearance reveals to the will-intellect union, or specifically to the intellect component, the nature of the will. And there is no other way to gain
this knowledge, just as there is no way to gain knowledge of one's own will
or character except by noting that portion of the world of appearance consisting of one's bodily actions.

Schopenhauer often suggests, as we have seen, that what is true of the
world (the macrocosm), or as he sometimes says "life," is equally true of
"man" (the microcosm). He writes in 1814, for example, that "the purpose of the farce in which everything essential is irrevocably fixed and
enacted" is "that man may know himself, may see what it is that he wills
to be, has willed, hence wills and therefore is." Instead of claiming that
"man" has an immediate knowledge of "himself," Schopenhauer argues that
only by looking outward into the world and life does "he" come to know
"himself": "*This knowledge must be given to him as a knowledge from outside.*"[39]
We come to know ourselves only empirically, that is, only by taking note
of what we do under various conditions; and in no other way—in no so-
called immediate way—do we come to know the sort of will or character
that we are. So, as I said above, following Hamlyn, we may know that we
will immediately or in virtue of self-consciousness (though even this is not
certain), but we can know what we will or the nature of our will only by
looking outward into the world of appearance, specifically, into our bodily
actions. Schopenhauer concludes the note just quoted thus: "Life is to

man, that is to the will, precisely what chemical reagents are to the body. Only in these is there revealed what it is, and it is only to the extent that it reveals itself." In short, only by your works can you know yourself.[40]

What is needed now is a reconsideration of a few things. The proposition, "The world is the self-knowledge of the will," allegedly expresses the single thought imparted in the whole of Schopenhauer's main work. It is supposed to be the answer to the question that philosophy has long been seeking. But if so, then—contrary to what one might expect—that question is not "What is the world in itself?" or "What is the world in reality?" For the answer to these (equivalent) questions is that the world is will. Nor is the question "What is the world of, or in, appearance?" For the answer to this question is that "the world" is (my) representation or that it is a vast set of objects subject, in various ways, to the principle of sufficient reason (hence subject to temporal, spatial, and causal dimensions). Consequently, "the world" that is allegedly the self-knowledge of the will designates neither the world in itself alone nor the world of appearance alone: It designates both at once. The expression "self-knowledge" has reference to the world as appearance or representation, and the expression "the will" has reference to the world as reality or the world in itself. In short: The double-sided world (in which we live and have our being) is that in which or that whereby the nature of the will (that is, what the will wills) is known by the will illuminated by the intellect. As Schopenhauer once put it, "through the addition of the world as representation, developed for its service, the will obtains knowledge of its own willing and what it wills, namely that this is nothing but this world, life, precisely as it exists."[41] If there were no world as representation, that is, no knowing subject and no known objects (which include normal perceptual objects, Ideas, and bodily actions), the will would have no way of knowing itself or its nature; it would be, in such a case, truly blind—just as it was prior to the advent of the brain (and thus the intellect), indeed, as we shall see, prior to the advent of human reason. Along the same lines, Schopenhauer will frequently say that the world is "the mirror of the will," or the visibility or "objectity" of the will, thereby indicating that the world is that in which the will appears and comes to be known.[42]

Frequently, especially in Book 4 of *The World as Will and Representation*, Schopenhauer ties up the thought of the will's knowing itself with morality. What the morally virtuous person recognizes is the unity of the will in all living creatures, and this recognition explains his or her compassion (*Mitleid*, pity) for them. Such a recognition is absent from the egoistic person, in whom "the will fails to recognize itself."[43] Near the very end of Book 4, without mentioning the single thought, Schopenhauer explicitly states that "the world is the self-knowledge of the will."[44] And he uses here exactly the same words he had used in his note of 1817: *die Welt ist die*

Selbsterkenntniß des Willens. With obvious reference to salvation or liberation from the will to life, he adds a bit later:

> But we now turn our glance from our own needy and perplexed nature to those who have overcome the world, in whom the will, having reached complete self-knowledge, has found itself again in everything, and then freely denied itself, and who then merely wait to see the last trace of the will vanish with the body that is animated by that trace.[45]

Once the will has been stilled and all striving has ceased,

> We see that peace that is higher than all reason, that ocean-like calmness of the spirit, that deep tranquillity, that unshakable confidence and serenity, whose mere reflection in the countenance, as depicted by Raphael and Correggio, is a complete and certain gospel.

For then "only knowledge remains; the will has vanished."[46] This final state of being, this cessation of the will whereby only knowledge remains, is accomplished only by the ascetic, who has come to see the world and life for what it is and who has renounced it for the sake of peace and serenity. Such a state of being could not be accomplished unless the subject of knowing and the subject of willing were "identical,"[47] so the whole notion of salvation or liberation depends on that "identity" first mentioned in the dissertation of 1813. What it is that actually denies the will— whether the intellect or the will itself—is difficult to determine (as we shall see in chapter 7). The issue is surely related to, and perhaps identical with, the difficult issue noted above, namely, what part of the "I" knows the will as it appears in the world of appearance: Is it the intellect or is it the will itself, or (somehow) simply the "I"? In other words, the miracle *par excellence* pertains not only to the will's knowledge of itself (as the world, and as self-consciousness) but also to salvation or liberation from the world.

The single thought, if it is to express the entirety of Schopenhauer's main work, cannot simply be that the world is the self-knowledge of the will (or that it is the mirror of the will). For that proposition fails to reflect the undeniable teleological nature of the will evidenced by its self-objectification, which Schopenhauer increasingly emphasizes in Books 3 and 4. In general, the first two Books of *The World as Will and Representation* characterize the affirmation of the will to life in that they portray the world as we know it under the governance or domination of the will to life; and the latter two Books characterize the denial of the will to life, and thereby indicate the purpose that the will has in objectifying itself in nature and finally in the human intellect in the first place. In short, a complete account of "the world" has to include not only self-knowledge of the will (that is, the will-intellect's knowledge of the nature of the will in its self-affirmation) but also the will's telos or aim in seeking knowledge of its inner nature (that is, the possibility of denial of the will to life).

For the expression of the entire single thought, I suggest therefore this proposition: The double-sided world is the striving of the will to become fully conscious of itself so that, recoiling in horror at its inner, self-divisive nature, it may annul itself and thereby its self-affirmation, and then reach salvation. Without the element of striving for self-knowledge, we omit the teleological nature of the will; and without the mention of the will's self-divisive nature, we omit the essential quality of the will to devour and feed upon itself as manifested in all of nature.[48] *The World as Will and Representation* is the account of the will's effort, first, to know itself explicitly and, second, to annihilate itself. It seems then safe to say that Schopenhauer was perfectly correct when he wrote to the publisher Brockhaus that the "series of thoughts" contained in his main work "has never come into any human head"!

A final question remains: Why did Schopenhauer not refer to the single thought—either in its shorter version favored by Malter or in its longer version suggested by me—when he advised his first admirers how to understand his philosophy? In none of his letters does he ever mention a single thought; he never says that the world is the self-knowledge of the will; he never alludes explicitly to the preface of the first edition of *The World as Will and Representation*. What he does do is quite different: He tells these admirers to read Kant, to whom he claims allegiance ("I am a metaphysician of Kants [*sic*] school"),[49] and he urges them to read *On the Will in Nature*:

> In this small essay the real core of my metaphysics is laid out more clearly than anywhere else, and it is especially suited to bring forth the so necessary conviction that the inner essence of all things, hence the sole reality in the world, thus the thing in itself, is precisely that, in us so familiar and yet so mysterious, which we find in our self-consciousness as the will and which is completely different from the intellect.[50]

All in all, I suspect that Schopenhauer did not refer to the world as the self-knowledge of the will for three reasons: One, it is a difficult thought to understand, at least apart from understanding the entire *The World as Will and Representation*; two, it might be interpreted in a way that makes Schopenhauer sound like Hegel; and three, by 1836, or even earlier, Schopenhauer had come to believe that the truly novel contribution of his entire philosophy (hence the single thought) consists of emphasizing the priority of the will over the intellect in the human being, along with claiming that the essence of the world and nature is identical with the essence of the human being.[51]

TWO

From Perceptual Knowledge
to Metaphysical Inquiry

In Book 1 of *The World as Will and Representation* Schopenhauer puts forth, among other things, a characterization of the world from the standpoint of perceptual or intuitive knowledge (*anschauliche Erkenntniß*). He announces in the first sentence that "the world is my representation" (*die Welt ist meine Vorstellung*),[1] and then proceeds to analyze the world as representation and to clarify what representing amounts to. The total account, with the world as representation on the objective side and representing on the subjective side, constitutes Schopenhauer's theory of perceptual knowledge—or, for short, his perception theory. What the term "representation" designates cannot be positively affirmed from the start, but what it does not refer to, in perception theory, can be determined: It does not refer to so-called things in themselves or to "abstract" representations (that is, concepts) or to "pure" representations (that is, Ideas). The most that one can positively affirm at this point is that by "representation" Schopenhauer means "perceptual" or "intuitive" representation.[2]

I shall examine Schopenhauer's conception of the world as (perceptual or intuitive) representation, not so much for its own sake, but for the sake of determining whether that conception leads into metaphysics. In more precise terms: Does his perception theory, once completed, ineluctably raise the original question of metaphysics, "What is the world besides representation?"[3] I am not asking whether Schopenhauer believes perception theory to point to an answer to the original metaphysical question, for about that there can be no doubt: He does not.[4] Yet Schopenhauer suggests that his account of the world as (perceptual) representation leads us, perhaps in various ways, to engage in metaphysical inquiry, and it is this very suggestion that I shall focus on. Several critics contend that Schopenhauer, in light of his general theory of knowledge, should (like Kant) deny the possibility of metaphysical knowledge—meaning thereby knowledge of the thing in itself—and in due course (see chapter 5) I shall entertain that contention. But here the issue is something else, something prior: What, if anything, in Schopenhauer's perception theory leads unavoidably or at least "naturally" into metaphysical inquiry (not into metaphysical solution)? Are there, in Schopenhauer's hands, any conceptions of perceptual representation or any accounts of the perceiver (or representer) that raise, not answer, the original question of metaphysics? This is the main issue in the present chapter, and it recurs, in a slightly different form, in the next chapter. Along the way, a few additional problems and puzzles will be discussed, though only insofar as they bear on the main issue.

If a person really brings into "reflective, abstract consciousness" the fact that "the world is my representation," Schopenhauer states, "philosophical discernment has dawned on him."

> It then becomes clear and certain that he knows [*kennen*] no sun and no earth, but only an eye that sees a sun, a hand that feels an earth; that the world around him is there only as representation, i.e., only in reference to another, the representer, which is he himself.[5]

What this philosophically discerning individual will realize, Schopenhauer maintains, is that he does not know (perceptual or intuitive) objects such as the sun or the earth or even the table directly in front of him; he will realize instead that he knows nothing but his sensory organs such as the eye or the hand.

In making this two-part assertion Schopenhauer misstates his own position in two ways, for what he actually means to say goes thus: First, the individual knows (and this is only one sense of "knows") changes in his sensory organs, not those organs themselves; and second, the individual knows (in a second sense of the term) perceptual objects quite definitely, that is, he sees the sun, he feels the earth, he touches the table, and so on. What Schopenhauer holds in fact is that only changes in one's sensory organs, and not perceptual objects, are "immediately known." Perceptual objects are only "mediately (or indirectly) known," which is to say that they are represented by the representer on the basis of "immediately known" (i.e., sensed) bodily changes, or, equally, that they are representations constructed out of sensations. Schopenhauer's main point may be put negatively: We do not have a direct or immediate knowledge of perceptual objects. This, above all, is what the philosophically discerning person realizes, and the philosophically naive person (i.e., the "realist") fails to recognize.

Instead of sticking with the eminently plausible distinction between sensations and representations—whereby the former are not and the latter are perceptual objects—Schopenhauer sometimes takes sensations, as well as perceptual objects, to be representations.[6] As a consequence representations already fall into two radically different classes: (1) mediate or indirect or even "objective" ones, that is, normal perceptual objects like chairs and tables; and (2) immediate or direct or "subjective" ones, that is, sensed bodily changes or sensations. That this generous extension of the term "representation" causes difficulties can easily be seen when we ask which class Schopenhauer has in mind when he asserts that the world is "my" representation. Does he mean that the world is my mediate (indirect, "objective") representation, hence the set of normal perceptual objects around me? Or does he mean that the world is my immediate (direct, "subjective") representation, hence the set of sensations I have? Or does he mean both, indifferently? The answer to this query bears immensely on the meaning of, to say nothing of the solution to, the metaphysical question, "What is the world besides representation?"

I am going to suppose that Schopenhauer's initial statement in Book 1 should read: The world is my mediate (indirect, "objective") representation. My chief reason for this supposition, or perhaps recommendation, is that only perceptual objects are actually represented (*vorgestellt*), and that sensations, being merely received and "given," are not represented. Strictly speaking, something is a representation only if it is represented. But it cannot be denied that Schopenhauer frequently regards sensations as representations as well. Just to complicate matters still further, Schopenhauer advances a third conception of "the representation," according to which it consists of the correlation of the knowing subject (the represent*er*) and the known object (the "objective" representation). In sum, then, there are three distinguishable conceptions of the world as representation in Schopenhauer's thought: (1) the objective (the representation is the perceptual, mediate, or indirect object); (2) the subjective (the representation is the sensed bodily change, or the sensation); and (3) the correlative (the representation is the correlativity of the knowing subject and the known, perceptual object).[7] Now we continue with the objective conception.

That which represents perceptual objects is the knowing subject (or represent*er*) that everyone of us "living and knowing" (i.e., animate) beings is; in other words, perceptual objects are representations of the knowing subject (or represent*er*). From this it follows, Schopenhauer holds, that there can be no perceptual object independent of the knowing subject; there can be no representation, understood as object, except in relation to the represent*er*. This line of thought constitutes the fundamental tenet of Schopenhauer's epistemological or transcendental idealism.

Several commentators have remarked that Schopenhauer simply asserts, but offers no arguments for, idealism in the opening passages of *The World as Will and Representation*; and they might add that he surely should defend idealism in light of the fact, which he acknowledges,[8] that (at least) Westerners typically maintain the "realistic" position that perceptual objects are immediately known and that they exist prior to and independently of being perceived. But perhaps Schopenhauer's neglect to defend by argument idealism can be explained by reference to, say, "the philosophical climate of his day."[9] This suggestion, urged by the commentators just cited, goes thus: Schopenhauer simply takes idealism for granted, believing that nearly every philosophically sophisticated person of his time (which was, after all, the heyday of German idealism) would find the doctrine wholly uncontroversial. In support of this explanation it might be pointed out that when Schopenhauer does come to adduce some considerations in favor of idealism (in 1844, in the second volume of *The World as Will and Representation*) he explicitly refers to "the philosophy of modern times," mentioning the idealistically minded thinkers, Berkeley, Kant, and even Descartes.[10]

But actually Schopenhauer does not think that idealism, as he conceives it, can be or needs to be proved. In Book 1, volume 1, he writes: "No truth is more certain, more independent of all others, and less in need of proof than this one, that everything that exists for knowledge, and hence this whole world, is only object in relation to the subject, perception of the perceiver, in a word, representation."[11] And in volume 2, where Schopenhauer purports to defend idealism (not very successfully, it must be admitted),[12] he again suggests that no defense is really needed or possible:

> "The world is my representation" is, like the axioms of Euclid, a proposition which everyone must recognize as true as soon as he understands it, although it is not a proposition that everyone understands as soon as he hears it. To have brought this proposition to consciousness and to have connected it with the problem of the relation of the ideal to the real, in other words, of the world in the head to the world outside the head, constitutes, together with the problem of moral freedom, the distinctive characteristic of the philosophy of the moderns.[13]

Some pages later Schopenhauer actually calls "the world is my representation" an axiom,[14] hence he implies that, like any axiom, it—and thus "no object without subject" and "no representation without representer"—cannot be proved and, being self-evident, does not need to be proved.

Schopenhauer errs in calling these propositions "axioms," since they are for him "definitions" (to continue with Euclid's terminology). In other words, for Schopenhauer "the world is my representation"—like its two equivalent formulas, "no object without subject" and "no representation without representer"—is an analytic, or definitionally true, proposition.[15] It is for this reason, and for no other, that this "truth" is so certain and in need of no proof. Regarding this issue—the first and fundamental truth about the world as representation—nothing about "the philosophical climate of the day" is relevant.

A second, and secondary, truth about the world as representation is that perceptual objects are "conditioned by" the perceiving subject in three specific ways: temporally, spatially, and causally. Schopenhauer calls time, space, and causality the "formal" features of perceptual objects, apparently indicating by "formal" that these three features derive from the subject's "forms" of perceiving. That perceptual objects exist in time and space, and that their states change in accord with causal law (hence with causal necessity), follows from the multifaceted principle of sufficient reason—that synthetic proposition knowable a priori that, in different ways, governs the specific "formal" features of all objects of knowledge, whether perceptual representations or abstract.[16] The proposition that perceptual objects are conditioned temporally, spatially, and causally by the perceiving subject does call for "a proof," but that proof has already been given by Kant, hence Schopenhauer does not bother to repeat it; so here reference to "the philosophical climate of the time" may be relevant. But the proposition that the world is my representation calls for no proof at all, for it is, in Schopenhauer's judgment, an analytic, definitionally true proposition. Indeed, Schopenhauer remarks that "in general no object without subject can be conceived without involving a contradiction,"[17] which is to say that "no object without subject" expresses an analytic proposition knowable a priori.

Nevertheless, the question arises as to what interpretation or "understanding" of the fundamental proposition of Schopenhauer's idealism will make it certain or self-evident. By Schopenhauer's own admission, "the world is my representation" can be heard without being understood and thus without being recognized as true. So what explication will make the alleged definition, "the world is my representation," and its equivalent assertions, fully understood and thus self-evident? Janaway puts forth a reasonable answer: "No object without subject" means, he says, "no experienced content without an experiencer"[18] (just as "no subject without object" means "no experiencer without an experienced content").[19] Accordingly, objects are to be understood as "contents of mental states."[20] A slightly different way of expressing this interpretation would be to say that, for Schopenhauer, object is identical with representation, and that just as there can be no representation without a representer—this being a self-evident linguistic truth—there can be no object without a subject. This account has two chief merits: It makes "no object without subject" (and also "no subject without object") self-evident; and it conforms to Schopenhauer's suggestion (in the passage from *The World as Will and Represen-*

tation, volume 2, quoted above) that the world as representation is "the world in the head."

On the other hand, this interpretation has a number of drawbacks. First, it entails that Schopenhauer simply begs the question as to whether "perceptual object" and "experienced content" (or "content of a mental state") designate, or even mean, the same thing. It may be true, however, that he does simply beg this crucial question, that is, possibly he does just stipulate that perceived chairs and tables exist *as objects* only in the mind or head of the perceiver. And there is some sense in which he believes this to be the case, but he does not simply stipulate it to be true, or so at least I shall try to establish. (Actually, "experienced content" and, say, "mental content" are ambiguous, as will be seen in my third point below.) Second, this interpretation makes Schopenhauer's version of idealism unbelievably radical, yielding the result that the whole vast world of perceptual objects, hence the entire world of objects examined by the natural sciences, exists only as a set of "pictures" (*Bilder*) in the head or brain. But, in fact, this position is sometimes suggested.[21] Third, and this sums up the first two points, this account acknowledges no difference between "immediate representations" (that is, felt or sensed changes in one's sensory organs) and "mediate representations" (those, in my judgment, genuine perceptual objects outside the organism). For Schopenhauer, an "experienced" or "mental" content must not be conflated with a perceptual object.

Nevertheless, the interpretation under consideration cannot be conclusively refuted, indeed, there is a lot of evidence supporting it—especially, I would point out, in the second volume of *The World as Will and Representation* and other later works. I doubt, however, that that interpretation would occur to anyone who read only the first volume in its original edition. To be sure, Book 1 of the first volume espouses a strong version of idealism with regard to perceptual objects or intuitive representations, but it conveys the undeniable impression that, though certainly "ideal" in some fundamental sense, they exist outside the head and in fact outside the skin of the perceiver: They are "outer things" (*Außendinge*). Hence, they are not "experienced contents" of consciousness—certainly not *in* consciousness—or sensed changes of sensory organs or immediate representations or sensory representations. These things are, in a word, sensations; and sensations are not to be identified with perceptual objects. It is true that there can be no sensations without sensing beings, and also true, according to Schopenhauer, that there can be no perceptual objects without perceiving beings; but the latter truth is not to be identified with the former truth.

I propose to advance, therefore, an alternative interpretation of "the world is my representation" or, equally, of "no object without subject," where "representation" and "object" refer to "outer things" such as this sheet of paper, the chair in the corner, and so on, and not to "inner things" such as sensations, felt changes on sensory organs, or the like. This interpretation, like Janaway's, must satisfy three main conditions: One, it must retain a strong version of idealism, so that the very existence (and not just the properties) of perceptual objects depends on the workings of the knowing or perceiving subject; two, it must insure the correlativity of subject and object, so that neither "precedes" the other; and three, it must render self-evident the formulas of Schopenhauer's idealism. The first condition will be met by understanding a perceptual object as the creation of the knowing subject, according to which the subject functions as an artist and its object is its own artwork; the second condition will be met by realizing that just as there can be no artwork without an artist and no artist without an artwork, so there can be no object without the subject and no subject without the object; and the third condition will be met by noticing that both artwork and artist arise simultaneously and correlatively, there being no artwork until the artist has created it and there being no artist until he or she has created the artwork. Moreover, the parallel continues, just as the artist does not create the artwork out of nothing, but only out of some sort of material, so the knowing subject does not create the known object out of nothing, but only out of sensory material, which is to say that it "transforms" the material of sensation into perceptual objects.

Perceptual knowledge, according to Schopenhauer, takes its start from changes felt on that peculiar representation called the animal or human body (*Leib*),[22] which is also denominated "the immediate object."[23] (One's own body [*der eigene Leib*] is a peculiar representation because, at least in perceiving outer objects in contrast to actually perceiving it, it is not represented; for the same reason one's own body is not itself a genuine object upon perception of outer objects, though it is a genuine object when it itself is perceived.) After insisting, contra Kant, that "all perception [*Anschauung*, intuition] is intellectual," that is, a matter of the intellect or the understanding rather than merely a matter of the senses (one does not "sense" perceptual objects), Schopenhauer remarks that "one could never arrive at it, if some effect were not immediately known, and thus served as the starting-point." "But this," he adds, "is the effect [*Wirkung*] on animal bodies. To this extent these are the *immediate objects* of the subject; through them the perception of all other objects is transmitted [*vermitteln*]."[24] In other words, the starting point of perceptual knowledge, hence the condition of the subject-object correlation in perception, consists of sensed or felt bodily changes, which the subject's faculty of understanding construes as effects of perceptual objects: "The changes, which every animal body experiences, are immediately known, i.e., sensed, and in that this effect is at once related to its cause there arises the perception of the latter as an object."[25] The sole function of the understanding is "to know causality"; hence, upon the experience of bodily changes (at least on sensory organs), it automatically takes those changes to be effects of some cause, i.e., of some perceptual object. According to this account (which will have to be modified significantly), perceptual objects are causally efficacious objects, but they are such, of course, only in virtue of the work of the understanding.

Without bodily changes immediately known (felt, sensed), Schopenhauer holds, there would be no perception, no perceptual knowledge, no representing of perceptual objects, hence no polar relation of subject and object; indeed, there would be no world as representation. Consequently, when Schopenhauer claims that this system starts neither from the object (as with "realism") nor from the subject (as with Fichte's "idealism") but from the representation, "which contains and presupposes them both,"[26] he could be referring to the body itself (the so-called immediate object)[27] or to the sensed bodily changes (the sensations or, alternatively, the immediate representations). Actually, however, he is referring there, as the context makes clear, to the subject-object correlativity. (Once again we see that Schopenhauer applies "representation" to several very different things.) Moreover, without the subject's faculty of the understanding (*Verstand*), whose sole function is allegedly the relating of effects (i.e., sensed data) to their causes (i.e., perceptual objects), there would be no perception either. Indeed, Schopenhauer writes, "there would remain only a dull, plant-like consciousness of the changes of the immediate object [i.e., the body] which followed one another in a wholly meaningless way, except insofar as they might have a meaning for the will as pain or pleasure."[28] Continuing with his thesis that perception is a function of the understanding, hence is intellectual, rather than merely a function of the senses, Schopenhauer remarks:

> As with the emergence [*Eintritt*] of the sun the visible world comes about, so with *one* stroke the understanding, through its single, simple function transforms [*verwandeln*] the dull meaningless sensations into perception. What the eye, the ear, the hand senses is not perception; it is mere data.[29]

When bodily changes (at least on sensory organs) are felt, there is sensation, but sensation is not yet perception; for the latter to occur, the understanding's (intellectual) function of construing sensed-bodily-changes as effects of perceptual objects outside the body (in space and time) must be drawn into the total account.[30]

This superficial survey of perception prompts two difficult questions: What is the nature of the perceptual object that allegedly causes sensed-bodily-changes (i.e., bodily changes that are sensed)? And what is the nature of the mind or understanding that allegedly construes bodily changes (i.e., sensed-bodily-changes) as effects of the perceptual object? To begin with, it is certain that perceptual objects are not things in themselves; for, according to Schopenhauer, there can be no causal relation between things in themselves and anything phenomenal, including sensed-bodily-changes. Secondly, it is certain that perceptual objects are not "objects in themselves," that is, "objects" that are not represented; for, Schopenhauer incessantly claims, there can be no such "objects." But if perceptual objects are neither things in themselves nor "objects in themselves," then what are they? They seem to be terribly elusive "things." In order to discern their nature more distinctly, one might bring to bear on the issue a certain conception of the mind or understanding, and then proceed with the following line of thought: We know things only as they appear to us, not as they are in themselves; things appear to us with certain formal properties (for example, temporality, spatiality, and causality) in virtue of the perceiving mind's forms of knowledge, but how things are independently of these forms remains hidden. This position, or something very much like it, is often attributed to Kant, and if rightly so, then for Kant (1) the mind is a sort of grid that filters sensory data in ways whereby we know things only as they appear (hence we know only appearances) and (2) things as they are independently of the way they appear remain hidden. Does Schopenhauer, except for denying the ultimate unknowability of things in themselves (albeit with qualifications of various sorts), maintain the same position? Answer: Sometimes he does, and sometimes he doesn't.

The grid model conception of the perceiving mind, as it may be called, occurs only in Schopenhauer's later writings, when (I submit) he was trying to align himself closely with Kant and, at the same time, make his position readily understandable. In the essay, *On the Basis of Morality* (appearing in 1841), Schopenhauer declares his opposition to Kant's notion of the moral law knowable a priori, but he avows acceptance of Kant's "theoretical knowledge a priori of space, time, and causality." He then remarks:

> The latter depends on the fact that they [space, time, and causality] express the mere forms, that is, the functions, of our intellect, by means of which alone we are capable of apprehending an objective world, and in which such a world *must* therefore present itself. These forms legislate absolutely for that world, so that all experience *must* always conform to them, just as everything seen by me through a blue glass *must* be presented blue.[31]

This analysis leaves open the possibility that the "objective world," thus anything in it, does not have the forms—space, time, and causality—that legislate how it must be presented to us, just as what is presented to us as blue in virtue of seeing it through a blue glass may not itself be blue. On the other hand, this analysis also leaves open the possibility—later to be denied—that the "objective world" is in fact temporal, spatial, and causal, just as possibly that which appears blue when seen through a blue glass is in fact blue. Be this as it may, in the passage just cited Schopenhauer seems to adopt the grid model of the intellect, and the question of the thing in itself comes to the fore: Are things in themselves the way they appear? Whether this question can be answered, indeed, whether the thing in itself can be discerned (Kant says no; Schopenhauer says yes, albeit with qualifications, and albeit on a path different from representation), is a further issue. But clearly metaphysical inquiry—as the question of the thing in itself—has arisen.

In the second, supplementary volume of *The World as Will and Representation* (1844) Schopenhauer proposes again a sort of grid model of the mind or "cognitive faculty." He writes:

> If our perception, and thus the whole empirical apprehension of things that present themselves to us, is already determined essentially and principally by our cognitive faculty and by its forms and functions, then it must be that things present themselves in a manner completely different from their own inner nature [*selbst-eigenes Wesen*], and that there they appear as through a mask. This mask enables us always merely to assume, and never to know, what is hidden beneath it; and it then gleams through as an inscrutable mystery [*Geheimniß*]. Never can the nature [*Natur*] of any thing pass over into knowledge wholly and without reserve.[32]

In every instance of perception, it is claimed, there is something of the thing perceived that never appears to the perceiver in virtue of the mask of the cognitive faculty, for it determines how things are perceived, how they appear. And how they appear is necessarily, and not just possibly, "completely different" from "their own inner nature." This is to say, perhaps with Kant, that things are in themselves different from the way they appear, and that the reason for this difference rests with the forms and functions of the "cognitive faculty." Again, then, the mind is conceived as a grid (or mask), and the question of the thing in itself surely arises.

Finally, in *Parerga and Paralipomena* (1851), after referring to "the medium wherein *experience in general* presents itself," Schopenhauer briefly sketches dianoiology (the theory of understanding); he concludes by mentioning "our attributing the color of a glass to the objects that are seen through it," which is said to be comparable to, in short, how things appear to us.[33]

Is Schopenhauer entitled to propose (as he does only, I think, in later writings) the grid model of the perceiving mind? Isn't that model inconsistent with other basic features of his perception theory, and more generally his representation theory? Surely Schopenhauer does not intend to claim that in perceiving an object the knowing subject imposes upon *it* the forms of time, space, and causality; for there is no perceptual object until these forms belong to it (and in fact there is no subject prior to the object). Otherwise, there would be "objects in themselves," somehow existing prior to their being perceived by the subject—and this idea, which Schopenhauer attributes to Kant, has been flatly denied.[34] Again, otherwise, there would be objects that are not representations, that is, objects that have not yet appeared to the knowing subject with temporal, spatial, and causal determinations—and this Schopenhauer calls "a dreamed-up monstrosity" (*ein erträumtes Unding*).[35] For him, being a perceptual object and being a representation with temporal, spatial, and causal properties are one and the same. Consequently, Schopenhauer cannot suppose that the perceiving mind makes objects appear, or makes out of objects representations with temporal, spatial, and causal properties. Does he suppose then that the subject imposes the forms of time, space, and causality on things in themselves (or on those mysterious "things presenting themselves," mentioned in the passage from *The World as Will and Representation*, volume 2, cited three paragraphs above)? Surely not; for no thing in itself interacts with or presents itself to the knowing subject, since otherwise the two would have to be related according to some version of the principle of sufficient reason—and that too Schopenhauer insistently rejects. Only objects imbued with the forms of time, space, and causality relate to the knowing subject.

Perhaps Schopenhauer maintains this: In perceiving an object the subject imposes upon certain sensory data the forms of time, space, and causality such that (somehow) the perceptual object, for the first time, emerges or arises. In other words: The gridlike mind filters sensory data in its three characteristic ways such that (somehow) temporally, spatially, and causally determined perceptual objects appear. But where do these sensory data come from? What causes them? The answer (if there is one) cannot be things in themselves, for things in themselves do not cause anything; and it cannot be perceptual objects, either as "objects in themselves" or as normal things like chairs and tables, for there are no "objects in themselves" and there are no chairs and tables until after (allegedly) the subject has worked over sensory data and made them appear. All in all, then, Schopenhauer is not entitled to propose the grid model of the perceiving mind, hence he is not entitled to introduce any inquiry into the thing in itself on the basis of a gridlike mind.

Nor is he entitled to maintain that perceptual objects are the causes of sensed-bodily-changes or, as he sometimes says, sensations. Yet he does so time and time again. In the second edition of *The Fourfold Root* (1847), for example, he asserts that from sensation on "the immediate object" or body "there certainly arises the perception of all other objects as the causes of such sensations [*Anschauung der übrigen Objekte, als Ursachen solcher Empfindungen*], whereupon those causes present themselves as objects."[36] But not only is this assertion contradicted by the claim that no object can be a cause[37] and by the declaration that "the law of causality is related exclusively to changes,"[38] it is simply unintelligible in its own right. If a perceptual object is exemplified, for instance, by the book I see before me now, and if this perceptual object is supposed to be the cause of sensations on the basis of which I see the book, then (like any cause, which always precedes the effect)[39] it must exist prior to its effects (the sensations), hence it must exist prior to my seeing it—and that means that this perceptual object will have existed independently of my seeing it, like those (Kantian) "objects in themselves" that Schopenhauer calls "dreamed-up monstrosities." Consequently, Schopenhauer has no entitlement to regard the mind as a sort of causal projector of perceptual objects, which objects (allegedly) cause sensations "in" the mind.

Is there perhaps a third model of mind in perception that will, first, extricate Schopenhauer from the difficulties just pointed out and that will, second, make sense? To satisfy these conditions, it cannot be maintained that a perceptual object (at least as something that one actually perceives) is the cause of sensations, and this—to reiterate—is so for two reasons: One, no object is ever a cause; and two, such an "object" would have to exist, as a perceptual object, prior to being perceived (and that is impossible). Nor can it be said that a perceptual object both arises from the mind's working on sensory data and also causes those sensory data, for then one and the same thing would apparently be both the "effect" (or result or outcome or the like) of sensory data and the cause of those very same data. Now, in fact, Schopenhauer does occasionally suggest a model of the perceiving mind—the artistic model—that promises to avoid the difficulties cited above, that firmly establishes a definite form of idealism, and that opens *one* door into *one* form of metaphysical inquiry.

On the artistic model of mind, the understanding creates the perceptual object out of data furnished by the senses. Schopenhauer remarks that in the essay "On Vision and Colors" "I have explained how the understanding produces [*schaffen*, creates] perception out of the data furnished by the senses."[40] Out of the raw, relatively indeterminate, and meaningless data of the senses the understanding creates the vast marvelous world of perceptual objects.

> If anyone standing before a beautiful landscape could for a moment be deprived of all understanding, then for him nothing of the whole view would be left but the sensation of a very manifold affection of his retina, resembling the many blobs of different colors on an artist's palette. These are, so to speak, the raw material from which just a moment previously his understanding created that intuitive perception. In the first few weeks of life the child feels with all his senses; he does not intuitively perceive, does not apprehend; he therefore stares stupidly at the world.[41]

Only when the child begins to use understanding does he or she become aware of, or indeed create, an objective world. In order to do its work, the understanding must have building materials (i.e., sensory data); so the understanding does not create the perceptual world *ex nihilo*, nor does it create objects solely out of itself (as Fichte, according to Schopenhauer, supposed). It is not surprising then that, in the second edition of *The Four-fold Root*, Schopenhauer calls the understanding *der werkbildende Künstler* (the work-forming artist), "whereas the *senses* are merely the assistants who hand up the materials,"[42] for the understanding, like the artist, is highly creative: It is the creator of the entire perceptual world and its world is its creation. Consequently, the subject-object correlativity is retained—no object without subject and no subject without object—for the subject, seen now as the understanding, does not exist prior to its creative activity, just as the object does not exist prior to being created. Someone exists as an artistic creator only upon creating something, hence the creator and the creation arise mutually and simultaneously upon the creative act, just as the perceiving subject and the perceived object arise equally upon the act of perception.[43]

To say therefore that "the world is my representation" is to say that the world is the creation of my understanding. And the sort of representation in question is not "an experienced content of consciousness," which would make the representation "immediate" or in fact sensation, but rather a construction of the understanding outside the body in space, which makes it "mediate" or "indirect." The proposition, "the world is my representation," is still analytic a priori, just as the proposition, "the created thing is the creative artist's production," is analytic a priori. The best term for expressing the understanding's work, and indeed for designating the subject's relation to its object, is *vorstellen* (which is, of course, the word Schopenhauer selects). Unlike passive sounding terms, such as "experience," "be (or become) conscious of," "be (or become) aware of," and so on, the word *vorstellen* clearly suggests that activity on the part of the subject's understanding without which it would have no perceptual objects. So with regard to the knowing subject and the known world in general, we may state Schopenhauer's position thus: *Das Subjekt stellt die ganze anschauende Welt vor: diese ganze anschauende Welt ist die Vorstellung des Subjekts* (the subject puts the entire perceptual world forth; this entire perceptual world is the putting forth of the subject). So, it may be said, Schopenhauer does present an "argument" for (transcendental) idealism, though only in the sense of analyzing what he takes to be a definitional truth.

Although I have distinguished the causal projector model of the mind from the artistic model, Schopenhauer combines the two such that two very different conceptions of perceptual objects result: the causal conception according to which these objects cause sensory data, and the creative or constructive conception according to which perceptual objects are intellectual constructs created out of sensory data. But now, as Gardiner has pointed out, we are faced with a serious difficulty:

> It may . . . be asked how perceptual objects can at one and the same time be regarded as produced by our minds operating in a certain way upon the data of sensation, and as causing or giving rise to those data; and it is hard to see how Schopenhauer could have satisfactorily answered this question.[44]

Janaway raises essentially the same issue when he claims that "Schopenhauer . . . seems committed to having empirical objects as both the prior conditions and the consequences of the understanding's operation upon sensations."[45] On the one hand, the table I see in front of me is the cause of sensations "in me," and, on the other hand, it is a construct of my understanding out of those sensations. The former view presupposes that the table exists prior to the sensations, hence prior to my seeing it; and the latter view suggests that the (constructed and perceived) table exists only after the sensations occur. After Janaway entertains a possible way out of the difficulty—from the objective standpoint, one can say that empirical objects causally act on other empirical objects, including the human body, and from the subjective or idealistic standpoint, one can hold that empirical objects are all constructed by the subject out of received sensations—he rejects this last-ditch response by concluding: "Schopenhauer is apparently committed to the view that the very same object has two roles: the table I see is both the cause of mere sensations in me, and a mind-dependent construct which transforms sensation into cognition by featuring as an objective mental content. It is hard to see how this is any more coherent than the Kantian version involving things in themselves as causes."[46] But is it really true that "the very same object" is both the cause of sensations and the construct out of sensations?

I am going to say "no" to this question, and make a distinction between the material body (which figures in the causal account of sensations) and the actual perceptual object (which the understanding creates out of sensations). It will be urged that this distinction has precedence in Schopenhauer's philosophy with regard to the human character, whereby the material body parallels the intelligible character and the perceptual object parallels the empirical character.

Suppose that sensations, and not simply bodily changes (which may or may not be sensed), have to be caused.[47] It does not follow that they are caused by the constructs created by the understanding out of sensations. They can be caused by changes in material bodies, which changes are in turn caused by other changes in material bodies, the ultimate effect being changes on the sensory organs that typically (but not always or necessarily) are sensed by the animal or human subject. A material body itself is a set of causal powers (or, as it will turn out, a set of "natural forces"), just waiting, as it were, to effect changes on the animal or human body as a result of changes that it (the set of causal powers) reacts to. For example, a material body to which one later attributes the quality of being red is that which causally responds to normal light cast on it and which then causally produces a change in the animal or human eye that is sensed as red. Indeed, as Schopenhauer puts it, "'the body is red' means that it produces the effect of red color in the eye."[48] But this claim has to be emended thus: "The body is red" means that it is a set of causal powers such that when normal light is shone on it, which is a change, it causally produces in the eye a change that is sensed as red. What I have called causal powers and have identified as the qualities of material bodies, Schopenhauer calls "modes of operation" or "kinds of effect" (*Wirkungsarten*). The forms and specific qualities of bodies (*Körper*), he writes, are "nothing but the peculiar and especially determined mode of operation [*Wirkungsart*] of bodies, and this precisely constitutes their difference."[49] If we eliminate from a material body its particular mode of operation—that is, its particular set of causal powers to produce changes on animal and human bodies—we are left with "mere activity in general, pure acting as such, causality itself, objectively conceived."[50] We are left, in other words, with matter, for "matter is throughout pure causality; its essence is action in general."[51]

In line with the thesis that for Schopenhauer the world is the macranthropos (the great human being), I want to explore the idea that "the object" should be understood as parallel to "the human being" or, more specifically, to "the human character."[52] A human character must be conceived in a dual manner: as "intelligible" or as "empirical." As intelligible, a human character is the underlying, never changing quality in virtue of which given motives are the causes of resultant actions. As empirical, a human character is the total complex of actions that, occurring in space and time, are caused by the motives to which the intelligible character or underlying quality of the agent in question is susceptible. A human being as an agent is then empirically the sum total of its actions or effects (its *Wirken*), and it is intelligibly the underlying quality that connects motives causally to its actions. In a parallel fashion, an object must be conceived in a dual manner: as "intelligible" and as "empirical." As intelligible, an object is the underlying "mode of operation" or, better, set of natural forces in virtue of which given changes in other objects are the causes of resultant effects in still other objects, for example, in a human body. And as empirical, an object is the total complex of effects that, occurring in space and time, are caused by the changes to which the intelligible object in question is susceptible. An object is then empirically, or perceptually, the sum total of its effects, and it is intelligibly the underlying set of natural forces that connects changes in other objects causally to, say, the human body.

Strictly speaking then no object (whether as material or as perceptual) is the cause of sensations, just as no character (whether as intelligible or as empirical) is the cause of actions. Emerging motives are the sole causes of human actions, and emerging objective changes are the sole causes of sensations. Yet neither set of cause and effect can obtain without some underlying "connector"—a set of natural forces in the case of objects, and an intelligible character in the case of human agents. In an analysis of perception we run up against a set of natural forces, and in an analysis of human action we run up against the agent's intelligible character; and although we have no insight into the nature of either "connector," we do know that both exist and that neither belongs to the world as representation. We know therefore that the world as representation—in both perception (where causality proper operates) and human actions (where motivation operates)—points to the existence of something other than representation, hence to something "metaphysical," but it gives us no information about the nature of that to which it points. If we are to gain any information about the nature of that to which the world as representation points, then we shall have to pursue a nonrepresentational route; for on the route of the representation, everything has been exhausted and we have led up to a dead end. Now, if the question of the thing in itself is the question of the nature of that to which representation points but offers no answer, then representation theory—regarding both perception and human action—does raise, but does not answer, the question of the thing in itself. Consequently, when Schopenhauer says that on the path of the representation we do not arrive at the thing in itself, he must mean that on that path we do not gain information as to the nature of the thing in itself, but not that we do not lead up to the question of the thing in itself.

In this very long, perhaps overly long, discussion an effort has been made to determine whether Schopenhauer's representation theory, specifically his account of perception, raises the problem of the thing in itself. And it has argued for an affirmative answer, at least insofar as the problem of the thing in itself may be construed as the problem of inquiring into the natural forces figuring in perception. Since nothing has yet been said about will in Schopenhauer's account of perception, since no mention of the term has even been made, it is false to maintain that "Schopenhauer thought that the justification for thinking that the thing-in-itself is to be identified in such and such a way is itself the justification for thinking that there is such a thing at all,"[53] or that "his arguments for the existence of thing-in-itself and for its identification with the will come to the same thing."[54] It is also wrong to suggest that the question of metaphysics arises only with regard to natural forces operating between "outer objects,"[55] for that question arises in perception, where "outer objects" and the body of the perceiver stand in a causal relation. In short, I am arguing, the question of the thing in itself, *construed as the question of natural forces*, arises first of all in Schopenhauer's account of perception. But it also arises in regard to the causal relations between "outer objects," as the next chapter shows. Before taking up that matter, however, it is worth noting that on at least one conception of the representation, presented already in Book 1 of *The World as Will and Representation*, Schopenhauer hints at another route into metaphysical inquiry.

For the most part, and especially in the criticism of Kant, Schopenhauer takes the terms "object" and "representation" not only to refer to the same thing, but to have the same meaning; regarding perception or intuition, at any rate, the two terms are usually treated as synonyms. Accordingly, the world as representation is identical, in meaning, with the world as (perceptual or intuitive) object. But in the course of developing the subject-object relationship Schopenhauer puts forth a second, and subtly different, account of the world as representation. He maintains, as briefly noted already, that

> the world as representation . . . has two essential, necessary, and inseparable halves. The one half is the object, whose forms are space and time, and through these plurality. But the other half, the subject, does not lie in space and time, for it is whole and undivided in every representing being.[56]

Several pages later, where Schopenhauer summarizes what has gone before, he states: "We started neither from the object nor from the subject, but from the *representation*; for the division into object and subject is its first, most general, and most essential form."[57] But if the representation and the object are identical—as the first account has it—then starting from the representation *is* starting from the object, and not from both at once.

Ignoring for the moment the idea of the "immediate representation," that is, the felt or sensed bodily-change—as well as the other things Schopenhauer designates by the term "representation"—we find here two distinct conceptions of the world as representation: (1) the objective conception, according to which the world consists exclusively of perceptual objects, otherwise called "mediate (or indirect) representations," outside which the knowing subject lies and, as it were, views the world (like the eye that sees everything except itself); and (2) the correlative, or two-halves, conception, according to which the world as representation is a whole, one half of which is object and the other half of which is subject, in which case—if the world is representation—both object and subject are members of the world. Conceptions (1) and (2) are, strictly speaking, incompatible; for in (1) the representation is only the object, hence not also the subject, but in (2) the representation is both the object and the subject. How important is this inconsistency?

That it is merely verbal, and thus not really significant, may be defended by drawing a distinction between the assertion, "The world is representation," and the phrase, "the world as representation." To assert that the world *is* representation is clearly to imply that it is representation for a representer, object for a subject. And to speak of the world *as* representation is to refer to the subject-object correlation required for all perceptual knowledge, without actually asserting or even suggesting that the subject is a member (an object or representation) in the world. In other words, "The world is representation" means that the world is object for the subject, but only the object exists in the world; and to speak of "the world as representation" is to refer to the subject-object correlation present in every instance of perceptual knowledge, to which there might be accompanied the reminder that—contrary to what is suggested—the subject does not actually inhabit the world of representation, i.e., the world of objects.

According to this defense, Schopenhauer is guilty at most of a verbal, wholly insignificant, inconsistency: Whether we say that the representation is object (for the subject) or that it is object-and-subject makes no real difference. There remains, however, the untidy fact that Schopenhauer uses the objective conception of the representation to criticize some rival theories and he uses the correlative conception of the representation to criticize others; indeed, on occasion he uses both to criticize the same theory. For example, in his effort to refute the (alleged) Kantian distinction between representation and object of representation, Schopenhauer flatly denies any such distinction on the ground that the two are one, thereby insisting on the objective conception of the representation. When he tries to demonstrate the absurdity of the controversy about "the reality of the external world" and at the same time to undermine the debate between idealism (of a sort) and realism (of a sort), he appeals to both the objective and the correlative conceptions.

Both realism and idealism assume, Schopenhauer holds, that the knowing subject and the known object are related in accord with the principle of sufficient reason, specifically, with the law of causality. "Realism," he writes, "posits the object as cause, and places its effect in the subject. The idealism of Fichte makes the object the effect of the subject."[58] Since realism maintains that independently existing objects act causally on the knowing subject, producing in it representations, it errs in two ways: One, it supposes that "objects" stand in a causal relation to the subject— whereas in fact no causal relation can obtain between the two, for "the object as such everywhere presupposes the subject as its necessary correlative" (whereby appeal is made to the correlative conception); and two, it supposes that "objects" differ from the representations that they (allegedly) cause in the subject—whereas in fact "representation and object . . . are but one"[59] (as the objective conception points out). So Schopenhauer uses one conception of the representation to refute one aspect of realism, and another conception to refute the other aspect. He could argue, however, that the objective conception of the representation, no less than the correlative conception, precludes the possibility of any causal relation between the realist's "object" and the knowing subject, since the knowing subject, not being a member of the world and thus not being an object, cannot enter into any causal relation at all. But, in fact, he does appeal to the correlative conception, thinking perhaps that as two halves logically related the subject and the object obviously cannot be causally connected.

The idealism of Fichte, Schopenhauer notes, does not actually claim that the knowing subject acts causally on the object, but rather that the subject somehow produces or creates the object purely out of itself: "The object can be produced from the subject or [like the web of the spider] spun out of it."[60] Its erroneous suppositions are that the subject (considered the thing in itself or the self-existent being) precedes the object and that the subject and its produced object are connected according to some form of the principle of sufficient reason, presumably (though it is hard to tell, Schopenhauer indicates) the law of causality. The first error is corrected by observing that subject and object are logical correlatives and therefore "have meaning" only in reciprocal, not causal, connection; and the second error is corrected by observing that the principle of sufficient reason does not pertain to the subject, but only to "the form of objects."[61]

Skepticism assumes, according to Schopenhauer, that "in the representation we always have only the effect, never the cause, and so never real *being*; that we always know only the action [*Wirken*] of objects."[62] Its skeptical note arises from the consideration that the action of objects—that is, of the representations of the knowing subject allegedly caused by the objects—may have no resemblance to the real being of objects, or at least that we can never know that they do. Both realism or "realistic dogmatism" (which asserts that there are objects outside our perception of them) and skepticism (which assents to realism's assertion) are corrected, first, by realizing that object and representation are the same, and, second, by observing that "the *being* of perceptual objects just is their *action*."[63] There can be therefore no question about a resemblance between alleged objects outside the knowing subject (that is, between so-called objects in themselves) and their alleged effects (that is, so-called representations) in the subject, hence there can be no basis for espousing skepticism. Notice that skepticism's original error is the realist's "dogmatic" (i.e., merely assumed) thesis that perceptual objects exist "in themselves," and that this error is corrected by Schopenhauer's objective conception of the representation.

Some aspects of the false doctrines of realism, idealism, and skepticism are corrected, on Schopenhauer's account, by the objective conception of the representation, that is, by the thesis that the representation and the object are one and the same. Other aspects are corrected by the correlative conception of the representation, that is, by the thesis that the subject and the object mutually entail each other and, taken together, make up the representation. Believing himself to have definitively refuted the three prevalent epistemological (and ontological) theories of his time, Schopenhauer concludes thus:

> All previous systems started either from the object [realism and skepticism] or from the subject [idealism], and therefore sought to explain the one from the other, and this according to the principle of sufficient reason. We, on the other hand, deny the relation between object and subject to the dominion of this principle, and leave to it only the object.[64]

It follows, incidentally, that causality pertains only to representations as identical with objects (or actually to their states); it may not be applied to representation as comprising both object and subject. In sum, the world as representation, that is, as object-subject correlation, has no cause and it causes nothing.

But now back to metaphysical inquiry. As we have noted several times, the question that supposedly leads into metaphysics is "What is the world besides representation?" Now when the representation is identified with the object, as on the objective conception, the answer is simply "the knowing subject"—and with that fully satisfactory answer, the area of metaphysics has not been broached.[65] Or, similarly, if we ask "What is the representation of?" the answer is again that it is the representation of the knowing subject—and again no metaphysical inquiry is introduced. Finally, if we ask "What is the content of the representation?" then, on the objective conception, the answer is apparently sensation—and once more nothing about metaphysics appears to arise.

On the other hand, when the representation is said to be the subject-object correlation, and the operative expression is "the world *as* representation" in place of the assertion, "the world *is* representation," then there does seem to be some justification for wondering whether the world is something besides representation. For notice now what one would be wondering: Is the world exhausted by the subject-object knowing relationship? Is the world nothing more than a world of knowledge, consisting of two interdependent halves? Is representation or knowledge all there is? More poignantly, am *I* nothing more than a knowing subject, on the one hand, and merely a representation or perceived object on the other? Schopenhauer's answer is no. I suggest therefore that with the correlative conception of the representation there is a natural tendency to wonder about the "something else," the "other than representation," particularly with regard to oneself. And if to wonder about this is to initiate a metaphysical inquiry, then the very notion of the world *as* representation tends to prompt that inquiry. In short, if the world as representation is merely the world as knower and known, and if the human being feels a natural reluctance to restrict the world to mere knowledge—which Schopenhauer no doubt believes—and if to wonder what "more" the world is is to raise a metaphysical inquiry, then the very idea of the world *as* representation does naturally lead into metaphysics. But this is so, however, only on a very special, or even unique, conception of metaphysics—one that has no obvious relation to a thing in itself or "ultimate reality" or the essence of the world or anything of the like. Metaphysics, for Schopenhauer, concerns first and foremost nothing but the nonrepresentable side of the world and experience; it concerns precisely that which cannot be incorporated within the world as representation—and that, given his narrow, though multifaceted, notion of representation, covers quite a lot.

THREE

From Science to Metaphysics

Schopenhauer opens Book 2 of *The World as Will and Representation* with this sentence: "In the first book we considered the representation only as such, hence only according to the general form."[1] What we have learned, he suggests (though he does not repeat it here), is that (1) the very existence of the perceptual representation is conditioned by the knowing subject ("No object without subject" or, equally, "The world is my representation"); (2) the perceptual representation is subject to the three additional, yet still general, forms of all perceptual knowledge (every object is characterized by time, space, and causality); and (3) there is the knowing subject only in conjunction with the known object ("No subject without object"). With regard to the abstract representation or concept (*Begriff*) (as Schopenhauer does in fact state here), we have discovered that (4) its content (*Gehalt*) is the perceptual representation, hence that it has all content and meaning (*Bedeutung*) only through its relation to the perceptual representation, without which it would be worthless (*werthlos*) and contentless (*inhaltslos*). This simply means that every genuine concept or abstract representation has to be based on and traceable to a percept or perceptual representation, or to a set of them: The concept "dog" is genuine because it is based on the perception of dogs, but, Schopenhauer holds, the concept "absolute ego," for example, is bogus because there is, and can be, no perceptual instance of it or of its parts.[2] But now, focusing exclusively on the perceptual representation, "we shall demand to become acquainted with its content [*Inhalt*], its more precise determinations and the forms [*Gestalten*], which it presents to us."[3] The content of the abstract representation is the perceptual representation; so what is the content of the perceptual representation? This is the question that opens Book 2, and that presumably leads into the heart of metaphysics.

53

One might think that the answer has already been given, namely, that the content of the perceptual representation is the sensation or set of sensations out of which the understanding constructs the perceptual representation or object. Just as the content of the abstract representation (or concept) is the perceptual representation (or percept or object), so the content of the perceptual representation is the sensation or sensation-complex out of which that representation is fashioned. Indeed, if "content" means, say, basis or foundation—that on which or from which something depends for its existence or occurrence—then this line of thought makes perfectly good sense. By way of elaboration one could add that the *form* of the perceptual representation derives from the knowing subject (whereby there are objects, and those objects are subject to temporal, spatial, and causal determinations) and that the *content* of the perceptual representation derives from the sensation or sensation-complex out of which it is constructed (whereby every such representation or object is a particular something, for example, a chair rather than a dog or tree or anything else). Being object imbued with time, space, and causality accounts for every perceptual representation's formal aspects, and sensations account for its "material" aspects or its specific empirical content. Once the formal aspects (which derive entirely from the subject) are conjoined with the "material" aspects (which, apparently, do not depend on the subject, except as receptor of sensation) we have the entire thing, be it a chair, a dog, a tree, or whatever. Accordingly, all perceptual objects would be alike in virtue of their (common) formal aspects (time, space, and causality) and each would differ from every other in virtue of its (particular) material aspect (the various sensations). Then, one might think, the entire story has been told. But Schopenhauer does not proceed along this line of thought at all.

Significantly, he talks as if the topic of sensation had never been brought up in Book 1, saying, as noted, that "we considered the representation only as such, hence only according to the general form"—which means according to its formal (or a priori) aspects. Perhaps he has not actually "considered" the material (or a posteriori) aspect, that is, sensation, but he has mentioned it; and, as we have seen, it is sensation that, from the standpoint of perception, leads through causality to natural forces, and eventually, it will be argued, to the thing in itself. To be sure, nothing about sensation reveals the nature of the thing in itself, but its very existence—which is not reducible to the formal (or a priori) aspects of the perceptual representation—indicates something other than its "general form." It has to be admitted, I suggest, that in one sense sensation is the content of the perceptual representation; it is the material or a posteriori aspect of perceptual knowledge; it does not proceed from the knowing subject's faculty of understanding; it is the "starting point" of all perceptual knowledge and indeed of all perceptual objects; it is that without which there would be no such knowledge and no such objects. Yet, clearly, sensation is not the content that Schopenhauer is concerned with. He probably holds that it remains within the world as representation, hence it cannot be the "content" of that world, as "content" is here intended. In the present context, then, "content" must mean for Schopenhauer something beyond or other than representation altogether. And, in fact, this turns out to be the case.[4]

After contrasting the content of the perceptual representation to its form, Schopenhauer makes reference to something apparently unlike content or at least to something far different from sensation. He writes of the perceptual representation thus:

> It will be of special concern for us to obtain information about its genuine significance [*ihre eigentliche Bedeutung*], about its otherwise merely felt significance, by virtue of which these pictures [*Bilder*] do not pass by us completely strange [*völlig fremd*] and meaningless [*nichtssagend*, uninformative], as they would otherwise inevitably do, but speak to us directly, are understood, and acquire an interest that engrosses our whole nature [*unser ganzes Wesen*].[5]

Although he will continue to speak occasionally of the content (*Inhalt* or *Gehalt*] of perceptual representations, Schopenhauer is actually seeking to discover their significance or meaning (and by that he certainly does not mean their sensory basis). And whatever this meaning is, he suggests, it will be something that dispels their strangeness, meaninglessness, or uninformativeness and thereby renders them understandable or intelligible and, perhaps most importantly, interesting. But what reason is there for thinking that they are alien and unintelligible to us in the first place? And why, all of a sudden, are perceptual representations—which are, after all, the empirical objects of normal experience and natural science—called pictures or images (*Bilder*)? Have they no "reality," no *Wirklichkeit*? Of course they do; their very being is their acting, their *Wirken*, hence they are *wirklich*. Do they then lack "reality" in some other sense, in some deeper sense, of the term? Are perceptual representations simply phantasms or "objects" of imagination? (Recall that *Vorstellung* can mean imagination as well as representation.) Is the so-called real world in fact a "dream world"?[6]

Without pausing to entertain any of these questions, and without explaining what is meant by the "genuine significance" of perceptual representations, Schopenhauer launches into an examination of three areas of inquiry (*Wissenschaften*, sciences or disciplines) that might be thought to provide us with the sought-for information: philosophy, mathematics, and natural science. (Although we do not yet really know what we are seeking, we do gain some insight into the matter as the discussion goes along.)

"In the first place," Schopenhauer remarks, "we find philosophy to be a monster with many heads, each of which speaks a different language," yet—except for outright skeptics and thoroughgoing idealists—prior philosophers generally agree on "the significance of the perceptual representation": They speak of "an *object* that lies at the basis (*Grund*) of the representation."[7] But this will not do, Schopenhauer insists, for, again, "we do not at all know how to distinguish that object from the representation"; indeed, "the two are one and the same, since every object always and eternally presupposes a subject, and thus remains representation." Moreover, since the principle of sufficient reason, which has been appealed to here in connecting the "object" with the representation, pertains only to the connection of representations with each other, hence pertains only to "the form of the representation," it cannot be used to discover something nonrepresentable that is allegedly connected to—and, apparently, constitutes the significance of—"the entire, finite or infinite, series of representations."[8] What we are seeking then is something that is not a representation (and thus is not an object), something that is not connected to the entire series of representations by means of the principle of sufficient reason (which principle operates only between representations), yet something that constitutes the significance or "content" of the entire series of representations, whether finite or infinite, such that, once discovered, this series will be intelligible or understandable. Needless to say, all of this is far from clear; for to begin with, it is not clear why we should be seeking anything "beyond" representation at all, that is, it is not clear why the world as representation is not perfectly intelligible as it is. Schopenhauer seems to be asking, "Why is there a world (as representation) at all?" but he forbids us to understand "why?" in terms of cause or ground, that is, in terms of the principle of sufficient reason. But how else can "why?" be understood? What will turn out is this: The term "why?" gets construed as "what?" So Schopenhauer is actually asking: *What* is the world as representation? *What* is it that appears in the world as appearance? The formal, but wholly innocuous, answer is "the thing in itself" or even "the nonrepresentable."[9]

Mathematics, according to Schopenhauer, cannot provide us with the information or knowledge we desire either. For "this science will tell us about these representations only insofar as they occupy time and space, in other words, only insofar as they are quantities." Mathematics deals exclusively with the How-many and the How-much; "since however this is always only relative, i.e., a comparison of one representation with another, and indeed only in that one-sided consideration of quantity, this too will not be the information that we are essentially [*hauptsächlich*] seeking."[10] This brief consideration of mathematics[11] reveals something important, namely, that what is being sought cannot be relative. Every item of mathematics is relative to some other item, in virtue of which alone it has meaning, that is, in virtue of which alone it is what it is; hence what is being sought must be nonrelative, "absolute," independent, unconditioned, or, in a word, groundless (*grundlos*). In sum, we are looking for something that clarifies the whole series of representations and that needs no clarification by anything else; in the vernacular, we are seeking something "rock bottom."[12]

Natural science, Schopenhauer holds, may be divided into two main branches: morphology (the science of structures), which describes the abiding forms of natural things, and etiology (the science of causes), which explains the changes in material nature.[13] But neither leads us to what we are seeking. Morphology, Schopenhauer remarks,

> presents us with innumerable and infinitely varied forms that are nevertheless related by an unmistakable family likeness. For us they are representations that in this way remain eternally strange to us, and, when considered merely in this way, they stand before us like hieroglyphics that are not understood.[14]

Etiology employs the law of causality, showing that one state of matter produces another state; but "it does nothing more than show the orderly arrangement according to which the states appear in space and time, and teach for all cases what appearance must necessarily emerge at this time and in this place." Etiology concerns itself then with changes in matter, with the fact that one appearance causes another, and nothing beyond that. "But in this way we do not obtain the slightest information about the inner nature of any one of these appearances." It only leads up to this "inner nature": "This is called a natural force [*Naturkraft*], and lies outside the province of etiological explanation, which calls the unalterable constancy with which the manifestation of such a force emerges whenever its known conditions are present, a law of nature [*Naturgesetz*]." So etiology does provide us with laws of nature, that is, it tells us what states of matter "occasion" the manifestation of a natural force in what other states of matter, but "the force itself that is manifested, the inner nature of the appearances that arise in accordance with those laws, remain for it an eternal secret, something entirely strange and unknown, in the case of the simplest as well as of the most complicated appearance."[15]

We understand "the force by virtue of which a stone falls to the ground, or one body repels another" no better than we understand "that which produces the movements and growth of an animal"—this is one of Schopenhauer's most insistent claims.[16] Mechanics (or physics) is no more intelligible to us than physiology (both of which belong to etiology), for the former presupposes natural forces—such as matter (it is said here, though usually Schopenhauer does not regard matter as a natural force), weight, impenetrability, etc.—that, in their inner nature, are "just as strange and mysterious" as the forces operating in physiology (those forces lying at the basis of animal movements and growth). "Consequently," Schopenhauer states, "even the most perfect etiological explanation of the whole of nature would never be more in reality than a record of inexplicable forces, and a reliable statement of the rule [or causal law] by which their appearances enter into time and space, succeed each other, and make room for one another." Since etiology leaves unexplained "the inner nature of the forces that thus appear, . . . it could be compared to a section of a piece of marble showing many different veins side by side, but not letting us know the course of those veins from the interior of the marble to the surface."[17] And, in this regard, etiology—which does, of course, all that it can do, and which in fact gives us practical knowledge—leaves us dissatisfied.

As portrayed by Schopenhauer, the branch of natural science called etiology instructs us only how things (or, strictly speaking, how changes in matter) stand relative to each other. As such, it produces in us the feeling that one would have upon being introduced to a company of people, each member of which presents himself as a friend or cousin of another member. One becomes acquainted with every single member of the company, indeed, in a sense one becomes acquainted with the entire company—but only relationally. Thus, Schopenhauer claims, one will then surely ask: "But how the deuce do I stand to the whole company?"[18] One would know each member only in relation to another member, and so it is equally with knowing the world of representations by way of etiology. After all of etiology's explanations are completed, our representations "still stand completely strange before us, as mere representations whose significance we do not understand." Why this is the case is explained thus:

> The causal connection gives merely the rule and relative order of their [representations'] entrance in space and time, but affords us no further knowledge of that which so enters. Moreover, the law of causality itself has validity only for representations, for objects of a definite class, and has significance [*Bedeutung*] only when they are assumed. Hence, like these objects themselves, it always exists only in relation to the subject, and so conditionally.[19]

We know then that we have representations, that they are such and such, and that they are connected by certain causal laws whose general expression is the principle of sufficient reason. But, claims Schopenhauer, we are impelled to make further inquiry because we are not satisfied with this knowledge, because it does not suffice for us: "We want to know the significance of those representations; we ask whether this world is nothing more than representation."[20]

But exactly why are we not satisfied with our knowledge of representations, as provided by etiology? Is there something about us, or about some of us, that impels us to ask whether this world is nothing more than etiologically known representations? Do we just naturally feel that representations have a genuine meaning or significance somehow "beyond" themselves? Are we, as human beings inhabiting the world of which we have a great deal of etiological knowledge, inherently dissatisfied with that knowledge and therefore driven to seek information that would constitute the "otherwise merely felt meaning" of representations? What would be the case if we were limited to the knowledge of the world that natural science, particularly as etiology, provides? Schopenhauer offers some response to these inquiries in the immediate sequel.

If the world were not something more than representation, if it were nothing but a set of perceptual objects conditioned by the knowing subject, hence simply a world of temporally, spatially, and causally interlocked objects, every single one of which is governed by the principle of sufficient reason, then, Schopenhauer claims, "it would inevitably pass by us like an empty dream, or ghostly vision, not worth our consideration." If, however, the world is something more than representation, if the world as representation does have a "meaning," then, says Schopenhauer, "this much is immediately certain": "This something about which we are inquiring must be by its whole nature completely and fundamentally different from the representation" and "the forms and laws of the representation must be wholly foreign to it."[21] What this means, first of all, is that "this something about which we are inquiring" will not be subject to any version or aspect of the principle of sufficient reason (including even the subject-object division), hence it will not have temporal or spatial or causal properties (and it will not be either a knowing subject or a known object). What it means, secondly, is that "this something" cannot be discovered by applying to the world as representation as a whole the principle of sufficient reason as if "this something" were the ground (*Grund*) or the cause (*Ursache*) of the world as representation; in short, whatever relation may hold between the world as representation and, say, the world as "other than representation," it will not be a relation that conforms to or arises out of the principle of sufficient reason.[22]

Schopenhauer likens his philosophy to "a Thebes with 100 gates,"[23] meaning that its core can be approached by entering many different portals. In nonfigurative language this signifies that many different considerations lead up to the original metaphysical question, "What is the world besides representation?" Two considerations derive from representation theory, one from the account of perceptual knowledge and the other from an analysis of causal explanation of natural occurrences. (Both, it should be noted, concern causality.) Perception—the construction of objects out of sensation, which the understanding (allegedly) takes to be the effect of changes in the natural world—presupposes the existence of causal powers or natural forces inherent in objects; but no account of perception informs us as to the nature of these powers or forces, every one of which (somehow) lies beyond, yet appears in, the world as representation. In short, natural forces are not appearances, they are not representations, they are not perceptions; yet without them there would be no appearance, no representation, no perception. Consequently, if metaphysics is conceived as an inquiry into the nature of those natural forces required for perception—as it is in fact here conceived—then perception theory does lead into metaphysics at least as an area of inquiry. Now, assuming that natural forces constitute the inner nature of perceptual objects, and that this inner nature is what they are in themselves, then the inquiry into natural forces amounts to an inquiry into what perceptual objects are in themselves. And that inquiry, though suggesting nothing as yet about will, is metaphysical inquiry.

It is not perception, however, that Schopenhauer emphasizes as the topic leading directly into metaphysical inquiry; it is causal explanation of natural occurrences, which he finds incomplete and therefore in need of metaphysical elucidation. What he calls etiology offers causal explanations, informing us (on the everyday level) that, for instance, water boils when heated to a certain temperature and (on a more sophisticated level) that, for instance, bodies of certain sorts are attracted to each other at certain rates of speed. What is presupposed in the first explanation is the nature of water, and only given it do we have a causal explanation connecting the introduction of a certain degree of heat and the resultant boiling; with that same heat and a different "substance," say, mercury, there would be no boiling or at least no boiling at the same time. What is presupposed in the second causal explanation is, at bottom, the (apparently) universal force of gravity. In every case of causal explanation of natural occurrences, some state (of something) will be said to result causally in another state, yet what counts as the cause and what counts as the effect will depend necessarily on the nature of the "something" (the "substance") in question— or rather on the natural forces that it exhibits. But, insists Schopenhauer, those natural forces are left unexplained, unfathomed, hidden.

Appropriately, then, Schopenhauer often uses the Latin expression, *qualitae occultae* (or, in the singular, *qualitas occulta*), for natural forces (*Naturkräfte*; in the singular, *Naturkraft*). The term originated in the Scholastic or medieval period of philosophy, prior to the advent of "modern science," and it was applied to every type of thing that undergoes causal change. This excessive use of the term's application Schopenhauer recognizes and opposes,[24] noting that whenever natural forces have been reduced in number, some having been reduced to other (genuine) ones, "a real advance has been made."[25] But he never abandons the idea that there remain many, many separate and distinct natural forces, that is, forces that cannot be reduced to any other more "original" ones; and he never supposes that natural science (or "cosmology") will one day reduce all previously cited ones to one ultimate force.[26] A word or two will be said about this matter later in this chapter and also in chapter 6 (on the Platonic Ideas), but for the most part critical comments will focus on the internal inconsistency of Schopenhauer's own account of causality, causal explanation, and related issues. For the present we need to gain a better understanding of what, in Schopenhauer's view, the sciences can and cannot accomplish, and what they do and do not deal with. We return, first, to the notion (or notions) of content (*Inhalt* or *Gehalt*).

To the extent that the sciences can be assigned any content (*Inhalt*) at all, Schopenhauer claims, it is nothing more than "the relation of appearances of the world to one another according to the principle of sufficient reason, and on the guiding line of the Why, which has validity and meaning only through this principle."[27] So far as the natural sciences are concerned, the Why applies only to the occurrence of some change at a particular time and place, and the Because refers to the occurrence of a preceding change, with the entire process taking place only upon the presupposition of a natural force (whereby general laws of nature are arrived at). An example, taken from the second edition of *The Fourfold Root*, is this: "The attraction of the thread by the amber at this moment is the effect; its cause is the preceding friction and the present proximity of the amber, and the natural force, acting in and presiding over this process, is electricity."[28] No natural force is either a cause or an effect, but it is that without which there would be no cause and no effect—and, indeed, no causal explanation. On the other hand, explanations in the nonnatural sciences or even in "metascience" make no appeal to natural forces. Schopenhauer writes:

> Explanation [*Erklärung*] is the establishment of that relation [of appearances]. Therefore, explanation can never do more than show two representations standing to each other in the relation of that form of the principle of sufficient reason ruling in the class to which they belong. If it has achieved this, we cannot be further asked the question Why, for the relation demonstrated is that which simply cannot be represented differently, in other words, it is the form of all knowledge.[29]

Schopenhauer continues by claiming that we do not ask why the following fundamental propositional truths hold: in arithmetic, $2 + 2 = 4$; in geometry, the equality of the angles in a triangle determines the equality of the sides; in, say, physics (or metascience or formal natural science), any given cause is followed by its effect; and in logic, the truth of a conclusion is evident from the truth of the premises. These propositions exemplify the "roots" of the principle of sufficient reason; they simply express the ways in which "representations" (of various sorts) are related necessarily, that is, in conformity with that principle; hence, once they are arrived at, they cannot be "represented differently," which implies that there can be no further explanation demanded of them. (As we shall see in a moment, to demand an explanation of these propositional truths would be, in effect, to demand an explanation of the principle of all explanation, that is, the principle of sufficient reason itself, and that, Schopenhauer will insist, is—from the standpoint of science and of the world governed by that principle—nonsense. It is not nonsense, however, from the standpoint of philosophy or actually of metaphysics. But more on this later.)

After referring to the job of explanation in the sciences (namely, that of establishing "the relation of appearances of the world to one another") and after citing four typical examples for which we do not demand an explanation (namely, those noted in the previous paragraph) Schopenhauer writes: "Every explanation not leading back to such a relation of which no Why can further be demanded, stops at an accepted *qualitas occulta*; but this is also the character of every original force of nature."[30] Payne attaches a note to the word "not," in which he says that "Dr Arthur Hübscher of the Schopenhauer Society of Germany is of the opinion that 'not' should be deleted." Hübscher did not do so in his edition of Schopenhauer's works because the issue is not sufficiently clear, but he believes it to be an error made in haste by Schopenhauer (*wie sie öfter bei ihm vorkommen*); in the Diogenes edition (volume 1, p. 121), however, the term "not" has been deleted. But that is surely an error, and indeed an error of the greatest magnitude.

For what Schopenhauer is saying here is clear enough and essential to his thought: Every explanation that does *not* lead back to a relation exemplified in the principle of sufficient reason—which really means every explanation of natural (empirical) science—stops at an accepted *qualitas occulta*, which, if genuine, i.e., not reducible to any other, is an original natural force. More fully, every explanation (every answer to Why) has to end with something, either with a version of the principle of sufficient reason (as do the four propositions quoted above) or—while presupposing the causal version of that principle—with an original natural force (as do the empirically discovered fundamental propositions of natural science). Hence, indeed, as the continuation has it: "Every explanation of natural science must ultimately stop at such [a *qualitas occulta* or original natural force], and thus at something wholly obscure; it must therefore leave the inner nature [*Wesen*] of the stone just as unexplained as that of a human being; it can give as little account of the weight, cohesion, chemical properties, etc. of the former, as of the knowing and acting of the latter."[31] Every explanation of natural science, but not every explanation, must ultimately stop at an original natural force; those which do not simply lead up to and express in some fashion the principle of sufficient reason itself.

Incidentally, the next two sentences, which do not appear in the first edition of *The World as Will and Representation*, Payne translates as follows:

> Thus, for example, weight is a *qualitas occulta*, for it can be thought away, and hence it does not follow from the form of knowledge as something necessary. Again, this is the case with the law of inertia, which follows from the law of causality; hence a reference to this is a perfectly adequate explanation.[32]

But what Schopenhauer actually says, and means, is something very different. Gravity or weight, he claims, does not proceed from the form of knowing as something necessary; this, on the contrary (*hingegen*, i.e., unlike gravity), is the case with the law of inertia, which follows from the law of causality. Payne has overlooked the word *hingegen*, or rather he has translated it by "again" instead of (what it should be) "on the contrary" or "on the other hand."[33] I want to go into Schopenhauer's elucidation of what can be and what cannot be a *qualitas occulta* or original natural force because it supports conclusively my contention that "not" must be retained in the crucial sentence cited above.

Weight or gravity (*Schwere*) is a genuine *qualitas occulta*, Schopenhauer holds, whereas inertia (*Trägheit*)—he actually says "the law of inertia"—is not a *qualitas occulta*. Gravity is a *qualitas occulta* for the two required reasons: First, it is a force of nature that causal explanations of certain natural occurrences run up against and cannot explain further; and second, it can be "thought away," which means that it "does not proceed from the form of knowledge [i.e., the principle of sufficient reason] as something necessary." Inertia or the law of inertia is not a *qualitas occulta* because it cannot be "thought away"; it is logically entailed by the law of causality, indeed, it (like its partner, the law of the permanence of substance, i.e., matter)[34] is simply a corollary of the law of causality, which therefore gives it "a perfectly satisfactory explanation" (*eine vollkommen genügende Erklärung*). It follows that the law of inertia (just as the law of the permanence of matter) is, like its source (the law of causality), synthetic a priori; whereas the law of gravity is only synthetic a posteriori.[35] Thus the former is not, and the latter is, subject to empirical exceptions.

Now to wrap up the issue. The explanation of the law of inertia (every body continues at rest or in motion unless some cause intervenes)[36] amounts to showing that it follows logically from the principle of sufficient reason of becoming, that is, the principle of causality; hence, inertia is not a natural force but only, one may say, a corollary of causality that cannot be "thought away" any more than the law of causality can. Once this explanation—an explanation by, say, logical entailment—is provided, no further explanation of the law of inertia is possible and no demand for such is sensible. This does not contradict the fact that the principle or law of causality can be both "epistemologically explained" (namely, by demonstrating its universal validity to rest with the knowing subject's understanding, as Kant succeeded in doing) and "metaphysically clarified" (namely, by acknowledging its underlying basis as will, as Schopenhauer purports to do). The law of gravity cannot be explained by mere appeal to the principle of sufficient reason of becoming because it is not logically entailed by that principle; hence gravity, which many causal explanations lead to and presuppose without being able to explain, is a genuine natural force. So, indeed, whenever an explanation does *not* lead back to the sort of (logical) relation holding between inertia and causality, or rather between the law of inertia and the principle of causality, then that explanation does reach or presuppose some natural force—which holds for gravity. It follows, for Schopenhauer, that gravity requires immediately a metaphysical clarification (it must be a direct manifestation of will), while inertia receives immediately "a perfectly satisfactory explanation" of a nonmetaphysical sort (it is simply a logical entailment of causality, though then causality, like everything, needs finally a metaphysical clarification).

Schopenhauer really means it, then, when he says, "Every explanation not leading back to such a relation of which no Why can further be demanded [where "such a relation" refers to a logical entailment of the principle of sufficient reason] stops at an accepted *qualitas occulta*," that is, at an original natural force. Just consider what would be the case if "not" were lifted from the above sentence. Taken literally, every explanation leading back to a version of the principle of sufficient reason would stop at an original natural force; but this is nonsense, for then there would be no need for postulating natural forces. Consider then further what would be the case if there were no natural forces. Everything would be ultimately explainable by appeal to the principle of sufficient reason; everything would be exhaustively "form" and thus have no "content," which is to say that everything in the world would be fully explainable by reference to something else in the world (and arithmetic, in effect, would be "the holiest thing in the temple of wisdom");[37] the world would consist of nothing but relations or relational things, everyone of which would be explainable by deduction (after the manner of Spinoza); there would be no genuine natural forces, hence no Platonic Ideas, but only fleeting shadows on a cave wall connected by causal law; in sum, the world would be nothing in itself, but rather mere representation "not worth our consideration."[38] By no means then can the little word "not" be deleted from the aforecited sentence.[39]

As indicated above, Schopenhauer holds that causal explanation—the principal task of natural science—presupposes and thus leaves unexplained two things: the principle of sufficient reason of becoming, that is, the law of causality, and natural or original forces. More broadly still, explanation in all of the sciences is limited in two regards:

Two things are absolutely inexplicable, i.e., do not lead back to the relation expressed by the principle of sufficient reason: First, the principle of sufficient reason itself in all its four forms, because it is the principle of all explanation, which has meaning only in reference to it; and second, that which is not reached by it [i.e., by this principle], but from which arises that which is original in all appearances: it is the thing in itself, knowledge of which is by no means subject to the principle of sufficient reason.[40]

Schopenhauer notes that at this early point (section 15 of Book 1) he cannot go further into the thing in itself. But it is curious that he even mentions the thing in itself at this point at all; it is especially curious that he implies that explanations in mathematics and logic appeal to but leave unexplained the thing in itself. The fact of the matter is this: Although Schopenhauer wishes to say here something about explanation in all the sciences, hence in mathematics and logic as well as in the natural sciences (mechanics, physics, and chemistry), the "life sciences" (botany and zoology), even history, and no doubt the "human sciences" (which deal with motivation above all else), he really has in mind only causal (and motivational) explanation, hence only certain nonformal sciences. But even then he should not refer directly to the thing in itself, but only at most to natural forces, basic properties, and human characters. Explanations in what may be called the formal sciences rest entirely on the principle of sufficient reason (they deal with "form"); but explanations in the nonformal sciences depend on both the principle of sufficient reason *and* natural forces and the like (they involve both "form" and "content"). What Schopenhauer will argue later, of course, is that these forces are direct manifestations of the thing in itself, in other words, that they are "objectities of the will," so this must be the reason for mentioning the thing in itself at this early stage.

To state what Schopenhauer is really getting at, we must say this: Causal explanation of natural occurrences, which takes a change in the natural world to be the effect of a preceding change (called the cause), presupposes and thus leaves unexplained both the relevant natural force and the law of causality itself. Postponing for a moment comment on the difficulties and complications of this account, we want now to investigate how Schopenhauer proposes to pass from causal (or natural scientific) explanation to philosophical clarification. "*Philosophy*," he states, "has the peculiarity of presupposing absolutely nothing as known; everything to it is equally strange and a problem; not only the relations of phenomena [*Erscheinungen*], but also those phenomena themselves, and indeed the principle of sufficient reason itself, to which the other sciences are content to refer everything."[41] In other words, philosophy refuses to rest until the two "inexplicables" are finally clarified and rendered intelligible. Where natural science leaves off, Schopenhauer maintains, philosophy proper (metaphysics) takes its start—for which reason, incidentally, metaphysics, or at least a true metaphysics, will never interfere with or be refuted by the discoveries of natural science.[42]

Schopenhauer clarifies the law of causality—that version of the principle of sufficient reason operating in the natural world—by maintaining (with Kant) that it derives from the knowing subject: Changes in the natural world have to be effects of antecedent changes because the knowing subject can experience them in no other way. Since causality is a triadic, not just dyadic, relation, every explanation has to appeal to something beyond mere changes in the natural world: It has to appeal to that "third thing" in virtue of which one change (the effect) necessarily follows from a preceding one (the cause), that is to say, it has to appeal to a natural force. Only philosophy (as metaphysics) can clarify natural forces; and, according to Schopenhauer, natural forces—like the individual wills (intelligible characters) of human agents—manifest the will. A natural force is not a cause of a change in the natural world for the simple reason that it is not in time; and it is not the effect of the will because neither a natural force nor the will is in time; hence metaphysical clarification of that which natural science leaves unexplained will not employ any version of the principle of sufficient reason, and especially not that version that speaks of cause and effect.

It is argued in the preceding chapter that, according to Schopenhauer's account, perception can be understood only by appeal to "causal powers" in the object perceived, and that these "powers" can be clarified ultimately only by metaphysical considerations; in short, perception has to be understood as involving causality, and causality has to be understood as involving nonperceived, thus metaphysical, factors. In this chapter it has been pointed out that, according to Schopenhauer's account, causal explanation of natural occurrences—or, more strictly, of changes in the natural world—presupposes and thus leaves unexplained natural forces, the ultimate clarification of which is left then for metaphysics. (I have suggested that the "causal powers" involved in perception are in fact the "natural forces" involved in natural occurrences.) Thus we have located two portals, both from representation theory (specifically, from causality in two aspects of representation theory), that lead into the core of Schopenhauer's Thebes-like philosophy. It may then be said with reasonable certainty that Schopenhauer broaches the subject of metaphysical inquiry, and specifically, the issue of what the world is besides representation, by finding natural science inadequate to clarify natural forces—those mysterious *qualitae occultae* that natural science cannot do without, yet also cannot clarify. So the task of clarifying them is left to metaphysics.

It may be asked, however, whether natural science or, more broadly, causal explanation in general has to rely upon natural forces (as Schopenhauer conceives them). But this is not the question I shall try to answer, for to begin with I am not qualified to do so. I propose to examine instead one of Schopenhauer's few specific and detailed accounts of cause and effect for the purpose of determining whether and, if so, how any natural force is involved there. The account I have in mind occurs in *The Fourfold Root*, and it goes thus:

> Through it [i.e., the principle or law of causality] are mutually connected all the objects presenting themselves in the entire general representation, which constitutes the complex of the reality of experience, as regards the appearance and disappearance of their states [*Zustände*, conditions] and hence in the direction of the current of time. The principle is that, if a new state of one or more real objects appears, another state must have preceded it upon which the new state follows according to a rule [*regelmäßig*], i.e., every time the first exist. Such a result is called a consequence [*Ein solches Folgen heißt ein Erfolgen*]; the first state is called the *cause*, the second, the *effect*.[43]

So it is, properly speaking, the appearance and disappearance of the states of all objects making up the world as representation, and not the objects themselves, that are mutually connected "through" (*durch*) the principle of causality. And whenever a new state of "one or more real objects" comes about, at the same place in space where an old state had obtained or existed, the old or preceding state is the cause of the new, or newly appearing, state, which is the effect. Hence, apparently, the causal formula for this process is, "Whenever the preceding state S exists, then necessarily the subsequent state S' appears," according to which S is the cause of S' and S' is the effect of S. Schopenhauer continues thus:

> If, for example, a body ignites, then this state of burning must be preceded by a state (1) of affinity for oxygen, (2) of contact with the oxygen, and (3) of a definite temperature. As soon as this state was present, the ignition has to ensue [*erfolgen*] immediately, but it ensues only now. Thus also that state cannot have always been there, but must only now have appeared. This appearance [*Eintritt*] is called a change [*Veränderung*]. Therefore the law of causality is exclusively related to changes and it always has to do only with them.[44]

In this example the effect is the body's igniting (a state of burning), which comes about, say, at time t_0 (now), and the cause of this state is the complex state 1, 2, and 3, which came together for the first time here at time t_{-1} (just an instant before). Just before that, at time t_{-2}, at least one of the three causally contributing factors (presumably 3) was absent, else the ignition would have happened at time t_{-1} and not have waited until now, at t_0.[45]

Where, in this account (which derives from the dissertation of 1813, and which is retained in the second edition of *The Fourfold Root* in 1847), do we encounter any natural force? Nowhere. Is there then no "third thing" that connects the cause and the effect? Yes, there is, but in this account it is not a natural force (of, say, the body that ignites) but instead it is substance or matter—that ubiquitous, permanent, nonappearing and nondisappearing, noncausing and noncaused "substrate" whose states "enter" time and space in accordance with causal law. Here causality applies only to the appearing and disappearing states of matter, not to that which bears these states, matter itself and not to individual bodies or natural forces thereof. And causal explanation of a new state of matter consists of nothing but a description of the preceding state of matter (presumably, at this place in space). What will later be called the natural force of a specific body or the constitution (*Beschaffenheit*) of the particular thing that allegedly undergoes changes, whereby its constitution is made known,[46] is here, in this early account, incorporated into "the entire state" just preceding the new state of matter and thus made a part of "the entire cause."[47] In both the early account of causality, which I have just cited, and the later account, which occurs in *The World as Will and Representation* (even the first edition), causal explanation requires a "third thing"; but earlier it is absolutely permanent matter (and in fact causality takes on cosmic proportions) and later it is, chiefly, a natural force or the constitution of a particular, relatively persisting, but not permanent object or thing— whereby causality narrows considerably in scope. There is, furthermore, this difference: In the early account, causality involves only three factors (state of matter at t_{-1}, state of matter [now] at t_0, and matter itself) but in the later account, causality involves four factors—state of object O at t_{-1} (a lobster's being gray), state of object O at t_0 (its now being pinkish), contact with boiling water ("the cause" of the transition), and O's constitution or natural force (that "inner quality" that distinguishes O from many other objects).[48] Whenever a particular object completely perishes (ice ceases) and another "takes its place" (water appears), Schopenhauer typically reverts to the early account of causality, the cosmic account that has matter as the "third thing"—as indeed he must.

Why, we may then ask, does Schopenhauer so doggedly insist on natural forces or *qualitae occultae* in his later account of causality and of causal explanation?[49] There may be available to him, or to anyone for that matter, good philosophical reasons for doing so, but there are also good philosophical reasons for his abandoning the old Scholastic practice. Although he claims that natural forces give to causes their causality, that is, they provide causes with the capacity to produce effects (they give *Wirkungsfähigkeit* to *Wirken*),[50] the "cash value" of this claim may only be that whatever actually happens was potentially about to happen—and on a normal interpretation this assertion is a mere tautology ("That which was not, but now is, was potentially") and not a genuine philosophical proposition. (Schopenhauer does regard natural forces as "latent powers" just awaiting their chance to get manifested, to reveal themselves in appearance.) As we have seen, he also holds that objects simply are what they do (under various conditions); he urges this contention particularly in opposing realism and skepticism, as was noted in the previous chapter. If we hold of any given object that "its being is its acting," and if we submit it to hundreds of tests in order to determine how it acts, then we have pretty much exhausted its "being." We shall then say of it: "It is that which acts in manner M upon condition C, in manner N upon condition D, and on and on." But we shall not then add that it is some "that which" that lies hidden "in" or "behind" all of those sets of conditions and reactions; we shall not say that it is or has some inner "constitution" or "natural force" in addition to those sets of conditions and reactions. There is thus no need or legitimacy to speak of any "capacity" (*Wirkungsfähigkeit*), potentiality, "latent power," or the like. Why did Schopenhauer not fully adopt this line of thought (he does accept it in large measure) and dispense with natural forces altogether?

To put it another way, why did Schopenhauer not adopt a thoroughgoing "phenomenalism" (a thing is simply the sum of its qualities, actions, or reactions, without a "core," inner nature, or "natural force")? Is it because he thinks that natural science has to rely on natural forces? Young, in defending an affirmative answer, writes thus:

> Is it true that natural science is committed to forces? Schopenhauer's argument is simply that there cannot be laws without forces to ground them and here, surely, he is right. It is true that Hume denied that *anything* can be said to ground the regularities in nature . . . but then *Hume's* business was to be skeptical about the rationality of science. The scientist, on the other hand, committed to the rationality of his enterprise, to the rationality, in particular, of projecting past regularities into the future, must assume some feature of reality to ground these regularities, to make them, in other words, *laws* rather than *mere* regularities.[51]

Many things could be said about this analysis and Young's subsequent argument (which certainly should be examined), including these: Scientists today talk more about models than about either laws or regularities; there may be no significant distinction between laws and, say, generalities in (modern) science; there may be no one enterprise going by the name "science" and no one homogeneous group going by the name "scientists"; and so on. And although Young may have discerned Schopenhauer's argument for retaining natural forces from the standpoint of (his view of) the science of his times, I am pretty confident that Schopenhauer retains natural forces for quite different reasons.

Beyond the fact (which really impressed Schopenhauer) that, for example, after three thousand years a dry seed can germinate and produce the sort of plant from which it came,[52] which does seem to point to an undeniable "vital force" (a cousin of the natural forces of physics, chemistry, etc.), Schopenhauer holds on to the doctrine of natural forces for two chief reasons: One, they are identical with, or at least closely aligned to, the Platonic Ideas—so, in Schopenhauer's mind, to give up the forces would compel one to give up the Ideas (horror of horrors! he would think); and two, the supposed forces in nature are parallel to the intelligible characters in human beings—and if the former were dropped, then there would be strong grounds for dropping intelligible characters (again, catastrophe!). Reserving the first point for later discussion (see chapter 6), I want to develop here the second point briefly.

The issue, in general terms, concerns moral freedom. Schopenhauer supposes, I suggest, that if natural forces were denied to natural bodies, if causal explanation of changes in natural bodies made no appeal to forces, and if those bodies were simply and solely what they do (yielding a sort of "reductive phenomenalism"), then parallel propositions would have to be made about human agents. The results would then be: Human agents have no intelligible character; motivational explanation would be restricted to motives and actions; and human agents would be exhaustively what they do ("human phenomenalism," as one might call it, would obtain). In other words, the human character would be only empirical with no intelligible aspect, every action would be fully explainable by the principle of sufficient reason of acting or willing (that is, by the law of motivation), and absolute fatalism would reign.[53] There would be no moral freedom, no responsibility, no escape from egoism (hence no possibility of compassion, *Mitleid*), in short, no "ethical significance" anywhere in the world. If we deny natural forces to bodies in nature, then we deny intelligible characters to human beings—so, I think, Schopenhauer supposes. In this connection, it is to be remembered that Schopenhauer typically characterizes natural forces as parallel to intelligible characters, and in fact elucidates them in no other way,[54] and that he regards Kant's distinction between the empirical and intelligible characters as "among the most admirable things ever said by man."[55] Actually, I think, Schopenhauer adopted the doctrine of the (Platonic) Ideas and the notion of the intelligible character prior to his acceptance of natural forces.

Suppose we were to conclude that Schopenhauer errs in thinking that the explanatory mode of natural science requires the supposition of natural forces; suppose we agreed, in other words, that Schopenhauer has no real justification for introducing the notion of natural forces (at least as he conceives of them) on the basis of the (alleged) incompleteness of causal explanation. Would there then be no route from natural science to metaphysics? No, for Thebes has 100 gates; so even if one or two are closed, many remain open—not only those pertinent to special phenomena that cannot be clarified by empirical means (a prime example being compassion, *Mitleid*), but the huge gate pertinent to the world as representation as a whole.

Schopenhauer believes (reasonably enough, it seems) that every particular representation is relative to some further representation, or to several further representations. "Everything is dependent on something else for its very existence"—to state in a succinct formula the principle of sufficient reason, the principle that governs the world as representation. Hence dependency and relativity mark the fundamental characteristic of all possible objects of experience and all kinds of representations studied by the various sciences. Logic deals with judgments, which are based on other judgments; mathematics deals with numbers and figures, which are what they are only in relation to other numbers and figures; the "human sciences" deal with actions, all of which depend on motives; and natural science studies empirical objects, whose states are causally connected to other states. Every object of inquiry in the sciences, and indeed every object of normal human knowledge, depends for its existence and its nature on something else. To say this is simply to repeat the part of the principle of sufficient reason that states

> all our representations stand to one another in a natural and regular connection that in form is determinable a priori. By virtue of this connection nothing existing by itself and independent, and also nothing single and detached, can become an object for us. It is this connection that is expressed by the principle of sufficient reason in its universality.[56]

Not only is every knowable representation or object relative to some other representation or object, but, according to Schopenhauer, additional forms of relativity (dependence, contingency) arise. It turns out that the notion of relativity (dependency, contingency) occurs on three levels, the last of which impels us to engage in metaphysical inquiry.

First, every particular representation or object is relative to, conditioned by, and dependent on some other representation or object. This is a logical consequence of the principle of sufficient reason (as stated in the passage just quoted), and it enunciates the mode of explanation provided by mathematics (which only compares one representation with another) and natural science (which only points out how one representation stands to another). (Recall the passage concerning the company of people one encounters, each one of whom is known only as the friend or cousin of another.) Second, the entire series of representations, thus the whole empirical world of objects, is relative to the knowing subject. This proposition simply restates the (idealistic) principle of all knowing, as expressed by "No object without subject" or "The world is representation." To call the world representation is, in effect, to relegate it to relativity; it is to make it dependent on something, which means (in Kant's idiom) that the world is not the thing in itself, which means (in Scholastic language) that the world lacks aseity (i.e., being in and for itself, or unconditioned being) and which means (for Schopenhauer) that the world lacks "content" or "meaning." Having established that the world is representation for the subject, one could direct the inquiry into, say, the unconditioned by concluding that the knowing subject is the ultimate item of existence, that is, that the subject (the ego, *das Ich*) is the thing in itself upon which everything depends while it itself depends on nothing else (Fichte's view). Although Schopenhauer grants, of course, that the objective world is dependent on the knowing subject, he argues (contra Fichte) that the subject is also dependent on objects: "No subject without object." Hence he refuses to regard the knowing subject (the ego as knower) as the thing in itself.

Through an examination of the world subject to the principle of sufficient reason, we have learned that it consists of two relata—known objects and the knowing subject. We have also discovered that they are mutually related, so that in fact the world (of representational knowledge) is a correlative world of subject and object, that is to say, neither exists on its own and each exists only in relation to the other. The conclusion then might be, as the dissertation of 1813 strongly suggests, this: There is no thing in itself, no unconditioned (noncontingent, "absolute," independent) being. But, as we know, Schopenhauer does not draw this conclusion; in fact, from the premises just cited, he concludes that there has to be something in itself.

He reasons, I think, as follows. Just as every particular representation exists only in relation to some other representation, and just as the entire series of representations exists only in relation to the knowing subject (which in turn exists only in relation to representations), so the world *as* representation—construed now as the whole subject-object correlation— exists only in relation to something nonrelational, i.e., to the thing in itself. Notice, as mentioned in the previous chapter, the switch from the world *of* representations, whose relatum would simply be the knowing subject, to the world *as* representation, i.e., the world as subject-object correlation, which has no relatum—except for something beyond all representation, thus except for (in a word) the thing in itself. The overall conviction has to be that for any set of mutual relata there must be some nonrelative foundation; so the metaphysical question here goes thus: What does the whole world as mutually dependent representational elements have as its ultimately nondependent basis? Putting Schopenhauer's apparent argument for the necessity of metaphysical inquiry, and in fact for the necessity of presupposing the thing in itself, into a sort of logical form, we get this: From the fact that O exists only in relation to S, and S exists only in relation to O (i.e., O and S are correlative), it follows that the O-S correlation is relative to something further, and finally to something nonrelative. The argument, however, is not valid: Affirming the O-S correlation and denying a relatum for it (especially, a nonrelative relatum for it) does not constitute a self-contradiction. Just because every representation presupposes another representation, and just because the world of representations presupposes the knowing subject (which in turn presupposes the world of representations), it does not logically follow that the world as representation—that is, the whole subject-object correlation—presupposes something else.[57]

But consider this. Every appearance (*jede Erscheinung*) is related to some other appearance, and every appearance presupposes that to which it appears, hence every appearance is doubly relative, and that to which appearances appear is also relative. Now if we proceed to call the entire series of appearances (*die ganze Reihe von Erscheinungen*) "the appearance" (*die Erscheinung*), as if it were one thing, then we shall be inclined to demand a relatum for it, just as we demanded a relatum for every particular appearance; and if we continue by insisting that that to which "the appearance" appears, i.e., the knowing subject, is just as relative as "the appearance" itself, and then unite the two into a new "appearance," then—recalling the dictum that appearance presupposes something more—we shall conclude that the whole world as appearance demands something more. This, I suspect, is the process of thought present in Schopenhauer's mind. But what is true of a single appearance is not necessarily true of the series of appearances, and what is true of the series of appearances is not necessarily true of the relation between that series and that to which it appears. In Schopenhauer the word "appearance" is applied to three very different things: an individual object, the infinite series of objects, and the subject-object knowing correlation. Now, from the fact that the first appearance is relative, indeed, doubly relative, and that the second appearance is relative (to the subject), it does not follow that the third appearance is relative at all. Kant makes the entire series of appearances relative, saying that "the sensory world" does not subsist for itself, hence it is not, but needs, the thing in itself.[58]

Schopenhauer allows the Fichtean point that this series is relative to the knowing subject, but then he makes this correlation "the representation" or "the appearance" and draws the conclusion that it needs the thing in it-self.[59] In the briefest possible manner, his thought is this: A set of relata is a relatum of something, and indeed finally of something nonrelative. His apparent argument for this thought is invalid, but the thought neverthe-less might be true. More likely, I suggest, it might be taken to be true by metaphysically inclined individuals, that is, by individuals who cannot be-lieve that "life and the world" is merely a cognitive matter (as cognition is characterized by the sciences). It will turn out, I suggest further, that, for Schopenhauer, metaphysics is not actually an inquiry into the "something else" of representations, but an inquiry into what the world as representa-tion is—with no reference to anything beyond the world. Schopenhauer has saddled himself so much with Kant's terminology that he cannot ac-curately state his own unique brand of metaphysics. He should have es-chewed all talk of the thing in itself, at least as that to which "the appear-ance" stands in a (properly understood) *relation.*

Nevertheless, Schopenhauer persists in characterizing metaphysics as, at least in large part, the inquiry into the thing in itself. He never ceases to praise Kant's distinction of appearance (*Erscheinung,* phenomenon) from the thing in itself, calling it "Kant's greatest merit."[60] He even suggests that discovering the nature of the thing in itself, in place of leaving it unknow-able, is that which modern philosophy has long set as its central task. These facts alone, to say nothing of numerous passages throughout Schopen-hauer's works, lend support to the understandable (but, I think, dubious) interpretation that Schopenhauer's chief entry into metaphysics is the path of discovering not that to which *the appearance* is ultimately related and on which it is finally based, but that which is the inner nature of *indi-vidual appearances* (or perceptual objects). In his "Criticism of the Kantian Philosophy," the appendix to *The World as Will and Representation,* volume 1, Schopenhauer remarks that Kant was led to distinguish appearance from the thing in itself by developing a distinction made by John Locke. "The latter had shown," Schopenhauer writes, "that the secondary quali-ties of things, such as sound, odor, color, hardness, softness, smoothness, and the like, founded on the affections of the senses, do not belong to the objective body [*objektiver Körper*], the thing in itself."[61] They belong to, or actually exist only in, the perceiver. Locke supposed, however, that certain qualities inhere in individual things themselves, for example, such quali-ties as extension, shape, solidity, number, and mobility; and these qualities Locke called "primary," believing them to be qualities of the thing in itself. What Kant showed is that so-called primary qualities—all of which are based on space, time, and causality—derive from, and belong to, the per-ceiver, no less than the secondary qualities do. So what then is left of the object, of the thing in itself? Nothing that we can ever know, Kant concluded, but there must be something—hence the doctrine of the unknowable thing in itself, the unknown *x* that, as it were, "effects" qualities in the perceiver but which itself is not a quality.[62]

According to this overall picture, evidence for which can be found in many passages,[63] Schopenhauer purports to solve the central problem of modern philosophy by giving a name to Kant's unknown *x*, and that name is will (the reality we all find ourselves to be in self-consciousness). This interpretation derives from an examination of modern philosophy's concern with the so-called real dimension of perceptual objects, that is, that which remains of perceptual objects once all their "ideal" or mind-dependent qualities have been removed. Thus Schopenhauer fits neatly into the mainstream of epistemology and metaphysics that has dominated the philosophical tradition from Descartes to Kant. Schopenhauer's contribution to modern philosophy may then be summarized in these three sentences: He accepted Kant's notion of the thing in itself; he denied Kant's claim that it is unknowable; he asserted that it is will. But this, I fear, is overly neat.

I doubt that Schopenhauer was initially led into metaphysics (understood as the inquiry into *what* the world is) by seeking to denominate, that is, give a name to, the unknown *x* of perceptual objects, otherwise known (or unknown) as the thing in itself. To begin with, perceptual objects or intuitive representations do not hide, conceal, or disguise anything about themselves: They are objects for the subject, they are representations of the representer, indeed, they are constructs of the representing subject out of the data of sense—nothing more, nothing less. They are exactly what they reveal themselves to be, they are exactly what the knowing subject makes them be, thus of perceptual objects there is no unknown *x*—indeed, the very idea is preposterous. To assume the unknown *x* would be to suppose that perceptual objects in themselves may differ from perceptual objects, and that supposition Schopenhauer has ridiculed many, many times.

Secondly, only in works written long after the original publication of *The World as Will and Representation* (1818) does Schopenhauer portray an approach to metaphysics as the search for the unknown *x*, that is, for "the objective body" once its entire set of qualities have been removed from it and transferred to the perceiving subject. Those passages in the appendix to *The World as Will and Representation*, volume 1, where Schopenhauer traces Kant's distinction of appearance from the thing in itself back into the earlier periods of modern philosophy, were—as pointed out in endnote 61— all added after the first edition. In the first edition he says nothing about Descartes with regard to Kant's distinction, and he says nothing about Locke with regard to primary and secondary qualities.[64] There is no mention at all of an unknown x, certainly not of an x that is the perceptual object set off from its qualities. In later works, I suggest, Schopenhauer was trying to bring his own thought into line with the modern tradition, particularly into line with Kant's thought about the thing in itself as the unknown x. To be sure, by 1818 and even earlier (as shown in *Nachlaß*, volume 1) Schopenhauer refers again and again to the thing in itself, frequently noting that Kant took it to be unknowable, but he applies this notion to the one inner essence of the world as appearance, not to the unknown x of any single perceptual object—and not even, I would add, to the ground of the whole world as appearance as its ultimate relatum, at least when "relatum" or "relation" is properly understood.

Earlier I reported Schopenhauer's comment that if the world were nothing but representation "it would inevitably pass by us like an empty dream, or a ghostly vision not worth our consideration,"[65] and I raised the question, "What does Schopenhauer find so unsatisfactory about the world as representation?" To ask this question is not exactly the same as asking, "What does causal explanation leave unexplained?"—but the two questions, at least in Schopenhauer's mind, ultimately run together. In addition to the principle of causality itself, causal explanations leave unexplained natural forces; and this fact provides a clue as to the unsatisfactoriness of the world as representation. For a key feature of natural forces is their invariableness, in virtue of which alone laws of nature can be explained.[66] A key feature of representations, on the other hand, is their variableness, which accounts for Schopenhauer's reference to them as pictures or images (*Bilder*) passing by us in a meaningless fashion. They come and go, they appear and disappear, they arise and vanish—and because of this, above all else, they are strange, uninformative, and meaningless. What is unsatisfactory about the world as representation is therefore its mutability, its constant change, its movement, and even the death of its every member. And the only thing that can dispel the unsatisfactoriness of the world as representation is something that does not change.

On this note we return to Schopenhauer's acknowledged predecessors: Kant, Plato, and "ancient Indian wisdom." Immediately after praising "Kant's greatest merit"—the distinction of appearance from the thing in itself—Schopenhauer does not, in the first edition of *The World as Will and Representation*, go into a long discussion of modern philosophy's concern with the perceptual object once all its mind-conditioned qualities have been removed. (As mentioned above, this he does only in later writings.) What he does do is something very different: He claims that Kant's distinction amounts to a new way of stating "the same truth" that Plato affirms, namely, "This world that appears to the senses has no true being, but only a ceaseless becoming; it is, and it also is not; and its comprehension is not so much a knowledge as an illusion."[67] Then Schopenhauer alludes, as he has before,[68] to Plato's simile of the cave:

> Men, firmly chained in a dark cave, see neither the genuine original light nor actual things, but only the inadequate light of the fire in the cave, and the shadows of actual things passing by the fire behind their backs. Yet they suppose that the shadows are the reality, and that determining the succession of these shadows is true wisdom.[69]

They are mistaken, of course, just as they are who take the work of Maya (in the *Vedas* and *Puranas*) to be reality. And we who take representations to be reality are equally mistaken.

Very earlier on, as far back as 1814, Schopenhauer entertains the thought that the world subject to the principle of sufficient reason—that is, "the world" of the dissertation of 1813—consists only of finite, temporally determined, and thus relatively unreal objects. He even says that "the principle of sufficient reason is nothing but the finiteness, or rather emptiness, of all objects," to which he then adds: "By virtue of that finiteness every object has only an apparent existence, like a shadow we cannot grasp, for every object exists only to the extent that its nonexistence still lies in the future and not in the present, but with the infinity of time this is immaterial."[70] Somewhat later, but still in 1814, he arrives at this thesis:

> *Plato's* doctrine that no visible and palpable things, but only the *Ideas*, the external forms, *really exist*, is only another expression of *Kant's* doctrine that *time* and *space* do not appertain to *things in themselves*, but are merely the form of my intuition.[71]

He seems very pleased with this discovery, noting that many philosophical critics make a point of emphasizing how fundamentally Plato and Kant differ, not only in ethics but also in metaphysics. Schopenhauer, however, will directly oppose this interpretive judgment, indeed he remarks: "The identity of these two great and obscure doctrines is an infinitely fruitful thought, which is to become a mainstay of my philosophy." In his exuberance he goes so far as to assert that "Kant's thing in itself is nothing but the Platonic Idea."

Throughout 1814 Schopenhauer jots down several comments on the will "in us," remarking once that "*the body* (corporeal man) *is nothing but the will that has become visible* (or object)."[72] Not surprisingly, then, he tends to identify not only the thing in itself and the Idea but also the will. In one passage he writes that "the will is the Idea,"[73] but later he amends this claim: "This is incorrect; the adequate objectity of the will is the Idea, but the phenomenon [*Erscheinung*] is the Idea that has entered into the *principium individuationis* [i.e., into time and space]. The will itself is Kant's thing in itself."[74] Somewhat later, though probably still in 1814, Schopenhauer discusses the movement of clouds, the changing forms of a brook, and the crystallization of ice on a window pane—all being "the feeblest echo of that will which appears and objectifies itself more completely in the plant, still more completely in the animal, and most completely in man"—finally summarizing his considered position thus:

> We . . . have to distinguish three things: (1) the will to life itself, (2) its perfect objectity which are the (Platonic) Ideas, and (3) the appearance of these Ideas in the form whose expression is the principle of sufficient reason, i.e., the actual world, Kant's phenomenon, the *Maya* of the Indians.[75]

Therewith we have the philosophical system that Schopenhauer was never substantially to alter.

But to get at the root of what I have called "Schopenhauer's dissatisfaction with the world as representation," we have to return to the years of 1812 to 1814 and consider his "philosophy of the better consciousness."[76] The human consciousness, Schopenhauer supposes, has a choice between two forms: the empirical (temporal) or the better (free, even atemporal). From the empirical consciousness, nothing of genuine value can be discovered: no true knowledge, no real virtue, no pure aesthetic contemplation. The world of the empirical (temporal) consciousness is the world of chance, error, and folly, the world of wickedness and sin, the world of sham "art" and philistinism.

> How . . . can this surprise us, for indeed this very world (i.e., our empirical, sensuous world of the understanding in space and time) has its origination only through that which, according to the utterance of our better consciousness, ought not to be, but is the wrong direction from which virtue and asceticism are the return journey and, in consequence of this, a peaceful death is the release (like that of ripe fruit from the tree and Plato, in the *Phaedo*, therefore calls the entire life of the sage a long dying, i.e., a breaking away from such a world)?[77]

Referring back to this paragraph, Schopenhauer writes a bit later:

> On a previous sheet I have explained why this world is bound to be so full of misery, conflict with itself, error, folly, and wickedness, because it exists through that which ought not to be. For this very reason, the *understanding*, as also being conditioned by that which ought not to be, namely, temporality, can *never* know the true nature of things.[78]

At this stage in his thought, Schopenhauer regards temporality specifically as that which "ought not to be," and he believes the temporal consciousness as that which ought not to be chosen.

It is the temporal consciousness that makes us finite (and death the most dreadful thing imaginable), that makes us self-centered (and real virtue unthinkable), and that makes us subjective or personal (and aesthetic contemplation impossible). How there can be a transformation from the temporal (empirical, "subjective") consciousness to the "better" (free, "objective") consciousness cannot be characterized in positive, discursive language, for all such language belongs necessarily to the empirical world and the empirical consciousness.[79] But Schopenhauer makes an effort to clarify such a transformation in the field of art, particularly regarding still-life paintings and architecture (which, note, do not suggest change):

> My explanation is perfectly applicable also to these, when it is borne in mind that, if our temporal consciousness completely dominates us and we are in this way abandoned to desires and thus gravitate toward vice (i.e., negation of the better consciousness), our entire nature is subjective, that is to say, we see in things nothing but their relation to our individuality and its needs. But on the other hand, as soon as we *objectively consider*, i.e., *contemplate*, the things of the world, then for the moment *subjectivity* and thus the source of all misery has vanished. We are free and the consciousness of the sensory world stands before us as something foreign that no longer bears us down. Also we are no longer involved in considering the nexus of space, time, and causality (useful for our individuality), but see the Platonic Idea of the object. . . . This liberation from the temporal consciousness leaves the better, eternal consciousness behind. . . . Therefore the *purely objective contemplation of any object* (only not of the ugly or the disgusting) results in this stirring of the better consciousness, but in particular this results from a contemplation of vegetable or inorganic nature (landscape), of the human form, and of architecture. This happens because these objects have the quality of drawing our attention to them, and thus of drawing us from the subjective into the objective mood. That they have this is due to the fact that the eternal forms of nature are based on a necessity that is impenetrable to our understanding but yet in some mysterious association with our innermost being, which may well lie beyond all explanation.[80]

Perhaps no positive account of the better consciousness and aesthetic contemplation can be given, as Schopenhauer has claimed, but it is at least clear that what appears to consciousness (whether individual, temporally, spatially and causally determined things or the eternal Ideas of those things) depends entirely on the form of consciousness (empirical in the former case and "better" in the latter) that one adopts.

What prompts Schopenhauer's dissatisfaction with the world as representation and what, equally, induces him to characterize objects subject to the principle of sufficient reason as unreal (as mere "pictures," ceaselessly flitting before us like shadows of a flame or clouds) can probably be described only by reciting his entire philosophy, ranging from his views on death, objectivity, freedom, virtue, renunciation of the (subjective) will, aesthetics, and so on. But I venture this short summary: That which comes and goes, appears and disappears, originates and perishes, stands in a necessary relation to an individual knower and willer, whose total existence is subject to the vicissitudes of life, to suffering and misery, to vanity and worthlessness (such that, as one form of pessimism has it, nonexistence would be preferable to existence); consequently, and all in all, the world as appearance is humanly unsatisfactory, and something other than it (say, its "content" or "meaning") must be sought—the search for which is metaphysics.

FOUR

From the Body to the Will

It would not be an exaggeration to dub Schopenhauer *the* philosopher of the body. To a greater extent than anyone before his time, and even since then, he makes the body—that is, one's own body (*der eigene Leib*)—the primary focus and indispensable condition of all philosophical inquiry.[1] If required to give a single answer to the philosophizing subject's question, "What am I?" Schopenhauer would surely reply, "I am body," though, he would just as surely add, "in more than one way." He therefore deposes the mind from the throne of philosophical investigation and installs in its place—the place the mind has occupied since at least the time of Descartes—the body, which plays the crucial role in theory of knowledge (both as the sensation-locus from which perception originates and as the brain whose counterpart is the intellect or the understanding), in ethics (as that which must be surpassed for moral virtue), and in metaphysics proper (as the key for penetrating the "essence" of the world). Amplifying this last point, which is a fundamental issue of the present chapter, it is only because one is body that access to the "meaning" ("essence," "content") of the world as perceptual representation can be gained.

On this very note, Schopenhauer commences the most important section of *The World as Will and Representation*, section 18 of Book 2. He writes: "In fact, the meaning that I am looking for of the world that stands before me simply as my representation, or the transition from it as mere representation of the knowing subject to whatever it may be besides this, could never be found if the investigator himself [that is, I myself] were nothing more than the purely knowing subject (a winged cherub without a body)."[2] But this investigator—the seeker of the "meaning" or the "something else" of the world as representation—is not a purely knowing subject; fortunately, he is "rooted in" that world, and as such he finds himself in it "as an *individual.*" Schopenhauer expands on this remark by asserting that "his knowledge, which is the conditioning bearer of the whole world as representation, is nevertheless conveyed entirely through a body, whose affections, as shown [in Book 1], are for the understanding the starting point of the perception of that world." The affections referred to here are sensations, that is, felt or sensed bodily changes that the understanding takes to be effects of changes in the external, natural world and out of which the understanding constructs external, natural objects. (Exactly what the understanding does with sensations—does it regard them as effects of perceptual objects, or does it use them to construct perceptual objects?— has been discussed in chapter 2, so it need not be considered here.) The chief point here is that the knowing subject is not a mind wholly separated from body, as Descartes seems to have held, but (let us say for the moment) an embodied mind; this amounts to a flat rejection of mind-body dualism.

Although Schopenhauer says that the *meaning* of the perceptual world could not be "found" unless one were oneself "rooted in" that world— hence unless one were an individual (in time and space, subject to causality), and, further, unless one's knowledge of the world were conveyed through a body susceptible to changes experienced as sensations—he should say (for he certainly believes) that the perceptual world could not be known at all, indeed, that it would not exist as the perceptual world unless these bodily conditions obtained. The knowing subject must be embodied, first of all, if sensations, from which perception arises, are to occur, but, and this is the point stressed, it must also be embodied, if the meaning of the perceptual world is to be "found." For the latter project, Schopenhauer probably wants to insist, the body must be something more than the mere conduit through which, in virtue of its affections (sensations), the perceptual world exists and is known. In other words: If the body were merely the locus of sensations—out of which the understanding constructs the perceptual world and thereby makes it a known world— then the philosophical subject, whose body this is, would have no conceivable reason for believing that the perceptual world has a meaning, to say nothing of "finding" its meaning to be will (or, for that matter, anything else). The body of the philosophical subject must be something more than sensation-locus, and in fact it must be known as something more, if, in short, metaphysical inquiry is to proceed. But the question is: What more?

The import of this question can be clearly recognized by considering the general argument that Schopenhauer proposes, or seems to propose, in his effort to establish that, in short, "the world is will." The argument goes thus: "I know my body in two ways, as representation and as will; I know outer bodies in only one way, as representation; but I may infer (or somehow conclude) that outer bodies are also will." If this really is Schopenhauer's argument (about which there can be doubt), then one thing may be said for certain, namely, that it has no plausibility at all unless I know my body as representation in the very same way that I know outer bodies as representation, and that my body known as representation must be exactly the same sort of representation as those outer bodies known as representation. If, for instance, I knew my body as representation in a nonperceptual manner and thus my body were for me a nonperceptual sort of representation, and I knew outer bodies solely in a perceptual manner and thus outer bodies were for me only perceptual representations, then the whole argument would break down. Whether it does or not depends equally, I suspect, on the conception of the knowing "I" in the two cases, which is to say: The "I" that knows my body as representation must be the very same "I"—or at least the very same kind of "I"—that knows outer bodies as representation. We cannot have, in one case, the purely knowing subject and, in the other case, the individual or embodied knowing subject; otherwise the proferred argument will not be valid. Finally, the will that I allegedly know my own body as, must be the same sort of will that is subsequently attributed to outer bodies: Will in me cannot be of, say, kind A and will in outer bodies of kind B—not at least if the argument is to conform to strict rigor. These are the issues that I shall critically discuss in this chapter. Along the way, I shall recite—and try to clarify—Schopenhauer's sequence of thought early in Book 2 of *The World as Will and Representation*.

After remarking that "the investigator" is not a purely knowing, bodiless subject but an individual, embodied knowing subject, and that "this body" undergoes affections (sensations) on which perception is based, Schopenhauer continues with this curious statement: "For the purely knowing subject as such, this body is a representation like any other, an object among objects."[3] What he is getting at is this: If the investigator were what he or she is not, namely, a purely knowing subject, then "this body" would be what it is not, namely, "a representation like any other, an object among objects," and that is to say that it would be an indirect or mediate object (constructed by the understanding out of sensations and placed in the temporal, spatial, and causal nexus). In the previous sentence "this body" refers to the body as undergoing sensations rather than to the body as constructed out of sensations, hence it refers to the body as (apparently) the "immediate object" rather than to the body as a "mediate object." My body is for me a mediate or indirect object only when I know it through the senses and thus perceive it, for example, when I touch, look at, smell, hear, and perhaps even taste it or a portion of it. Perceiving my own body as a mediate object requires the immediate object as source of sensations, but what I represent and perceive is the former and not the latter. And this is perfectly possible: My body, or at least the body, can be for me a mediate object.[4] When this occurs, I am the purely knowing subject and the body is for me indeed "a representation like any other, an object among objects." As the immediate object, on the other hand, the body is not a representation or an object in the same sense that all outer bodies are; in fact, as such, the body is not really, or strictly speaking, an object at all.[5] Every outer object, however, is a genuine object, that is, a mediate object, or, equally, a normal representation, and only as such can it be known by me—in which case I am a purely knowing subject at least with regard to it.

Now, and this points up a serious problem with the aforecited argument, if there is to be a true parallel between knowledge of this body and knowledge of outer bodies or objects, then both sorts of knowledge have to be mediate or indirect, and both things known have to be mediate or indirect, that is, normal perceptual objects or intuitive representations (*anschauliche Vorstellungen*). But then, this body (conceived as truly "a representation like any other, an object among objects") cannot be known any more "intimately" than any other mediate object; it remains for its knowing subject (which is, as noted, the purely knowing subject) just as mysterious and alien as any mediate object. Hence knowledge of it can give no clue to the meaning (essence, content) of the world of nature. As a matter of fact, Schopenhauer fully recognizes this fact (though he believes he can find a way of circumventing the difficulty). Speaking directly of the body as mediate object, he writes:

> Its movements, actions are so far known by it [*ihm*, i.e., to the purely knowing subject] in just the same way as the changes in all perceptual objects, and they would be for it [*ihm*] equally strange and incomprehensible if their meaning were not unravelled for it [*ihm*] in an entirely different way. Otherwise, he [*er!*] would see his conduct [*sein Handeln*] follow on presented motives with the constancy of a law of nature, just as the changes of other objects follow upon causes, stimuli, and motives. But he would no more precisely understand the influence of the motives than the connection of any other effect appearing before him with its cause. He would then also call the inner, to him incomprehensible, essence of those manifestations and actions of his [!] body a force [*Kraft*], a quality, or a character, just as he pleased, but he would have no further insight into it.[6]

This passage starts out with the purely knowing subject (*das rein erkennende Subjekt*) and this body (*dieser Leib*), which were just referred to in the previous sentence, but it proceeds (perhaps as early as the second half of the first sentence and certainly in the second sentence) to the investigator (*der Forscher*) and his body (*sein Leib*) and either his or his body's conduct (*sein Handeln*).[7] But, at this point, the subject is supposed to be the purely knowing subject and the body is supposed to be this body as a mediate (perceptual) object, hence the masculine pronoun should not be used and, more importantly, no mention should be made of *his* body or *his* conduct. Whatever body and whatever conduct the purely knowing subject knows must be alien, as outer bodies or objects and changes in those objects are, hence they must not be regarded as *his* or even *its*: They are certainly not the body or conduct of the purely knowing subject, for this subject—which only looks into but does not inhabit the world of bodies and conduct or changes—has no body and carries out no conduct. Moreover, the purely knowing subject does not wonder about the meaning of anything; only the investigator does.

What then is the significance of Schopenhauer's shift from the (neutral) purely knowing subject and this body to the (masculine) investigator and his body? I suspect this: It allows Schopenhauer to persuade the reader, without benefit of argument or defense, that one and the same body is intimately tied to and yet an object of one and the same knowing subject. Consequently, it may be said that the knowing subject has a twofold knowledge of the body, vaguely put as knowledge of it both as representation (like every outer object) and as will (unlike any outer object). And from that, Schopenhauer claims, it is perfectly reasonable to transfer this knowledge to other bodies, that is, outer objects, and thereby to hold that they are not only representations but also will. I shall argue that this line of thought should not persuade the reader, but for now I want to continue with a close analysis of the text.

After stating the propositions that would be true if the investigator of the sought-for meaning were a purely knowing subject—basically, that the investigator would have no insight into his own conduct—Schopenhauer continues thus:

> All this, however, is not the case; on the contrary, the answer to the riddle is given to the subject of knowing appearing as an individual, and this answer [*Wort*] is *will*. This, and this alone, gives him the key to his own appearance, reveals to him the meaning, shows him the inner mechanism [*das innere Getriebe*] of his essence, of his doing, of his movements.[8]

Insofar as there is an argument, it may be summarized in this manner: If the investigator of the meaning of the world as representation were a purely knowing subject and, accordingly, the body (*Leib*) were a perceptual object like every other perceptual object, then he would find (say) the movements of the body just as mysterious as the changes in other bodies (*Körper*); but it is not the case that the investigator finds those movements mysterious and meaningless (for he finds them to rest with will), hence it is not the case that the investigator is a purely knowing subject (rather, he is "the subject of knowing appearing as an individual," i.e., an embodied knowing subject) and it is, accordingly, not the case that the body is for him just another perceptual object (rather, it is "his own appearance," whose meaning or essence is revealed as will).

But, as we have noted, the body must be for the investigator a perceptual object and he must be a purely knowing subject, for otherwise the alleged knowledge of the body's essence (will) could not be, by way of inference, transferred to "other bodies," all of which are perceptual objects or intuitive representations. In short, if there is to be, for the investigator, a genuine analogy between his body and other bodies (or objects), then his body must be conceived in the same way that other bodies are—and that is as a genuine perceptual object. It may be conceived in another way as well, but for the analogy to go through, it must be conceived as a perceptual object. As a matter of fact, Schopenhauer acknowledges, without really heeding, this point in the following passage:

> To the subject of knowledge, which through its identity with the body appears as an individual, this body is given in two completely different ways: once as representation in understandable perception [*verständige Anschauung*], as object among objects, subject to the laws of these objects; but then also simultaneously in a completely different way, namely, as that which is immediately known to everyone, and is denoted by the word *will*.[9]

This simply means that "this body" is given to the individual (embodied) subject of knowledge as a mediate or indirect object and as will. But what the passage means and whether it really expresses what—in light of other passages—must be Schopenhauer's position are two different things. Is it really the case that the individual, as the subject of knowledge, knows the same thing, namely, it is said, this body, as representation and as will? If it is for him a representation, hence a mediate or indirect object, then apparently that it is not also for him will; for, strictly speaking, no representation that is a mediate or indirect object is ever known as will, and this fact pertains to "this body" or to any body. In general, whenever one knows anything as a representation or as a mediate or indirect object, then one is a purely knowing subject, not an individual (embodied) knowing subject. Something, it seems, has gone badly wrong.

Let us, however, try to put all of this in the clearest (and best) possible light. To the individual (embodied) subject of knowledge, this body—with which this subject of knowledge is somehow "identical"—is given (1) as representation and, simultaneously, (2) as will. In virtue of (1), this body is given as a normal perceptual object, as a mediate (indirect) object constructed by the understanding out of sensations, thus as an intuitive representation subject to the relevant aspects of the principle of sufficient reason (i.e., it is in time and space, subject to causality); in virtue of (1), in other words, this body is given in exactly the same way that the tree outside the window or the fan across the room is given. (This is the import of the phrase, in the passage just quoted, "as representation in understandable perception.") In virtue of (2), this body is given as will, which is to say (using the first person) that I am immediately aware of it as the "subject" of pains and pleasures, as the pursuer of goals and the avoider of threats, as mover or agent, indeed, as the source of all things volitional (in the fullest sense of the term). Given in this way, the body is totally different from everything represented by the understanding, hence from everything perceptual and "mediated by" or known through sensation. With the rarest of exceptions, this body is never given to me merely as representation— the only sort of exception occurring when I revert to the purely knowing subject and look upon my own body as if it were "another body" (as perhaps occurs upon a feeling of "disembodiment"). And never is this body given to me as will wholly apart from being given as representation. In almost all cases, then, this body is given to me, simultaneously, as representation and as will. One remarkable feature of this account is that it contains no reference to the body as immediate object; it will make an appearance later, however, and in fact a striking appearance, but then, I think, the whole picture of the twofold knowledge of one's own body changes drastically. But for now I want to follow Schopenhauer's subsequent remarks.

Actually, he holds, I never know either the body as representation or the body as will "as a whole"; each of these is "given" to me, as the embodied or individual subject of knowing, only in segments or, perhaps better, in "slices." For this reason, it seems, Schopenhauer turns the discussion away from the body as representation and as will to individual bodily movements (or actions) and individual acts of will. Continuing to speak of the subject of knowledge as an individual, he puts forth this well-known passage:

> Every true act of his will is immediately and exceptionlessly also a movement of his body; he cannot actually will the act without at the same time being aware that it appears as a movement of the body. The act of will and the action of the body are not two objectively known states that the bond of causality connects; [they] do not stand in the relation of cause and effect, but are one and the same thing, though given in two entirely different ways, first completely immediately and then in perception [*Anschauung*] for the understanding. The action of the body is nothing other than the act of will objectified, i.e., entering into perception.[10]

Schopenhauer thus consciously opposes the traditional thesis that volitions (or, in his idiom, acts of will) antedate and causally produce bodily movements. "Only in reflection are willing and acting different," he writes, "in reality they are one."[11] They are "one," however, only in the sense that

the bodily movement manifests or reveals the corresponding act of will—
just as, I might add, the whole body is the manifestation of the individual
will, and indeed the whole world as representation is the manifestation of
the "world-will." In none of these cases is the will the cause of its manifestations; for it is not the case that the will and its manifestations are connected by any version of the principle of sufficient reason, including that
version called causality. In short, the world as representation is the will
manifested, objectified, made known. But only in one instance—that of
the bodily movement and the act of will, or, as Schopenhauer often says,
the body and the will—does this fact come to one's explicit awareness.

For the sake of clarification, it would be convenient if we could point to
something other than the body of which one also has a twofold knowledge. But none can be found: Knowledge of one's own body, in the twofold way noted, is unique. "With the exception of my own body," Schopenhauer writes, "only *one* side of all things is known to me, namely, that of
the representation."[12] And although in rare cases I might know my body as
a representation, I can never know it only as will (as was pointed out earlier). On this latter point Schopenhauer states his position most explicitly:

> The knowledge that I have of my will, although an immediate knowledge,
> cannot be separated from that [knowledge I have] of my body. I know my
> will not as a whole, not as a unity, not completely according to its essence,
> but I know it only in its single acts, and hence in time, which is the form of
> the appearance of my body, like every object; therefore the body is the con-
> dition of knowledge of my will. Accordingly, I cannot really imagine [*vor-
> stellen*] this will without my body.[13]

Two important assertions are made here: One, I know my will "only in its
single acts," that is, only in "slices" based on the temporal dimension of
the body (the will's appearance); and two, apart from the body in time I
would have no knowledge of my will at all, indeed, I could not even "imag-
ine" it. It would be more understandable if one could say that there is
something I know both as representation and as will, for example, my "action" both as bodily movement and as act of will, and my "organism" both
as body and as will; but this mode of linguistic expression does not conform to Schopenhauer's and it might suggest (quite wrongly) that what I
know in two ways is something other than what I know "it" as.

Schopenhauer supposes at this point that "the investigator" (the philosophizing I) of the meaning of the world as representation has come to
know the meaning of one representation, namely, his own body, and that
meaning is, in a word, will. The question now is simply this: Can the
twofold knowledge of his own body be reasonably extended to other "bodies," that is, to intuitive representations or "outer bodies," such that their
meaning will also be determined? The investigator may thus be portrayed

as saying to himself, "I know my body as representation and as will; I know 'outer bodies' only as representation; may I, however, infer that they too are will—and indeed will in essence, just as I am will in essence?" He is wondering, it seems, whether he may reasonably use an argument from analogy, specifically (in brief) this one: "My body is representation and will; 'outer bodies' are representation; therefore 'outer bodies' are also will." Now, arguments by analogy are notoriously weak; they yield at most a probable conclusion, and perhaps not even that.[14] But if they are to be even minimally convincing, one thing is absolutely necessary: The two things figuring in the analogy must be exactly alike in one regard (and the more regards alike the better). In the present case this means that "my body" must be a representation in exactly the same way that "outer bodies" are representations—else there is really no justification, from the very start, for inferring that "outer bodies" are will because "my body" is will. Is it true, then, that "my body" (*mein Leib*) is a representation in exactly the way that "outer bodies" (*äußere Körper*) are representations? Doubt has been cast on an affirmative answer above, which is to say that doubt has been cast on the claim that, from the one standpoint, my body is a representation like any other representation, an object among objects. Now we will consider the matter more deeply.

From one standpoint, of course, my body is for me a representation in exactly the same way that outer bodies (or objects) are representations for me: Both are mediate or indirect objects, both are normal objects of perception. As such, they are temporal and spatial objects constructed by the understanding out of sensation, and their changing states are governed by the law of causality. From this standpoint, moreover, my body—or, more accurately, this body—is a mediate or indirect object for me as the purely knowing subject, just as all outer bodies are mediate or indirect objects for me as the purely knowing subject. Consequently, my (or this) body is just as alien, meaningless, and incomprehensible as any outer object, which is to say that the so-called meaning of my (or this) body is just as hidden as the so-called meaning (essence, content) of outer objects: I, as the purely knowing subject, have no more insight into my own body as mediate or indirect object than I have into outer bodies; in other words, my body as normal intuitive representation is not also given to me as will. If I were ever able to arrive at the conclusion that the meaning of my own body is will, I would have to arrive at it by inference—not by something called immediate knowledge or awareness. In this case, we do have a true analogy between the knowledge of my own body and the knowledge of outer bodies—both are mediate objects and thus normal intuitive representations; but, in this case also, I do not know my own body under the conception of mediate object as will, hence I cannot use an argument by analogy to conclude that outer bodies are also will. It is not my own body as normal intuitive representation that I also know as will. This decisive fact precludes an inference to the conclusion that outer bodies, known only as normal intuitive representations, are *also* will. I do not even know that my body as intuitive representation is will in the first place.

Schopenhauer admits everything I have been saying, it may be observed, when he claims that for the purely knowing subject the body is a representation like any other and that for this subject the body's meaning (essence, content) is no more revealed than the meaning of any other representation.[15] On the other hand, he also claims that this body is given to one as a representation like any other and as will,[16] though this surely seems to contradict the former claim. In any case, perhaps the body should not be conceived as a representation in the sense of a mediate or indirect object "like any other," or at least not solely as such. And, in fact, Schopenhauer suggests this very supposition when (still in section 18 of Book 2) he writes that "the body, which in the previous Book and in the essay on the Principle of Sufficient Reason I called the *immediate object*, according to the one-sided viewpoint deliberately taken there (namely that of the representation), will here from another point of view be called the *objectity of the will*."[17] Accordingly, it might be declared, my body is given to me as immediate object and as will (not as mediate object and as will); hence it is the body as the immediate object, that is, as the appearance or manifestation of the will, that parallels or proves analogous to outer bodies. But although these provisions would allow an argument by analogy to get started, such an argument would overlook two things: One, the body as the immediate object is only the locus of sensations that do not affect the will, thus it—in this particular capacity—is not the manifestation of the will; and two, outer bodies are not known as loci of sensations at all. That Schopenhauer insists on these two claims can be easily confirmed.

After affirming the "identity" of acts of will and bodily movements— "Every true, genuine immediate act of will is at once and immediately also an appearing act [*Akt*] of the body"—Schopenhauer adds that "every impression [*Einwirkung*] on the body is at once and immediately also an impression on the will."[18] When an impression on the body is contrary to the will (one does not like it), it is called pain (*Schmerz*); when it accords with the will (one does like it), it is called pleasure or gratification (*Wohlbehagen, Wollust*). Pain and pleasure are not representations, Schopenhauer states, but "immediate affections of the will in its appearance, the body." And then, just following the universal claim that every impression on the body is an impression on the will, Schopenhauer (as was his wont) proceeds to qualify that claim: "There are only a certain few impressions on the body which do not rouse the will [namely, some of those of "the purely objective senses of sight, hearing, and touch"], and through these alone is the body an immediate object of knowledge, since, as perception in the understanding, the body is a mediate object like all other objects." Setting aside the curious sequence of ideas, this implies that the body is the immediate object only with regard to impressions on it that do not rouse the will as pain or pleasure.[19] But, as said above, from this conception of the body, that is, as the immediate object or, equally, as the locus of sensations that do not rouse the will, no parallel can be extended to outer bodies (for they are not, or at least are not known as, immediate objects or loci of sensations not rousing the will), and in fact the body as the immediate object is dissociated from the will altogether. One feels forced to conclude that from one's own body as object—whether mediate or immediate—nothing can be inferred about outer bodies, certainly nothing to the effect that their meaning (essence, content) is will. This should not really be surprising, given the fact that one's own body as object—again, whether mediate or immediate—belongs entirely to the world as representation and that, in Schopenhauer's view, no examination of anything as representation yields access to anything beyond or other than representation. Possibly, then, the attribution of will to outer bodies has to commence with a conception of one's own body in a totally different light, in one wholly unlike that of object; and possibly this attribution does not proceed by means of inference, or at least not by inference in accord with any argument by analogy (despite all that Schopenhauer suggests to the contrary). This twofold possibility will now be explored.

It would be well at this point to reconsider what Schopenhauer hopes to accomplish by examining one's own body (*der eigene Leib*); then we shall see, I think, that not even the most comprehensive account of the body as it figures in representational knowledge (or cognition) will provide any grounds for arriving at the desired goal. That goal is the determination of the meaning (essence, content) of the world of nature, of the world as representation, which includes, of course, one's own body as a representation. And, as Schopenhauer never ceases to insist, no matter how deeply or fully one goes into the world as representation, one can never discover its meaning. More broadly still, no matter how far we delve into the human being as representation—either as object of whatever sort or as subject of knowledge—we shall never, on this route, gain any information about, say, the essence of the human being. Consequently, only by examining one's own body as something other than representation or object (whether mediate or immediate) and oneself as something other than subject of knowledge, can we hope to find the meaning of the body, or of oneself, and thereby gain an insight into the meaning of the whole world as representation. All the talk about the body as representation, just as all the talk about oneself as subject of knowledge, is largely (if not entirely) irrelevant to the desired goal.

What then, if anything, do we know about the body other than that it can be made an ordinary object of perception (a mediate object, like every other object in the world of nature) and that it is the locus of sensations (the so-called immediate object, insofar as those sensations do not rouse the will)? First of all, we know that some sensations (that is, some felt impressions on the body) do rouse or affect the will. When they affect the will negatively, they are called pains; when positively, they are called pleasures or gratifications. Now if it is true, as Schopenhauer believes that it is, that pains and pleasures are not representations (thus that they are not literally known, represented, or "objective") but that they are most assuredly experienced or felt (thus that we are undeniably aware of them) then (1) we are not merely subjects of knowledge or representers, (2) the body is not simply an object or representation, and (3) the "world of experience" is not exhaustively a world of knowledge, cognition, known object and knowing subject of objects, that is, it is not merely a world as representation. From the fact that some sensations rouse or affect the will, in being felt negatively or positively, it follows that (I shall say) the human (also the animal) being is "something more" than an item in the world as representation, whether as subject of knowing or as object of knowledge. To suppose otherwise, Schopenhauer would say, is to deny what every animate being recognizes through experience nearly every moment of its life. And if the term "will" best characterizes the subject-side of pains and pleasures, then it is will that we animate beings are—besides, but somehow intermingled with, intellect.

The importance of the body stands out in this manner. Only in virtue of the body—which undergoes (*erleiden*) pains and pleasures, and which entails its counterpart, i.e., the will—do human beings have initial grounds (though not the only grounds) for attributing to themselves "something more" than intellect. In other words, we become conscious of ourselves as will, specifically, as the subject of unwanted or wanted sensations, because we are bodies—not bodies as objects, not bodies as known, but bodies as, say, "lived" (*erlebt*). It is thus through the body as "lived" that we are conscious of ourselves, initially, as will, from which it follows, not insignificantly, that we cannot bypass the body and claim access to the will. If by "immediate awareness of the will" one meant awareness that occurs apart from or independent of the body, then, in Schopenhauer's judgment, there would be no "immediate awareness of the will."

To a very large extent, metaphysics, for Schopenhauer, is the area of inquiry that recognizes and tries to clarify that aspect of the human being that is neither subject of knowledge nor object of knowledge; and this aspect, he holds, deals with will. Since this aspect of the human being cannot be denied, the actuality (not just the possibility) of metaphysics cannot be rejected. But metaphysics, for Schopenhauer, extends beyond (what might be called) "the study of pains and pleasures"—otherwise it would afford no insight into, say, the natural world. It also involves the study of human action—and this, Schopenhauer holds, does provide insight into the natural world.

The argument commences with the obvious fact that the body moves. And every one of its movements, Schopenhauer holds, conforms to the principle of sufficient reason of becoming, that is, to the general law of causality, which is to say that every bodily movement has "a cause." (Without a cause, the body, like everything in nature, would remain forever at rest, or if it were already in motion, it would never change direction or come to rest—both of these in virtue of the "law of inertia.")[20] We recall that a cause of a body's movement can take three different forms: a cause proper (a so-called physical cause), e.g., another body comes into contact with it and moves it; a stimulus, e.g., intense light makes the eye blink; and a motive, e.g., the sight of an injured child moves (motivates) the body, or, actually, the human being, to render assistance. When the body moves by way of a physical cause or stimulus, it moves in a passive sense: *It is moved* (by something else), and its movement is said to be involuntary (*unwillkürlich*). But when the body moves by way of a motive, it moves in the active sense: *It moves*, and its movement is then said to be voluntary (*willkürlich*).[21] When the body is moved by a cause proper, its movement will be explained in the manner of any inorganic body's movement (as in physics, mechanics, chemistry, etc.); and when the body is stimulated to move, its movement will be explained in the manner of any organic body's movement (as in biology, physiology, etc.). I shall run these two types of explanation together and say that the explanation of a body's movement, by both a cause proper and a stimulus, is causal; for in both cases the body is passive and acted on from without. But when the body moves, that is, when it is motivated to move, then its movement will be explained in the manner unique to conscious animal bodies; here the body is active and the motive moving it passes through cognition. In this latter case, the explanation of the movement will be motivational, the operative sort of motive for animals always being a presently perceived object but the operative sort of motive for human beings often being "abstract," i.e., thought and not presently perceived. The human being, on this score, differs from the animal only in virtue of the former's wider range of possible motives: Human actions are sometimes motivated by thought of the distant past and of the distant future, but animal actions are motivated only by perception of present objects. And so on.[22]

I have no wish to suggest that Schopenhauer's account of these truly complicated and deeply complex matters is satisfactory (indeed, I do not think that it is satisfactory).[23] But I do want to present a favorable picture of his conviction that, in a phrase, "motivation clarifies causation." His line of thought goes as follows. Nothing but one's own motivated bodily movement or voluntary action yields any clue for understanding, beyond the level of scientific understanding, changes or movements in nature (including movements of one's own body explainable by strict causality and stimulation). If one's own body were only caused (in the physical sense) or stimulated to move, then its movements would be just as mysterious as any movement or change in the natural world; but one's own body is also motivated to move (often by very abstract motives, on the basis of one's own individual, or even unique, character) and awareness of this fact (through, say, self-consciousness) allows one to understand in an extrascientific, hence metaphysical, way strict causality in inorganic changes and stimulation in organic change. For any voluntary bodily movement or action, there must be an operative motive in conjunction with the human agent's character or will; for any movement or change in nature, there must be a cause plus a natural force (or "inner constitution" of the thing that undergoes the change). Causal explanation of a natural change leads up to but leaves unexplained the required natural force; and motivational explanation of one's own voluntary bodily movement or action would remain equally unexplained except for the crucial fact that one knows it not only as a bodily movement but also as an act of will. Consequently, the meaning of one's voluntary bodily movements is revealed: One becomes aware that what connects the operative motive with the bodily movement is the "I so will it." So the initial riddle of why this motive and the bodily movement figure as "ground" and "consequent"—which is demanded by the principle of sufficient reason—is solved through the awareness that I so will this precise connection. Why do I so will it? Because, quite simply, that is the way I am: I am the will to connect this motive with this bodily movement. And no further "why-question" makes sense.

The result of this analysis can be expressed in more than one way; for example, one's action is both a bodily movement and an act of will, one's voluntary conduct is both a manifestation of one's character and an act of character, and, perhaps most generally, one's own body is both a representation and a will. Schopenhauer tends to favor the last-mentioned expression, and I shall follow suit. So the key metaphysical question arises anew: Can the recognition that one's own body is both representation and will be reasonably extended to other "bodies," that is, to intuitive representations (as they are usually called) or perceptual objects external to one's own body?[24] Schopenhauer does not think, I propose to argue, that logic or reasoning (certainly not reasoning by way of an argument by analogy) demands an extension of what we recognize about ourselves to outer objects. What he does think, I suggest, is that if we do not carry out this extension, then we shall have to acknowledge certain very unfortunate (and even deeply disturbing) theses. I shall again place the discussion in terms of the philosophical subject called "I."

First, then, I would have to adopt the position that Schopenhauer labels "theoretical egoism," by which he means the doctrine that I alone am truly real (being not only representation but also will), and thus that "everything else" is fundamentally unreal (being merely representation, devoid of will). In other words, I would have to deny "the reality of the external world."[25] By "theoretical egoism" Schopenhauer does not mean solipsism, at least as it is typically defined, namely, as the doctrine (in the radical version) that there are no minds other than my own or (in the moderate version) that I can never know for certain that there are other minds. What he does mean, as he makes quite clear, is the doctrine that denies reality (i.e., will) to everything other than my own body, including not only nonanimate objects such as chairs, trees, stones, and so on, but also animals and other human bodies. The crucial question for Schopenhauer is thus not, "Are there other minds?" or "Can I be sure that there are other minds?" or "Do I have any justification for attributing mind or intellect to other human (and animal) bodies?" but rather, "Are the things I know by way of perception, hence as intuitive representation, also will?" or "May I on reasonable grounds attribute to perceptual objects—nonhuman as well as human, nonanimate as well as animate—that which I find in myself through self-consciousness, namely, will?" The question of "other minds" is not the real issue, hence solipsism—as normally defined—is not the doctrine at issue.

Schopenhauer remarks that theoretical egoism, "which . . . regards as phantoms all appearances outside of its own individual [i.e., its own body]," can "of course never be refuted by proofs," but he adds that no one has ever seriously put it forth as a positive doctrine.[26] It always takes the negative, skeptical form of defying any proof of the reality of outer or external objects. "As a serious conviction," he writes, "it could be found only in a madhouse; as such it would then need not so much a refutation as a cure." He proposes, therefore, to treat "this skeptical argument of theoretical egoism . . . as a small frontier fortress." "Admittedly the fortress is impregnable," he adds "but the garrison can never sally forth from it, and therefore we can pass it by and leave it in our rear without danger"— meaning apparently that its "sallying forth" to do battle with us would amount to admitting our reality, and thus would contradict itself. In any case, this cursory discussion of theoretical egoism, called "the last stronghold of skepticism," is very strange: Why should Schopenhauer admit the irrefutability of this form of skepticism here when earlier (in section 5 of Book 1) he proposes a thorough refutation. There, it will be recalled, he rejects skepticism about the reality of the external world on the ground that individual perceptual objects are what they effect, that they are real in that they exercise an effect on other objects.[27] Obviously, then, "real" in the present discussion does not mean the same as "effective" (*wirklich*); it must mean, "are, besides representation (hence besides being effective) also something in themselves (hence also will)." Whether they are real in this sense is the question Schopenhauer is raising, and it cannot be given an affirmative answer "by proofs." Notice what this entails: No argument or proof can establish that, in short, the natural world is will. (It is not by way of reasoning that one may arrive at the metaphysical proposition that the external world is not only representation but also will.) Nor, of course, can it be directly known or "felt" that outer bodies are real, i.e., will, although it is directly known or "felt," according to Schopenhauer, that one's own body is real, i.e., will. (Metaphysics, at least regarding the external world, does not proceed by way of argument, proof, or deduction.) Consequently, the philosophical subject is confronted with two mutually exclusive alternatives: Either I extend the knowledge I have of myself as will to the natural world (in the absence of rational proof and of direct accessibility) or I adopt the "mad" position that the natural world is unreal.[28]

But adoption of the second alternative, with regard to a large portion of the natural, external world, is not only mad; it is, in Schopenhauer's judgment, evil. Theoretical egoism entails practical egoism, according to which "a man regards and treats only his own person as a real person, and all others as mere phantoms,"[29] and that doctrine, Schopenhauer holds, expresses the fundamental stance of an evil man. In other words, he who refuses to attribute to members of the external world that "reality" he finds in himself to be will endorses theoretical egoism, which is (from the theoretical standpoint) madness, and he thereby refuses to attribute to other persons and even animals this same "reality," whereby he endorses practical egoism, which is (from the moral standpoint) evil. Consequently, it may be said, theoretical egoism, in virtue of its entailment, namely, practical egoism, is a doctrine that no morally decent person will adopt.[30] (The objection that "even so, there is no reason to attribute will to nonanimate beings" will be entertained below.) When Schopenhauer claims that his philosophy will be metaphysics, aesthetics, and ethics, all wrapped up into one, or that his philosophy is "one thought," presentable in these three basic branches of philosophy, he has in mind ideas like the aforementioned one about egoism. And he would add, no doubt, that the theoretical egoist, being committed to practical egoism, has to deny the possibility of compassion (*Mitleid*) and, hence, the very possibility of genuine ethics, for he has to regard all conduct as egoistic and none as indicative of, say, one individual will's being identified with another.[31] So the adoption of theoretical egoism has truly momentous ethical ramifications.

Third and finally, the individual who refuses to attribute "reality," understood as will, to natural beings and natural occurrences, in short, to changes in both animate and nonanimate bodies, deprives himself or herself of a satisfactory understanding of the world as representation. This individual will be not only mad and evil (which may be set aside for the moment) but also condemned, indeed, self-condemned, to despair. He or she will have to accept the humanly distressing proposition that the natural world is utterly unintelligible. But, Schopenhauer holds, this consequence can be avoided, and one (if not the) fundamental task of philosophy is to show how the world can be made intelligible. Natural science cannot perform this task, and no philosophy modeled on natural science—that is, no philosophy restricted to explanation in accord with the principle of sufficient reason—can do so; only a philosophy that employs self-understanding as its starting point, and then applies it to nature, can succeed in rendering nature (the whole world as representation) understandable. Schopenhauer's commitment to this general strategy—briefly, world-understanding through self-understanding—cannot be exaggerated.

In a sense, of course, natural science can explain everything: It can, at least in principle, discover the cause of every natural occurrence. But, in another sense, it can explain nothing: It can tell us nothing about the "content" operating in natural occurrences. Thus Schopenhauer asks: "What is the use of explanations that ultimately lead back to something just as unknown as the first problem was?"[32] He is referring here to the problem of understanding the forces operating in natural occurrences and the "vital forces" operating in animate life and behavior. A new mode of explanation, or, better, clarification or understanding—one unique to philosophy—has to be devised if, in a phrase, we are to get to the bottom of things, that is, if we are to gain an insight into the world of nature. And that mode of understanding finds its place in oneself; it is, as noted, self-understanding.

Schopenhauer proposes, therefore, to inaugurate a new method of inquiry, one unique to philosophy proper and supplementary to that of natural science. Already in 1816 he expresses agreement with the policy of (say) natural philosophers who start out with what is best known and then proceed to what is less known, but he holds that they err in supposing that "what is most universal ["the so-called universal forces of nature"] is also the best known." Schopenhauer then sketches his own view of the matter:

> Just like those [others], I too intend to start from that which is best known. They, however, regarded the most universal phenomenon and the most imperfect and therefore simplest phenomenon as the best known, although they saw that it was wholly unknown to them. But instead of this, the best known to me is the phenomenon in nature which is nearest to my knowledge and at the same time is the most perfect, the highest power of all others, which therefore expresses most clearly and completely the essential nature of all, and this is the *life and action of man*. Those others finally tried to explain these as the ultimate thing from the forces of inorganic nature. I, on the other hand, learn from man to understand those forces, and here I

do not proceed in accordance with the law of causality which never leads to the inner nature of things; on the contrary, I consider directly the essential nature of man, the most significant phenomenon in the world. I find that, if I leave aside the fact of his being my representation, man is through and through *will*; will is left over as the in-itself of his true nature. What this is is immediately given to everyone, for everyone is this inner nature itself.[33]

Somewhat later, but still in 1816, Schopenhauer makes this telling assertion: "From yourself you shall understand nature, not yourself from nature. This is my revolutionary principle."[34]

This principle is not entirely revolutionary, however, for it, or something like it, began with Descartes' "subjectivistic turn" in philosophy (I know my mind better than anything else), it continues with Kant's "transcendental turn" (the fundamental laws of nature are discoverable a priori in the human understanding), and it finds some expression in Hegel's "spiritualist turn" (history and the world are to be comprehended in terms of spirit's striving for rationality and freedom); but the thoroughness and radicalness with which Schopenhauer carries this principle out is novel— to say nothing of the fact that, for Schopenhauer, it is the will, and not the mind (or intellect, understanding, reason, spirit), that one knows best and that one then uses for understanding the world of nature. I suggest then that Schopenhauer introduces into philosophy the "macranthropological turn," which is, of course, a central theme of this entire study.

In light of Schopenhauer's "revolutionary principle," which is stated in terms of understanding (*verstehn*) rather than in terms of fact, his chief metaphysical proposition should not be formulated in a categorical assertion to the effect that "Things in the world of nature are in reality will, just as the human being is in reality will." What Schopenhauer is actually presenting us with is this predicament: Either we attribute to the natural world that which we find in ourselves as will or we leave it—or rather its essence, content, or meaning—hidden in inscrutable mystery. To adopt the latter option would be to assent not only to Kant's doctrine of the unknowability of the thing in itself, but to the doctrine of the unintelligibility or nonunderstandability of the natural world. Actually, as we shall see later, Schopenhauer agrees with Kant that the thing in itself cannot be *known*, hence what it is cannot be asserted as a knowable fact, but he believes that the natural world can be fully *understood* (or interpreted, or rendered intelligible). He believes, in other words, that we can arrive at the "meaning" of the natural world, but only by assigning to it—both on the individual level and on the "cosmic" level—that which we know in ourselves as will. So far as knowing the natural world is concerned, we do know it as the world as representation: We know it as object for the knowing subject, hence as the world as governed by the principle of sufficient reason. How this works out constitutes the subject-matter of representation theory, the job of which is "representation analysis." But if we are to understand the "meaning" of the natural world (i.e., the content or essence of the world as representation), we have to leave representation theory behind and proceed to metaphysics, the task of which is "representation interpretation."[35] The same point can be made by saying that representation theory is concerned with knowledge of the "form" of the world (how it appears) and metaphysics is concerned with interpretation of the "meaning" of the world (what it is). Notice that the very word "meaning" indicates that interpretation (or understanding) is the aim of metaphysics, not knowledge (or cognition).

That we can never have knowledge of the content or meaning of the natural world can also be derived from the fact that all knowledge (cognition) is either direct (immediate) or indirect (inferential). We have direct knowledge of our own body, Schopenhauer suggests, in two respects: first, as the locus of "pure" sensations, that is, as the locus of those impressions on the body that do not affect the will; and second, as the will through impressions on the body that do affect the will and through immediate awareness of the will's participation in voluntary bodily actions. In a sense it can be said that we have direct knowledge of sensations, out of which we have indirect knowledge of outer objects (including the body as a mediate object, as an intuitive representation) in virtue of the principle of sufficient reason, hence by way of inference or construction. But we have no knowledge (or cognition)—neither direct nor indirect—of the content or meaning of outer objects, though, Schopenhauer holds, we do have direct knowledge of the content or meaning of our own body, namely, as will. If we were to have knowledge of the content of outer objects, it would have to be direct, but that has been ruled out, or indirect (i.e., inferable on the basis of the principle of sufficient reason), but that too has been ruled out because the content of outer objects is not related to their "form" (i.e., to their temporal, spatial, and causal dimensions) in accordance with the principle of sufficient reason. Consequently, we can have no knowledge (cognition) of the content, meaning, or essence of the world as representation; at most we can have an interpretation or understanding of that content, meaning, or essence. If it were otherwise, by the way, theoretical egoism could be refuted—either by direct knowledge or "by proofs," that is, either by immediate awareness of will in outer things or by employment of the principle of sufficient reason in some version or other.

The attribution of will to the natural world takes place on two levels: the individual and the general (or cosmic or universal). On the individual level, the predicament facing us goes thus: Either we understand the natural changes that a given object undergoes in the way that we know our own (voluntary) bodily movements to proceed, namely, as manifestations of our will or character, or we cannot understand natural changes at all.

Accordingly, Schopenhauer draws a close comparison between the "behavior" of a body of water or of a stone and the voluntary conduct of a human being:

> I consider the inner being that first imparts meaning and validity to all necessity (i.e., effect from cause) to be its presupposition. In the case of man, this is called character; in the case of a stone, it is called quality; but it is the same in both. Where it is immediately known, it is called *will*, and in the stone it has the weakest, and in man the strongest, degree of visibility, of objectivity.[36]

Somewhat later Schopenhauer expresses essentially the same position thus:

> The way in which the character [of a human being] discloses its qualities can be fully compared with the way in which every body in nature-without-knowledge reveals its qualities. Water remains water with the qualities inherent in it. But whether as a calm lake it reflects its banks, or dashes in foam over rocks, or by artificial means spouts into the air in a tall jet, all this depends on external causes; the one is as natural to it as is the other. But it will always show one or the other according to the circumstances; it is equally ready for all, yet in every case it is true to its character, and always reveals that alone. So also will every human character reveal itself under all circumstances, but the phenomena proceeding from it will be in accordance with the circumstances.[37]

What a motive is to a human agent, a cause is to water; the effect of a motive is a human action or voluntary bodily movement, and the effect of a cause is a natural occurrence; that which connects the motive to an action is the agent's character, and that which connects the cause to the resultant natural occurrence is the body's quality; the character of the agent is will, and the quality of the natural body is equally will. Thus:

> Only from a comparison with what goes on within me when my body performs an action from a motive that moves me, with what is the inner nature of my own changes determined by external grounds, can I obtain an insight into the way in which those inanimate bodies change under the influence of causes, and thus understand what is their inner nature.[38]

From motivation, and only from motivation, can one understand causation—not the other way around.

The knowledge (*Erkenntniß*) that "everyone possesses directly in the concrete" Schopenhauer calls "feeling" (*Gefühl*).[39] His choice of this term makes clear his belief that this is a special sort of knowledge, that it is not representational knowledge, that it is not knowledge by which a knowing subject stands sharply distinguished from its object. And, of course, it is not knowledge of a representation, of an appearance; instead it is knowledge of the essence or inner nature of one's own appearance, which essence is manifested in appearance or in representations, that is, in one's

actions and the "substratum" of these, the body. This is a knowledge unlike any other, hence, presumably, the reason for calling it "feeling." Again,
Schopenhauer reminds us that the will "becomes known [*kenntlich werden*]
to the individual himself not as a whole, but only in his particular acts."
One gets to know (or "feel") one's own will only empirically, as it is often
put, that is, bit by bit or "in slices." With every individual instance of a
motive's connection with its result, an action, one becomes immediately
aware of an "I so will it"; then, Schopenhauer writes,

> The reader who with me has gained this conviction will find that completely
> of itself [*ganz von selbst*] it will become the key to the knowledge of the inner-
> most being [*Wesen*] of the whole of nature, since he now transfers it to all
> those appearances that are given to him, not like his own appearance both
> in direct and indirect knowledge, but in the latter solely, and hence merely
> in a one-sided way, as *representation* alone.[40]

He will acknowledge that very will not only in appearances like his own,
that is, in other human beings and animals, but led by "continued reflection" (*fortgesetzte Reflexion*) he will come to recognize that will in every natural force—from the force that shoots and vegetates in the plant to that
which forms the crystal to, finally, gravitation. He will recognize that all of
these things differ only in appearance, but not in their inner nature or essence. "It is only this application of reflection [*Anwendung der Reflexion*]
which no longer lets us stop at the appearance, but leads us on to the *thing
in itself*." What the application of reflection reveals to us is truly remarkable. In Schopenhauer's graphic and almost lyrical language it is this:

> Appearance means representation, and nothing more. All representation, of
> whatever kind it may be, all *object*, is *appearance*. *Thing in itself* however is only
> the *will*; as such it is not representation at all, but *toto genere* different from it.
> It is that of which all representation, all object, is the appearance, the visi-
> bility, the *objectity*. It is the innermost, the kernel of every particular and also
> of the whole. It appears in every blindly acting natural force; it also appears
> in the deliberate conduct of the human being, and the great difference be-
> tween the two concerns only the degree of appearing, not the essence of that
> which appears.[41]

Once the philosophizing "investigator" acknowledges, presumably through
"feeling," that he or she is not a merely knowing subject, but, in virtue
of the body, is also a willing subject—one who undergoes pain and pleasure and performs voluntary actions—then he or she has discovered the
key for understanding (interpreting) the "meaning" of the world of nature. It is from self-knowledge, and only from self-knowledge, that world-
understanding has to proceed; it is from knowledge of the microcosm that
understanding of the macrocosm can alone be reached.

And what is it, precisely, that allows or even necessitates the passage of self-knowledge to world-understanding? It is, Schopenhauer says, the "application of reflection," hence it is a function or operation of human reason—that one faculty that distinguishes human beings from animals, and of course from all lower beings. For Schopenhauer, the faculty of reason accounts for the humanly unique functions of abstraction (the formation of concepts from percepts), language use (the tying of concepts to words), inference (drawing of conclusions from premises), and "overviewing" (the escape from the present, whereby motives of actions can be "abstract" rather than, with the animal, immediately perceived, and whereby the human being can survey and wonder about the whole of the world and life).[42] It is this last function of reason—the capacity to view the whole, as it were—that Schopenhauer has in mind when he speaks here of the "application of reflection."

Three observations about Schopenhauer's line of thought come to mind. First, the faculty of reason is in no way a faculty of "intuition"; one cannot legitimately purport to intuit the essence of the natural world, which reflects Schopenhauer's firm rejection of the so-called reason-intuition (*Vernunft-Anschauung*).[43] Second, the transference of self-knowledge to world-understanding does not take place by means of an argument from analogy, contrary to what I suggested earlier in this chapter and equally contrary to what Schopenhauer sometimes suggests himself. He does not really intend to argue that we find ourselves to be representation and will, we find other things to be representation, therefore we may infer that other things are, or probably are, will also. Granted, there is a hint of such an argument; but, I think, Schopenhauer takes a rather different course: The human being cannot know or even conceive of anything except—using the most general terms—representation and will, hence if he or she is to denominate the natural world as something other than mere representation, then he or she must call it will.[44] There simply is no alternative—except of course to leave it absolutely unknown or, backtracking now, to relegate it to mere representation. The third observation is this. If I find that my essence is will, then I find—given that essence is not subject to the principle of sufficient reason—that the one essence, the whole essence, the underlying "meaning" of the entire world as representation, is will. In a sense, then, there is no, and can be no, transference of what I find as my essence to other things; for to find the essence of anything is to find the essence of everything. To think otherwise would contradict the very notion of essence. Given this presupposition—the essence is the One in the Many—Schopenhauer does not need to rely on any separate argument by analogy or even on any transference from self to the world.[45] Nevertheless, he continues to talk of transference of immediate knowledge of will in oneself to (say) interpretation of other things as will.

A serious difficulty remains: When Schopenhauer attributes will to the natural world, indeed, to the inanimate as well as the animate world, has he not stretched the meaning of "will" so far beyond its rightful limits that it in fact loses all meaning? Critics often agree, albeit with some reluctance, to attribute will to all animals and possibly even to some plants (for example, to those which "bend" toward sunlight or which "extend" their roots deeper and deeper into the ground "in search of" water), but they refuse to apply will to wholly inorganic things like water, stones, crystals, and the like. Is Schopenhauer not guilty of the worst sort of anthropomorphism? Not surprisingly, Schopenhauer recognizes the difficulty, hence he offers a response to it. The following passage was written in 1816:

> I have greatly widened the extension of the concept of *will*, so that it encompasses appearances that people never [before] assigned to it. This results from the fact that I recognize its essential nature [*das Wesentliche desselben*], while people earlier stopped with its secondary determination, and thus [I] make the species into the genus. People recognized will only where knowledge accompanied it and therefore [where] a motive determined its expression. I say, however, that every movement, formation, striving, being, that all of these are appearance, objectity, of the will; for it is the in-itself of all things, i.e., that which remains of the world after one withdraws from it the fact that it is our representation.[46]

In the past, Schopenhauer holds, people have employed the term "will" only to designate the conscious will, that is, the will found in animals and human beings, hence the will determined by motives. (And sometimes, but not here, he holds that "will" has been restricted to the rational, conscious will, that is, to the will found only in human beings insofar as "abstract" motives determine "its expression.") The conscious will, however, is secondary to the nonconscious will, and in fact the latter is the "essential nature" of the former and it extends far beyond the former. Since the term sought must designate what the entire world is besides representation (or appearance), that is, as he puts it, what the world is in itself, it must designate that which is common to everything in the world as representation. It must name, as it were, the ultimate genus. Yet if the word is to be meaningful and philosophically useful, certain conditions have to be met. First, "we must borrow its name and concept from an object, from something in some way objectively given, and therefore from one of its phenomena [*Erscheinungen*]."[47] Nevertheless, that which is to be named—as the thing in itself—is not an object and thus not a phenomenon. Second, the phenomenon or object from which the required name and concept are borrowed must be "none other than the most complete of all its phenomena, i.e., the most distinct, the most developed, the most directly enlightened by knowledge," and that, Schopenhauer asserts, is "man's *will*."[48] "I therefore name the genus after its most important species, the direct knowledge of which lies nearest to us, and leads us to the indirect knowledge of all the others."[49] Third, and most subtly, the term used to designate the thing in itself must be derived from that which we find, through self-consciousness, to be our own essence, hence it must be unique on this score, not arrived at by abstraction or inference, and not discerned by any knowledge gained through observation of the world as representation.[50] This condition, Schopenhauer believes, makes the proper term "will"—for it is what is known "absolutely and immediately," and thus "better than anything else"—and it precludes, for example, "force" (and, I would add, "drive" and "energy"). Force is above all the scientific concept that the metaphysical concept of will is supposed to clarify; and although force is in a way ubiquitous, it is precisely that which science leaves unclarified. And "drive" (*Trieb*) will not work; for it is "a graphic, useless word taken from the objective world."[51] In response to a critic's suggestion that "drive" might replace "will" for the purpose intended, Schopenhauer writes:

> How stupid! Here the issue is knowledge of the thing in itself, which can never be derived from appearance, representation, consciousness of other things; therefore however the concept of *drive* originates from *driving* [*trieben*], as a herd [of cattle], always indicating power from behind, there merely for spectators from outside. The will is revealed only to the self-consciousness and is its entire content.[52]

The only word suitable for characterizing the thing in itself, that is, the meaning of the entire world as representation, is one that designates that in oneself which is directly known by self-consciousness—and that is will and will alone.

By way of criticism one might well object to Schopenhauer's designation of the widest of all genera by the term that, strictly speaking, designates only its highest species; for this practice is one that he condemns in other philosophers, claiming, for instance, that Kant should never speak of reason or rationality apart from human reason because it is found only in human beings.[53] Another, and perhaps more significant, objection is this: The sort of will that I allegedly know directly in myself is not the sort of will that I attribute to nature, especially, to inanimate nature. The sort of will that I recognize in myself is "illuminated by knowledge," it is reflective and truly elective will, it is above all the sort of will that figures in, and only in, voluntary bodily movements, hence it is (in German) *Willkür.* But the sort of will that I attribute to inanimate nature is blind, it is wholly unreflective and nonelective, it is also the sort of will that figures in my nonvoluntary bodily movements, hence it is (in Schopenhauer's German) *Wille.* It is only with my voluntary bodily movements, and thus not with my involuntary ones, that I become conscious of the "I so will it" that (allegedly) connects motives—especially abstract motives—with bodily movements such that these movements do not appear to me as strange, meaningless, and incomprehensible. Schopenhauer fully acknowledges this distinction, indeed, he emphasizes the vast difference between *Willkür* and *Wille*.[54] But he seems not to grasp the problem generated by the distinction or difference. If I know immediately only *Willkür*, then I should attribute only *Willkür* to things known mediately; that, however, would result in the absurdity of holding that my own involuntary bodily movements and the movements of all nonrational (and nonelective) beings occur in virtue of rational, elective, and conscious behavior. And the question arises as to what *Wille* could mean to me; for I do not literally know it, but only *Willkür*. So either I should attribute *Willkür* to all things outside myself—which is absurd, and admitted by Schopenhauer to be absurd[55]—or I should attribute nothing discoverable in myself to them.

Schopenhauer talks as if we have, in the matter at issue, two things: that genus for which there is no name (and which belongs to all things) and the highest species thereof called *Wille*. But there are actually three: the two just mentioned plus *Willkür*. Or, to put it another way, there is only one known thing: *Willkür*. It is the only thing of which I am immediately conscious, it is the only thing that provides an insight into my own bodily movements (all of which must then be voluntary), hence it is the only thing that I should attribute to other movements in nature—but that, as noted, would be absurd. So far as I can see, Schopenhauer fails to take up this problem, no more than he takes up the problem about the disanalogy between my own body (the immediate object) and outer bodies (mediate objects). He *says* that he recognizes the essential nature of *Willkür* to be *Wille* (that is, that he recognizes the essential nature of the voluntary will to be just plain will), but he should say at most, I think, that unless we attribute to nature something like *Willkür* we must despair of ever understanding it at bottom. And perhaps that is precisely what he does hold: Either interpret the natural world as (say) *Willkür*-like or abandon hope of understanding it at all. And he believes, of course, that the former alternative is supported by empirical observation,[56] while the latter is humanly intolerable.

FIVE

From the Will to the Thing in Itself

At this point in his discussion Schopenhauer believes that he has established that the world is something besides representation and that the human individual is something besides the purely knowing subject. The world is will as well as representation, and the human individual is a willing subject as well as a knowing subject. Schopenhauer frequently claims that will is the essence of the world while representation is the world's mere "accident" (or incidental, contingent aspect) and that the willing subject is the essence of the human individual while the knowing subject is secondary and derivative (a mere tool of will appearing in an individual). In principle, these propositions generate no serious problems. But when Schopenhauer goes on to maintain that will is the thing in itself,[1] that the thing in itself is nothing but the will,[2] and further that as such will is totally different from representation,[3] then (at least according to many critics) important difficulties arise.

First, if will as thing in itself is totally different from representation—the former being free from every aspect of the principle of sufficient reason and the latter being subject to every aspect—then how can will as thing in itself be manifested in representation? How are we to understand this notion of manifestation? If something R (representation) has qualities t, s, and c (time, space, and causality) and something W (will as thing in itself) has none of these qualities, then what sense can we assign to the assertion that R is the manifestation (or objectity) of W? Is manifestation a relation? For Schopenhauer, it cannot be; for relations obtain only between representations, and not between representation and nonrepresentation such as will as thing in itself. (To suppose otherwise, we recall, was the great error Kant made, according to Schopenhauer, in holding that the thing in itself is the "ground" or even the "cause" of the phenomenon.) How then do representation and will as thing in itself "stand" to each other? This is the first major difficulty: The "relation" between representation and will as thing in itself, between appearance and reality.[4]

Second, if will is the thing in itself, hence not representation (appearance, object), and if everything knowable is representation, then how can it be said that we human beings know (are aware or conscious of) the will? The difficulty facing Schopenhauer on this score, according to several critics, can be put thus: If we know something, it is a representation (or appearance or object); if something is not and cannot become a representation, then we do not and cannot know it; so either will as thing in itself is representational (which Schopenhauer disallows) or it is not knowable (which, against Kant, he denies—in a way). But, the critics continue, Schopenhauer cannot have it both ways: Either he must construe will as thing in itself in a manner that it becomes (at least) something like a representation or he must deny its (human) knowability. This is the second important difficulty: the alleged knowability of the will as thing in itself.

In this chapter I propose to deal with these two difficulties, starting with the second, more-often cited one. If it cannot be overcome, then (many critics conclude) Schopenhauer cannot even begin to put forth a metaphysical doctrine.[5]

One of the fundamental problems with evaluating the second objection—that Schopenhauer, to be consistent, should eschew any claim to metaphysics—is that critics present their objection in terms that Schopenhauer does not use or they use terms in a sense foreign to Schopenhauer's meaning. This becomes quite clear in the argument urged by Copleston, who believes that Schopenhauer, according to Book 1 of *The World as Will and Representation*, has precluded the possibility of knowing "the noumenal." Copleston writes:

> It is really very difficult to see how, after laying down his theory of knowledge and his doctrine of the phenomenon [in Book 1], Schopenhauer can give any satisfactory formal justification for a metaphysic. Either all knowledge is knowledge of the phenomenal, in which case there can be no knowledge, at the very least no communicable knowledge, of the noumenal, or there can be knowledge of the noumenal, in which case knowledge is not essentially knowledge of the phenomenal.[6]

Copleston remarks further that

> the proper conclusion from Schopenhauer's epistemology, as from that of Kant, is agnosticism: a metaphysic is quite out of order. It is true that sometimes Schopenhauer admits a certain agnosticism in regard to the Will; but the question is, "how, on his premises, can there be any knowledge of the Will at all, whether real or partial?"[7]

By "the noumenal" Copleston means the thing in itself, apparently wholly removed from "the phenomenal," or the world as representation; but it is by no means obvious that Schopenhauer conceives "the thing in itself" in this manner. The statement about knowledge of the will (or the Will) being only partial may refer to Schopenhauer's belief that the will "becomes known to the individual himself not as a whole, but only in its particular acts."[8] But even so, it is not at all obvious that this will is identical with (Copleston's) the Will; in fact, this will is the will or character of an individual human being and the Will (apparently) is the so-called world-will. The remark about knowledge of "the noumenal" not being communicable may refer to Schopenhauer's (later) account of the mystic's "knowledge," but that "knowledge" may not be of the will.

Gardiner raises essentially the same issue, but he puts it in terms of a "dilemma" deriving from "the distinction drawn between nonperceptual awareness of ourselves as will and the perceptual knowledge we have of our own [bodily] behaviour." Of Schopenhauer he then writes:

> If he claims that in inner experience we are directly conscious of ourselves as will, it follows that the will falls within the range of our experience. But must it not then be "idea" [representation] in the Schopenhauerian sense of that which is presented to a knowing subject; and if so, how can he claim that our acquaintance with it gives us access to the thing-in-itself? For the latter by definition lies beyond the realm of appearance, beyond the illusory realm of representation which (following Indian thought) he sometimes called "the veil of Maya." If, on the other hand, the will is not idea but noumenal, how can he assert that we have experience of it?[9]

Again, there is mention of "noumenal," which is a term Schopenhauer does not use to express his own thoughts; he uses "noumenon" (in Greek and German) only to note that Kant misused this Greek expression[10] and to cite some sections in Kant's writings.[11] It may also be noted that, for Schopenhauer, "nonperceptual awareness" would be awareness that does not start from sensation, hence awareness of something that is not spatial (and not causally efficacious), but this does not necessarily entail that there cannot be an awareness of something nonspatial (and noncausal), whether that "something" is called an "idea" or not.

In any case, to escape the dilemma Gardiner devises (at least as he sees it), Schopenhauer will have to show that some experience (acquaintance, consciousness, "knowledge") is not representational, and then argue that nonrepresentational knowledge, not being of perceptual objects, is knowledge of one's will, which finally gives us access to the thing in itself. Among the problems that Gardiner calls attention to, the first is perhaps this: What could nonrepresentational knowledge be? Janaway raises this very question:

How can there be a way of knowing about oneself which is not a matter of representation? If there cannot be such a way, then Schopenhauer's grand strategy is fatally impeded—but has he himself not made the vehement assertion that there could be no knowledge (or cognition . . .) which was not the being present of some representation for the subject? It seems that he can only advance to knowledge of the thing in itself by denying this central part of the representation theory. Schopenhauer never really provides a satisfactory answer to this worry.[12]

In other words, if all knowledge is necessarily knowledge of representation, then knowledge of one's own will is also knowledge of a representation, hence one's own will is a representation—yet Schopenhauer constantly denies this conclusion. Furthermore, and equally significant, knowledge of one's own will as a representation opens no door to "knowledge of the thing in itself." So, in effect, goes Janaway's argument, about which I say more below.

Perhaps the chief point of these criticisms—that Schopenhauer should remain an agnostic about knowing the nature of the thing in itself—will prove in the end to be correct. For, at least in several later writings, Schopenhauer does appear to allow, or in fact to insist on, a sense in which "the thing in itself" is humanly inconceivable—using this last term in its literal meaning, namely, as that which cannot be put in concepts. Consequently, if metaphysics is defined as the study that purports to characterize, in concepts, "the thing in itself," then Schopenhauer does not believe metaphysics possible. On the other hand, if metaphysics is understood as a study purporting to characterize, in concepts, the inner nature of the world lying before us so that it will become intelligible (at least for the most part), then Schopenhauer cannot be regarded as agnostic concerning metaphysics. Throughout his philosophical writings, Schopenhauer sharply distinguishes "immanent" metaphysics, one that (say) "remains true to the world," from "transcendent" metaphysics, one that "goes beyond the world."

In a note written in 1815, Schopenhauer declares: "*My philosophy* will never in the least go beyond the realm of experience [*Erfahrung*], that is to say of the perceptible in the fullest range of the concept. For, like every art, it will merely repeat the world."[13] His philosophy, like art, has the task of "repeating the world," but, unlike art, it does so in abstract conceptual language (in which case it resembles science). Being based solely on experience, Schopenhauer's philosophy will say nothing about how or why or if the world came about or where it is headed—for all of this would amount to a transcendent metaphysics. Although Schopenhauer may now and again step over this self-imposed limitation,[14] he usually abides by it. Accordingly, whether Schopenhauer's philosophy does or can contain a metaphysics depends on what one means by "metaphysics": If one means an account of how or why or even if the world originated, then one must conclude that Schopenhauer does not put forth a metaphysics; but if one means an account of what the world is, or actually what the world is besides representation, then one must ascribe to Schopenhauer a metaphysics. For what the world is besides representation, he claims, is will, and that claim is a metaphysical one—where "metaphysical" concerns simply the other-than-representational. As noted above, Schopenhauer calls his metaphysics immanent in contrast to transcendent, "immanent" referring precisely to that which appears in appearance (or in experience), and "transcendent" referring to whatever may be wholly beyond appearance (or experience), hence wholly beyond that which may be expressed in language. (Language, for Schopenhauer, may become very abstract, but if it is to remain meaningful it must not denominate anything lying wholly beyond the realm of experience.)[15]

Whether metaphysics is possible, and of what sort, is hardly mentioned in volume 1 of *The World as Will and Representation*, but in volume 2, especially in the chapter called "On Man's Need for Metaphysics," the topic receives a fairly thorough treatment. In this extremely wide-ranging chapter, the central idea of which is perhaps that "man" is "an *animal metaphysicum*,"[16] Schopenhauer offers a definition of metaphysics:

> By *metaphysics* I understand every alleged knowledge that goes beyond the possibility of experience, and so beyond nature or the given appearance of things, in order to give information about that by which, in some sense or other, that [nature? or given appearance?] would be conditioned, or in popular language, about that which is hidden under nature and makes it possible.[17]

Given this definition, one might expect that Schopenhauer would deny the possibility of metaphysics, for as defined it would appear to be a transcendent inquiry. But, as later remarks make clear, "going beyond the possibility of experience" can, despite appearances, remain immanent.

Schopenhauer begins the heart of his account by agreeing with Kant that experience must be analyzed into appearance and the thing in itself, or what are, in other words, "the forms of knowledge and the being in itself of things,"[18] or, further, the forms of things experienced and the content of those very same things. From this starting point, a legitimate sort of metaphysics can arise—one that remains immanent and even, in a sense, experiential, in that it deals with things experienced and only with them. Specifically, Schopenhauer holds, this metaphysics deals with the "kernel" of the appearance, to which he adds this significant comment: "It is true that this kernel can never be entirely separated from the appearance, and be regarded by itself as an *ens extramundanum*; but it is known [*erkennen*, recognized] always only in its relations and connections to the appearance itself."[19] And then this:

Only the clarification and interpretation of this [appearance], in relation [*Bezug*] to its inner kernel, can give us information about it which does not otherwise come into consciousness. Therefore in this sense metaphysics goes beyond the appearance, i.e., nature, to what is concealed in or behind it . . . yet always regarding it only as that which appears in it, but not independently of all appearance. Metaphysics thus remains immanent, and does not become transcendent. For it never tears itself entirely from experience, but remains the mere clarification and interpretation thereof, as it never speaks of the thing in itself otherwise than in its relation [*Beziehung*, connection] to the appearance.[20]

Schopenhauer makes here two important points about his metaphysics: (1) It will say nothing about any "thing in itself" existing (subsisting, obtaining) wholly apart from experience or independent of all appearance, but only about (say) the thing in itself of appearance (hence, if by "noumenon" or "the noumenal" critics mean some "thing in itself" wholly apart from experience and appearance, then they are referring to something—or rather to a "nothing"—that Schopenhauer's metaphysics ignores); and (2) it is an interpretive endeavor, rather like a deciphering of a document whose script is not understood at the start or the decoding of a secret message that only after a number of unsuccessful tests finally proves to be sensible and intelligible. Concerning this second point, Schopenhauer writes: "Then there remains no doubt as to the correctness of the deciphering, since it is not possible for the agreement and consistency, in which all the signs of that writing are placed by this interpretation, to be merely accidental; nor is it possible for us, by giving the letters an entirely different value, to recognize words and sentences in this new arrangement of them."[21] This remark presupposes that we have a language to start with. I would like to suggest that we must first of all know how to talk about our own "kernel" before we can come to know how to "decipher" the "kernel" of nature: In the experience or recognition of the "identity" (yet difference) of the knowing and willing subject in ourselves, we find the "key" for understanding the "identity" (yet difference) of the world as representation and world as will. Hence again: The macrocosm is the microcosm writ large, and the microcosm is the macrocosm writ small.

Not being transcendent in at least two basic ways—that is, not being concerned with the origin or destination of the world and not dealing with anything that may "exist" apart from the world (as appearance)—Schopenhauer's metaphysics acknowledges several limitations. In fact, Schopenhauer makes an explicit point of granting that his solution to "the riddle of the world" does not by any means answer every possible question that the human mind might raise. (Incidentally, this "modesty" does not come forth in the first volume of *The World as Will and Representation*; there the reader is led to think that Schopenhauer believed himself to have solved all central philosophical questions, as is perhaps typical of youthful thinkers.)[22] Although his philosophy contains no doctrine incompatible with any obvious fact about the world, because "each one has been thought out in the presence of perceived reality, and none has its root in abstract concepts alone," and although "it contains a fundamental thought [*Grundgedanke*] that is applied to all appearances of the world as their key," which thus proves to be "the correct alphabet" for understanding the world,[23] his teaching, Schopenhauer notes, does not add everything up "in the sense that it leaves no problem still to be solved, no possible question unanswered."[24]

> To assert anything of the kind would be a presumptuous denial of the limits of human knowledge in general. Whatever torch we kindle, and whatever space it may illuminate, our horizon will always remain encircled by the depth of night.[25] For the ultimate solution of the riddle of the world would necessarily have to speak merely of things in themselves, no longer of appearances. All our forms of knowledge, however, pertain precisely to appearances alone; therefore we must make everything comprehensible through coexistence, succession, and relations of causality. But these forms have sense and meaning only in relation to the appearance; things in themselves themselves [*Dinge an sich selbst*] and their possible relations cannot be comprehended through those forms. Therefore the actual, positive solution to the riddle of the world must be something that the human intellect is wholly incapable of comprehending and thinking; so that if a being of a higher order came and took all the trouble to impart it to us, we should be able to understand absolutely nothing of his revelations. Accordingly, those who profess to know the ultimate, i.e., the first, grounds of things, thus a primordial being, an Absolute, or whatever else they choose to call it, together with the process, the reasons, the motives, or anything else, in consequence of which the world results from them, or emanates, or falls, or is produced, set in existence, "discharged" and ushered out, are playing tricks, are windbags, if not just charlatans.[26]

Since the human intellect is directed only to the world as representation, being nothing but the knowing subject of representations, it cannot reach out beyond the world as representation and purport *to know*, that is, *to have as object*, things in themselves. We should note well, then, that for Schopenhauer we human beings cannot know any thing in itself, we cannot know any thing as it is in itself; or, to put it conversely, nothing in itself can become for us an object (of knowledge).

This all-important conviction is repeated when Schopenhauer states in the chapter called "On the Knowability of the Thing in Itself"[27] that "there is a contradiction in the assertion that a thing is known according to what it is in and by itself,"[28] and that "being-known of itself contradicts being in itself."[29] In none of this, however, does Schopenhauer deny the possibility of interpreting the world as representation, that is, the possibility of "deciphering" it. On the contrary, Schopenhauer affirms this possibility, which is in fact the possibility of engaging in metaphysics, and he carries it out in terms of that which we find in ourselves (through self-consciousness) as will or, as he says more and more, as will to live (or will to life, *Wille zum Leben*).

In several of Schopenhauer's letters written after the publication of the second edition of *The World as Will and Representation* (1844), there appears an explicit treatment of the will, the thing in itself, knowability, and interpretation—all of which notions bear directly on (say) the possibility of metaphysics. I propose to cite a few particularly relevant passages:

> I have never written the history of the thing in itself, as it may be outside of time, but only of that of the thing in itself objectifying itself in time, where it arises [*auftreten*] as will to life. I have demonstrated the phenomenon of its affirmation and (entering into time) its negation. I have shown that the existence of the world is the appearance of its affirmation; therefore it is not that of its negation. "No will, no representation, no world—for us nothing."—Further than this negative truth I have not gone; otherwise I would have had to become transcendent. Thus I have interpreted [*auslegen*] only appearance and placed it in relation to that which appears, the thing in itself. I have never set myself the task, on the other hand, of constructing processes in the thing in itself; precisely that differentiates me from the 3 famous sophists whose whole philosophy is a construct of the so-called Absolute.[30]

Schopenhauer clearly avers in this passage that the thing in itself, objectifying itself in time, arises or appears as will to life. And he denies asserting anything about the thing in itself as it may be outside of time or apart from objectifying itself in time. He claims further that the existence of the world is the appearance of the affirmation of the will to life, and it is not the appearance of the negation of the will to life; with the negation of the will to life there is for us no appearance, no representation, no world, hence *for us* there is nothing. Finally, it is suggested that the thing in itself is that which appears in appearance (*das Erscheinende in der Erscheinung*).

In a letter written eight years later, to Julius Frauenstädt, Schopenhauer castigates the future literary executor of his *Nachlaß* for suggesting that he, like Kant, should have left undetermined what the thing in itself is.

> Then I could immediately throw my whole philosophy out the window. It is precisely my great discovery that Kant's thing in itself is that which we find in self-consciousness as the will, and that this [will] is completely different from and independent of the intellect, therefore without this is present in all things. But this will is thing in itself merely in relation to appearance: it is what this [appearance] is, independently of our perception and representation, which means precisely in itself; therefore it is that which appears in every appearance, the kernel of every being. As such it is will, will to life.

That it can get loose from willing is shown, in human beings, by the ascetics in Asia and Europe through the millennia. [*The World as Will and Representation*, I, section 70]. This getting loose, or rather its result, is for us immediately a transition into nothing (Nirvana = nothing); but all nothing is relative [*ibid.*, section 71].—Going beyond these cognitions is absolutely transcendent; therefore philosophy stops here, and mysticism begins. . . . The thing in itself you are always to seek only in appearance, as present merely in relation to it, not therefore in the cloud-cuckoo-land, where you seem often to contemplate it; thereinto we cannot go; that is to say, it is transcendent. You must always keep in mind what the intellect is, a mere tool of assistance for the paltry purposes of an individual appearance of the will. Hence Kant has demonstrated its limits, and I have, in addition, demonstrated the source of this limitation—he in a subjective, I in an objective way; because I with the will have won for myself a Πον στω [*pon stō*, foothold]. My philosophy does not undertake to clarify how a world such as this one has been able to come about, but merely to orient ourselves therein, i.e., to say *what* it is.[31]

Here Schopenhauer insists that Kant's thing in itself is the will, that it is "completely different from and independent of the intellect," hence that its presence in all things is not contingent on the intellect, but yet that "the will is thing in itself merely in relation to appearance" in that it is what appearance is, and thus "the kernel of every being." It seems then that we cannot speak of the thing in itself *and* appearance—as if they were two "things," hence possibly as if the former were the cause of the latter—but only of the thing in itself in appearance, that is, of that which appears in appearance; and this, says Schopenhauer, is the will to life. It seems further that this world "lying before us" (as it is often put) is the will to life made object, indeed, perceptual object, in virtue of the forms of the intellect, hence this world is the will to life presented to us temporally, spatially, and causally.

Frauenstädt persisted in claiming that it was an error to characterize the thing in itself as will on the ground that, according to Schopenhauer, the will is eliminateable while the concept of the thing in itself contains noneliminateableness, indestructibility, "since we understand by the *thing in itself* that which remains over after everything else, everything merely relative, transitory, appearing is eliminated."[32] In response Schopenhauer criticizes Frauenstädt for failing to take notice of the passages he had cited in his previous letter.

In vain, for example, I have written that you are not to seek the thing in itself in the cloud-cuckoo-land (i.e., there where the Jewish God sits) but rather in the things of this world—therefore in the table on which you write, in the chair under your worthiness. Moreover you say, "it remains a contradiction that I speak of the thing in itself in terms incompatible with the concept of the thing in itself." Quite right! with *your* concept of the thing in it-

self it is eternally incompatible, and this you make known to us in the following declared definition: the thing in itself is "the eternal, nonoriginating,
and nonceasing original being [*Urwesen*]."—*That* would be the thing in itself?!—I'll tell you what that is: that is the well-known Absolute, thus the
disguised cosmological proof on which the Jewish God rides. . . . You have
wanted to give him a new mask and title; only that this is stolen from the
Kantian closet do we raise a protest. Name him therefore like the others, in
your sense philosophizing comrades, e.g., the supersensuous, the divin-
ity, the unending, the unthinkable, or most prettily, with Hegel, "the Udea"
[*die Uedäh*].—We know however what is stuck under all of this: it is the
master of the Absolute, who, when one grabs it and says, "where did you
come from, fellow?" answers: "Impertinent question! I am the master of the
Absolute, who is liable to no accountability; that follows 'analytically from
my name.'"[33]

A bit later, in the same letter, Schopenhauer remarks that Kant gives the
meaning of the thing in itself (which he does not explain) and he (Schopenhauer) tells us what it is. He then writes:

> My philosophy never speaks of the cloud-cuckoo-land, but of *this world*; that
> is, it is immanent, not transcendent. It spells out the world lying before
> us, like a hieroglyphics-tablet (whose key I have found in the will), and
> shows its interconnection throughout. It teaches what appearance is, and
> what the thing in itself is. This [latter], however, is the thing in itself merely
> relatively, i.e., in its relation to appearance; and this [appearance] is appear-
> ance merely in its relation to the thing in itself. Beyond that *it* is a brain-
> phenomenon. What, however, the thing in itself is outside that relation I
> have never said, because I don't know it; but *in* that relation it is will to life.
> That this can be eliminated I have demonstrated empirically; and I have
> merely concluded that with the thing in itself its appearance must also fall
> away. Denial of the will to life is not the annihilation of an object or being,
> but mere not-willing, in consequence of a *quieter.*—Grasp it and note it!

Just as it makes sense to speak of appearance only in relation to that which
appears, namely, the thing in itself, so it makes sense to speak of the thing
in itself only in relation to appearance, as (say) the essence of appearance.
And the thing in itself in relation to appearance is will to life. This statement forms the core of Schopenhauer's entire philosophy (at least according to this letter). What the thing in itself may be otherwise, that is, wholly
apart from appearance, hence (one might say) what the thing in itself in
itself is, this can never be said, and Schopenhauer's philosophy says nothing about it. Also reiterated here is the claim that when the thing in itself
in appearance, that is, the will to life, ceases (as with extreme ascetics or
mystics), then appearance also ceases—and therewith the possibility of
philosophical discourse.

The most striking and puzzling aspect of Schopenhauer's account here—
and presumably the aspect that Frauenstädt found unacceptable—is the

suggestion that the thing in itself is relative to and dependent on appearance (just as, unproblematically, appearance is relative to and dependent on the thing in itself). We have been led to believe that the thing in itself is unconditioned being and that appearance (or representation) is conditioned being—not only by the knowing subject but also by the thing in itself. Is Schopenhauer now, in later life, denying this proposition? Has he changed his conception of the thing in itself? Doesn't the term "the thing in itself" just mean unconditioned or nonrelative being, hence being unconnected to appearance? And isn't Frauenstädt right in interpreting Schopenhauer as holding that when (if ever) the will is eliminated, as with the ascetics or mystics, the thing in itself remains over? No fully adequate response can yet be given to these concerns, but several things can be said. First, so far as philosophy goes, the thing in itself and appearance are conjoined such that the world is thing in itself in appearance, and as such it is the will to life, the will made visible, indeed, the will manifesting itself to the will ("The world is the self-knowledge of the will"). Second, the propositions "The world is appearance (or representation)" and "The world is thing in itself (or will)" express only the two aspects of the world, that is, of one and the same world; they do not point to two worlds or even two "things" constituting the world. These two propositions, in other words, are abstract and one-sided, which is to say that they simply characterize the world from two perspectives, either of which by itself is correct but incomplete—just as "I am knowing subject" and "I am willing subject" characterize the ego (*das Ich*), the subject that I am, from two perspectives.

These responses help solve the first difficulty mentioned at the beginning of this chapter, namely, how we are to understand the "relation" between representation and will as thing in itself. The solution is that the representation is will as thing in itself become object, become knowable or visible. Since representation and will are not, literally, two different things, they do not, literally, stand in a relation to each other. In fact, they are "identical" with each other, in the same way that a voluntary bodily movement and an act of will are "identical"—two sides or aspects of one and the same thing, expressible perhaps as "an action." The alleged comparison is not exact or perfect, however, for will as thing in itself is not subject to any form of the principle of sufficient reason, while an act of will is subject to the form of time. This small deficiency turns out to have a very favorable result: Only because an act of will has at least one feature fully in common with the world of nature, namely, the feature of time, can an act of will serve as the key to interpreting the world of nature (more about which below).

Do we now have enough information to answer, on Schopenhauer's behalf, the objections urged by Copleston, Gardiner, and Janaway? I think so, at least for the most part. Copleston's main point is that there can be no knowledge of the thing in itself (which he calls "the noumenal"), hence there can be no metaphysical knowledge. If he means that the thing in itself, apart from appearance (which he calls "the phenomenon"), can never be an object of knowledge (*Erkenntniß*), then he is perfectly right and in full accord with Schopenhauer's explicit position. Even if he means that there can be no knowledge of will as thing in itself, that is, that will as thing in itself cannot become an object understood precisely as will as thing in itself, then he is also right and, again, in full accord with Schopenhauer's view. (Actually, will as thing in itself is will that is not object, though when will—not now as thing in itself—does become object, it does so either as Ideas or as individual representations. This will be discussed in chapter 6.) But if he means that there is no justification for interpreting the appearing world (the world as representation, "the phenomenon") as being essentially will, then he is wrong. Nothing in Schopenhauer's "doctrine of the phenomenon" precludes such an interpretation, and indeed one thing that is "known," namely, individual acts of will, provides the key for the interpretation. An act of will is not "known" by way of sensory data; it is not a perceptual object; but it is a temporal object of which everyone is fully aware, Schopenhauer holds, in conjunction with (voluntary) bodily movements, which are full-fledged perceptual objects or rather, actually, changes in the (peculiar, it must be said) perceptual object called the body.

Gardiner holds that if we are directly conscious of ourselves as will, then "the will falls within the range of our experience," hence it must be a representation and therefore not the thing in itself. He adds, in effect, that no consciousness of anything representational can give us access to the thing in itself, given that the latter is by definition nonrepresentational, lying beyond the realm of appearance or representation. Now, to begin with, what we are directly conscious of is, again, acts of will, which is to say that we recognize "immediately" the "inner side" of those bodily movements that are voluntary or motivated (as opposed to being caused from without, by causes proper or stimuli). On the basis of this singular experience, whereby, it may be said—albeit with some latitude—we recognize that we are essentially will and only "accidentally" representation, we discover the key for interpreting the changes in the world of nature. Second, in reality there are not two realms—the so-called noumenal and the phenomenal—but only one world, the thing in itself in appearance. Yet, if "the noumenal" or the thing in itself is defined as what the world is, wholly apart from being appearance or representation, hence wholly apart from being knowable, then clearly it does not fall within the range of our experience (to use Gardiner's phrase). On this Schopenhauer insists time and time again. But if the thing in itself is always thing in itself only in "relation" to appearance, as (say) the kernel of appearance, and if we have a

recognition of the thing in itself of our own appearance—through immediate awareness of acts of will—then we may use this recognition as the
key for interpreting the world of nature. (This is not to say that an act of
will is one's own thing in itself, but only that immediate awareness of an
act of will is in effect "knowledge" or recognition [*Erkenntniß*] of oneself as
will, hence of one's own thing in itself in appearance—not totally or fully
or perfectly however. It is the same with "knowledge" of a perceptual object: Every single experience of a perceptual object is an experience of the
object, but no single experience exhausts the object, and perhaps not
even all actually possible ones do; more are always possible.) So, finally, do
we have knowledge of the thing in itself in the appearing world? No,
never. Do we have grounds for interpreting the thing in itself in the appearing world as that which we find ourselves to be through the immediate awareness of acts of will, hence upon performing voluntary bodily
movements? Yes, most assuredly.

Janaway suggests that there can be no knowledge about oneself that is
not a matter of representation, hence that Schopenhauer cannot advance
from self-knowledge to knowledge of the thing in itself. Well, that I am
now in pain is something "I know," and pain (Schopenhauer claims) is not
a representation; nor of course is pleasure, which I can also "know."
Consequently, it is not the case (for Schopenhauer at least) that there can
be no knowledge about oneself that is not a matter of representation. And
once I analyze what a pain or a pleasure is, I see that it has reference to
myself as will and makes no sense otherwise: A pain is an impression that I
do not want, a pleasure an impression I like—"want" and "like" referring
necessarily to will. Moreover, and once again, Schopenhauer never claims
that I have knowledge of the thing in itself or of anything as it is in itself—
when "thing in itself" is strictly defined, namely, such that being-known
contradicts it. But I do have knowledge of or at least I am aware of acts of
will, precisely in those cases when my bodily movements are voluntary; in
fact, it may be said, I recognize a bodily movement to be voluntary when,
and only when, I am aware simultaneously of its "other side" as an act of
will. Are acts of will representations? Not exactly: They are certainly not
representations in the same way that objects in the world of nature are,
that is, they are not perceptual constructs built up out of sensory materials. (Acts of will are more like pains and pleasures than like normal perceptual objects.) However, my bodily movements are exactly like changes
in bodies or objects in the world of nature. So, according to Schopenhauer, I "transfer" what I recognize about my voluntary bodily movements,
namely, that their "other side" is acts of will, to changes in bodies in nature—this "transference" being really a matter of interpretation.

Several things have gone wrong in these criticisms of Schopenhauer's
position. First, the critics impose upon his position terms and concepts

(particularly, "the noumenon" or "the noumenal") that are really only appropriate to Kant's philosophy (and even then only to a particular conception of Kant's philosophy). This practice is understandable, given Schopenhauer's frequently declared allegiance to Kant, but, despite what Schopenhauer may have thought, his position differs considerably from Kant's on many crucial issues—even, I would say, on the very meaning(s) of "the thing in itself." (As suggested in an earlier chapter, Schopenhauer would have been much better off if he had eschewed at least much of Kant's terminology, including "the thing in itself.") Second, the critics fail to see that Schopenhauer allows for a kind of awareness or recognition—a sort of "feeling"—that differs quite a lot from representation: Awareness of pains and pleasures, as well as awareness of acts of will, are not typical instances of representation, which is to say that they are not cases of perceptual or intuitive representation based on sensory data. Third, these critics overlook the fact that Schopenhauer's metaphysics is really an interpretive study, not literally a cognitive science; otherwise put, it is more a matter of decipherment than a matter of acquaintance. When one says that "I know (by way of interpretation) that the world of nature is will," one is not necessarily saying that "I know (by acquaintance) the will." (Interpretive knowledge differs from knowledge by acquaintance.) Fourth and finally, the critics seem to assume that Schopenhauer is a dualist; but actually he is an essentialist (the world is essentially will, and only accidentally representation) or, in a very unusual sense, a double-aspect theorist (the world, from one aspect, is will and, from another, representation— the former being fundamental). For Schopenhauer, it is not the case that there are two worlds, or even two realms (domains or whatever) of the world; for him, it is the case, however, that there are two basic ways of viewing one and the same world—that world lying before us—namely, as representation and as will. The term "as" cannot be ignored: *The World as Will and Representation* is a treatise about *the* world, on the one hand, *as* will and, on the other hand, *as* representation. One world; two ways of looking at it—one way interpretive, and the other cognitive.

Rather than critically examine the objections put forth by Copleston, Gardiner, Janaway, and others (as I have done), one might attempt to undermine the objections by denying their underlying presupposition, namely, that Schopenhauer believes the will to be the thing in itself (which is the tack taken by Julian Young). Young argues that, for Schopenhauer, three and not just two things (he even says "worlds") must be distinguished: the thing in itself, the will, and the representation or appearance.[34] Knowledge of the representation is normal intuitive or scientific knowledge; knowledge of the will is metaphysical knowledge; but there can be no knowledge of the thing in itself. Accordingly, it is no objection to Schopenhauer's scheme of things to argue, as do the aforementioned critics, that the thing in itself cannot really be known; for, according to Young, Schopenhauer himself urges, or at least should urge, this very contention. To put Young's interpretation a bit differently, Schopenhauer advances a trichotomic ontology, not a dichotomic one.

It could be the case, of course, that Schopenhauer simply contradicts himself, holding both that the will is the thing in itself and that the will is not the thing in itself;[35] or it might be that, for him, the will is in one sense the thing in itself but in another sense not (or not exactly, not fully) the thing in itself; or it could be that early on Schopenhauer takes the will to be the thing in itself but later he finds some important differences between the two. As a matter of fact, some of the crucial evidence that Young cites for his interpretation does not appear in the first edition of *The World as Will and Representation*, even when it stands in the first volume, for example, Schopenhauer's remark that "my path lies midway between the doctrine of omniscience of the earlier dogmatism [the claims of rationalist metaphysicians to be able to know by pure thought the character of ultimate reality] and the despair of the Kantian critique." Young calls this "a conclusion which affirms precisely the trichotomy I have proposed."[36] Possibly, then, Schopenhauer's conception of the thing in itself changes over time, meaning at first only the essence (meaning, content) of the world as representation—in which case it is the will—but meaning later something going beyond even the essence of the world as representation—in which case it would be wholly unknowable, indeed unthinkable, "in itself." It is very difficult to decide which of these possibilities, if any single one of them, actually holds, hence it is very difficult to evaluate Young's interpretation.

Nevertheless, as noted above, Schopenhauer devotes one chapter in volume 2 of *The World as Will and Representation*, "On the Knowability of the Thing in Itself," explicitly to the issue at hand, and I propose to examine it in some detail.[37] What Schopenhauer should maintain in this chapter is this: Will is the thing in itself (meaning the essence, content, or meaning) of the world as representation or world as appearance, and this proposition (through interpretation or decipherment) is something that human beings can know; human beings, however, are incapable of knowing (i.e., of being acquainted with) will as thing in itself in appearance; what they do know in themselves, besides those "affections" of their will called pains and pleasures, are acts of will, which being in time are partial appearances; indeed, only as appearances, at least in part, could they provide a key for interpreting outer, full appearances (temporal, spatial, and causal) as being will in themselves, as being will in essence;[38] there can be no knowledge, whether direct or interpretive, of any thing in itself, wholly apart from appearance.

Now, Schopenhauer does explicitly state that "there is a contradiction in the assertion that a thing is known according to what it is in and by itself, in other words, outside our knowledge." And why? Simply because "all knowing is essentially a making of representation" and "my making of representations, just because it is mine, can never be identical with the being in itself of the thing outside me."[39] What a thing is in and of itself is actually defined as what it is as unknown, hence to speak of knowing such a thing (which amounts to knowing it as unknown) is self-contradictory. Schopenhauer assumes, however, that some sort of being in itself must be "conceded" to every representation,[40] but he insists that "on the path of *objective knowledge*, thus starting from the *representation*, we shall never get beyond the representation, i.e., the appearance.[41] "So far," Schopenhauer adds, "I agree with Kant." Then there appears this famous (or, in the minds of some, including Young,[42] this infamous) passage:

> But now, as the counterpoise to this truth, I have stressed that other truth that we are not merely the *knowing subject*, but that *we ourselves* are also among the beings to be known, that *we ourselves are the thing in itself*. Consequently, a way *from within* stands open to us to our very own and inner essence of things to which we cannot penetrate *from without*. It is, so to speak, a subterranean passage, a secret alliance, which, as if by treachery, places us all at once in the fortress that could not be taken by attack from without. Precisely as such, the *thing in itself* can come into consciousness only quite [*ganz*] directly, namely, by *it itself being conscious of itself*; to try [*wollen*] to know it objectively is to demand something contradictory. Everything objective is representation, consequently appearance, in fact mere brain-phenomenon.[43]

In this passage Schopenhauer characterizes the objective world as a fortress that is impregnable from without, and he claims in effect that what the objective world is in itself can be discerned only by employing the subjective tactic of discovering what the human individual is in itself, hence the mention of "a subterranean passage." (Allusion is made once again to theoretical egoism—the impregnable fortress from without.) This amounts to saying, as Schopenhauer does say just below, that "we must learn to understand nature from ourselves, not ourselves from nature."[44] Self-knowledge, that is, knowledge of one's own willing, Schopenhauer expresses thus: The thing in itself is conscious of itself. This curious statement calls to mind the proposition that the world is the self-knowledge of the will (the "single thought"), and it is just as difficult to understand as the "single thought." But the following remarks may help.

The subject of knowing (the intellect) and the subject of willing (the will) are the two components of self-consciousness or inner knowledge: The former knows and the latter is known. (This knowing, however, is not "intuitive," that is, it is not a matter of *Anschauung*, for, as Schopenhauer notes, "all intuition is spatial," and the willing subject is not in space.)[45] Hence the principle of all knowing—the correlation of subject and object—is preserved in self-consciousness, which is to say that "although the two flow together into the consciousness of an I, . . . this I is not *intimate* with itself through and through . . . but is opaque, and therefore remains a riddle to itself."[46] The I would be intimate with itself, apparently, only if it were conscious of itself wholly apart from all forms of knowing—a conceptual impossibility. "But," Schopenhauer states, "the inner knowledge is free from two forms belonging to outer knowledge, the form of *space* and the form of *causality* which brings about all sense-perception [*Sinnesanschauung*]," yet "there still remains the form of *time*, as well as that of being known and of knowing in general." This means that the subject of willing is not known as located in space, and knowledge of it is not conveyed by sensation from which perception proceeds; but the subject of willing is a known object and it is known in time, which is to say that one knows one's own will (or willing) only in "slices," that is, in acts of will occurring in time.

> Accordingly, in this inner knowledge the thing in itself has indeed to a great extent cast off its veils [i.e., the forms of knowing], but still does not appear quite naked. In consequence of the form of time which still adheres to it, everyone knows his own *will* only in its successive individual *acts*, not however as a whole, in and by itself. Hence no one knows his character a priori, but he becomes acquainted with it only by way of experience and always imperfectly [*unvollkommen*, incompletely].[47]

It can be said, therefore, that I know my will only in the sense that I know, that is, I am directly aware of, individual acts of will, which are temporal (but not spatial or causal) appearances of my will. I am never directly aware of my will "as a whole," or a priori, or entirely free from the conditions contained in the principle of sufficient reason; I am never aware of my will free from time.

Are we now in a position to determine whether, in Schopenhauer's view, will is the thing in itself (as most commentators maintain) or will is to be distinguished from the thing in itself (as Young holds)? No final determination of this issue can be reached without a consideration of the Ideas (in the next chapter) and an examination of asceticism and mysticism (in chapter 7). But judging from what we have already surveyed, we can say with relative certainty a number of things. One, it makes no literal sense to speak of the thing in itself *simpliciter*, that is, apart from its relation to appearance; accordingly, the apt expression is "the thing in itself in appearance," and it designates the essence (content, meaning) of, say, the world as appearance; this essence goes by the name "will," which is to say that will is the essence or, if one likes, the thing in itself of the world as appearance. Two, it makes no sense to regard the thing in itself as an ontological item, an entity, an object, a thing: *Das Ding an sich ist kein Ding.*

We can speak only of what some thing is in itself, that is, what that (known) thing is in addition to being known, to being object or appearance or representation; and that, Schopenhauer claims, is will—whether we are referring to an individual thing or to the whole of nature, that is, whether we are referring to a single appearance (such as this chair) or *the* appearance (meaning the entire world as representation). Three, we are incapable of becoming acquainted with any thing as it is in itself, which is to say that we can never have direct access to the essence of any single thing or to the essence of the whole world as appearance. But on the basis of direct acquaintance with acts of will (in ourselves), we are placed in a position to interpret the essence of all appearance as will; in fact, we have to interpret it as such—or else revert to the despair of Kant's unknowability thesis without qualification.

These three contentions Schopenhauer should explicitly put forth, but he does so only in part and he occasionally denies (or seems to deny) some aspects of them when he proceeds toward the end of chapter 18 of *The World as Will and Representation*, volume 2. The first important passage goes thus: "With the emergence of an act of will out of the dark depth of our inner being into the knowing consciousness, there occurs a direct transition into appearance of the thing in itself lying outside of time."[48] An act of my will's becoming conscious is the atemporal thing in itself's entering into appearance, specifically, into time. In other words, this "atemporal thing in itself" is that which appears in the appearance otherwise known as an "act of will" (or so at least Schopenhauer seems to hold). "Accordingly," he adds, "the act of will is only the nearest and clearest *appearance* of the thing in itself," which suggests, of course, that the act of will is not identical with the thing in itself. Then, Schopenhauer remarks, "if all other appearances could be known so immediately and intimately by us, we would have to assign to them that which the will is in us," but actually no other appearance is so immediately and intimately known by us.

> Therefore in this sense I teach that the inner essence of every thing is *will*, and I call the will the thing in itself. In this way, *Kant's* doctrine of the unknowability of the thing in itself is modified in that it is not absolutely and completely unknowable, in that nevertheless the by far most immediate of its appearances, distinguished *toto genere* from all the rest by this immediateness, represents [*vertreten*] it for us.[49]

On the basis of this unique awareness, namely, awareness of an act of will, which has to be reckoned an object (only) in time and therefore a temporal appearance, Schopenhauer believes himself justified in holding that "the inner essence of every thing is *will*." He takes the act of will to be the temporal appearance of the atemporal will as thing in itself, but the will as thing in itself is never an appearance—indeed, the very idea is self-contradictory. Or, to put it differently, the will as thing in itself is by defini-tion nonappearance, nonobject, nonknowable (by acquaintance); but an individual act of will is an appearance, an object (albeit only a temporal object), knowable and known. Insofar as it can be said that the will as thing in itself "presents itself to us," it must be stipulated that it does not do so exactly, precisely, and wholly as it is, but only as an individual act of will, which (in contrast to outer appearance) is the "most immediate" ap-pearance of will as thing in itself. The act of will is therefore, for us, the representative or deputy (*Vertreter*) of the will as thing in itself, which en-tails that we "know" the latter only by "immediately knowing" the former (as one may "know" a gigantic business organization only by "knowing," in person, its highest-level agent, say, the chief executive officer).

Now, Schopenhauer continues, we can raise the question of "what that will, which presents itself in the world and as the world, is ultimately and absolutely in itself, i.e., what it is, completely apart from the fact that it presents itself as *will*, or in general *appears*, i.e., in general *is known*." He flatly asserts that "This question can *never* be answered, because . . . being-known itself contradicts being in itself and everything known is as such only appearance."[50] Actually, the question is very strange; it seems to be, "What is the will apart from presenting itself as will, hence apart from ap-pearing?" And the answer would seem to be forthcoming and obvious, namely, that it is nothing. For what else could will be except will? It would be what it presents itself as: It would be will and, necessarily, it would pre-sent itself as will. Is Schopenhauer supposing, on the other hand, that will might not present itself as will, and that will not presenting itself as will would be will as it is in itself? Precisely here, it seems (in accord with Young's account), Schopenhauer drives a wedge between the thing in it-self and the will; for he proceeds with the following remarks on the un-answerable question:

> But the possibility of this question shows that the thing in itself, which we know most immediately in the will, may have, entirely outside all possible ap-pearance, determinations, qualities, and modes of existence which for us are absolutely unknowable and incomprehensible, and which then remain as the essence of the thing in itself, when this, as explained in the fourth book, has freely abolished itself as *will*, has thus stepped out of the appearance en-tirely, and as regards our knowledge, that is to say, as regards the world of appearance, has passed over into empty nothingness. If the will were simply and absolutely the thing in itself, then this nothing would be an *absolute* one, instead of which it expressly results there for us only as a *relative* one.[51]

This seems to suggest that it is possible for the thing in itself to "freely abolish itself as *will*" and yet remain as something—albeit something that we human beings cannot know or grasp, and therefore something that philosophy (as an immanent metaphysics) cannot characterize, at least in "positive" terms. Not only is, say, the abolition of the will possible, Schopenhauer claims here, it is an actual, undeniable fact.

The final sentence in the long passage just quoted means that once willing has ceased, then the world "for us," that is, the world as representation or the world as known, has ceased, which is not to say, however, that absolutely everything must have ceased; indeed, it is suggested that the thing in itself, apparently meaning now ultimate reality or unconditioned being, remains. This consideration, which gives perhaps the best support for Young's thesis that will is not identical with the thing in itself, contradicts Schopenhauer's claim, cited earlier, that the thing in itself is thing in itself only in relation to appearance. He could mean, however, that it makes philosophical sense to speak of the thing in itself only in relation to appearance, but that beyond philosophy, hence with mysticism, the thing in itself wholly apart from appearance must be acknowledged—even though nothing can be said about it, at least "positively," for to do so would amount to transcendent metaphysics.

One of the more puzzling statements in the aforecited passage is that, in effect, "the essence of the thing in itself" can "freely abolish itself as *will*" (and then "remain" or "remain over," *übrig bleiben*). What could be meant by this subject-term? Does it make any sense to suppose that the thing in itself has an essence or that this so-called essence can abolish itself as will? Not really. What does make sense is the suggestion—however difficult it is to explain—that certain human individuals can, and do, cease selfish willing, in which case they adopt the incentive of compassion or pity (*Mitleid*) and thereby abandon egoism and, of course, malice. It also makes sense to suggest that certain individuals (those called geniuses) engage in aesthetic contemplation, whereby their knowledge becomes "objective" rather than "subjective" or will-governed, and they are said to contemplate the Platonic Ideas. In neither case, by the way, does the world cease to be; for with genuine moral virtue, one is aware of suffering in others that one views as if it were one's own; and with aesthetic contemplation, one becomes aware of the world as Idea, hence of the will become "pure" object. In both cases, then, knowledge continues, but it is "objective" knowledge, and the world remains, but it is a world in which selfishness, "subjectivity," or even individuality no longer reigns. "What happens to the world once affirmation of the (individual) will to live ceases?" is analogous to "What happens in the individual character once selfishness (etc.) ceases?" These two questions are even more than analogous; they are identical—the former stressing the objective side of what the latter stresses on the subjective side. For, after all, cessation of the will to life occurs only with and in human individuals; literally, the so-called "essence of the thing in itself" has nothing to do with the matter.

We seem to be faced with two positions concerning the will and the thing in itself: (1) The will is the thing in itself, which is to say that will is the essence of the world as appearance or that will is what the world is besides representation; and (2) the will is not the thing in itself, or rather will is not identical with the thing in itself, for will can cease and the thing in itself yet remain over. The two positions are contradictory, provided that "the thing in itself" means the same thing in both propositions. They are not contradictory, however, if (as I suspect) Schopenhauer has two different conceptions of the thing in itself. On the philosophical conception, one may speak (as Schopenhauer often does) of the "will as thing in itself," whereby will and thing in itself are identified; but here "thing in itself" is only a short-hand term for "thing in itself in appearance," which means, in effect, that thing in itself is thing in itself only in relation to appearance, being actually the essence of inner nature of (the world as) appearance. In a phrase, then, will is the thing in itself in appearance. What appearance is in itself, what it is that appears in appearance, what the essence of appearance is—all of these are answered by the word "will." Are we ever directly acquainted with will as thing in itself? No, which is to say that we are never directly acquainted with the essence of appearance. We are acquainted only with individual and successive acts of will or, somewhat more broadly, with our own will in temporal slices. (Strictly speaking, we are never acquainted with our own will as "the in-itself" of ourselves, which is what Schopenhauer means when he claims we do not become acquainted with our will or character as a whole or a priori: We know our character only temporally, empirically.) Consequently, the will we find in ourselves is not the essence of all appearance, that is, it is not (in this precise sense) the thing in itself; for the will we find in ourselves is itself an appearance, indeed, a temporal object—yet it is the most immediate and clearest appearance of the essence of all appearance, i.e., (in this precise sense) the thing in itself. On this ground alone, Schopenhauer holds, we may claim (by way of interpretation and understanding) that will is the thing in itself (in appearance), the essence of appearance. We thereby employ the term that fits our most immediate and clearest "object" of awareness to characterize that which, strictly speaking, never becomes an object of awareness, namely, will as thing in itself (in appearance). No other term is available to us for this characterization.

Schopenhauer's second conception of the thing in itself I shall call "mystical," and I shall say that on this conception "the thing in itself" signifies ultimate reality, the noumenon (if one thinks of Kant), or, to say it best, unconditioned being. "Unconditioned being" denotes that which is, by definition, not conditioned by any mode of knowledge or thought, hence it is not only not subject to time, space, and causality but, further, not even subject to "objectity" or "objectness." It is therefore wholly ineffable, completely "beyond" the reaches of knowledge, thought, and conceptualization; as such, it is wholly "beyond" the domain of philosophy. On this conception, one can "speak of" the thing in itself only in a negative fashion, as indeed the very term "unconditioned being" indicates: It is that which is not "objectified" by the human intellect in any manner whatever. In a very real way, the mystical conception of the thing in itself amounts to an insistence on the possibility of there being something that the human intellect cannot reach; or, in other words, it amounts to an insistence on the finitude of the human intellect. To this it should be added that Schopenhauer believes in a possible mysticism, which on his understanding provides positive evidence for, say, unconditioned (and unknowable) being and, in this sense, for the thing in itself beyond all relation to appearance. Nothing can be said philosophically about such a thing in itself (other than, perhaps, that it is the One in the Many, hence something totally indeterminate), but, Schopenhauer holds, when and if complete denial of the will to life occurs in any human individual, then this individual loses all individuality and, as it were, becomes one with the One—all division, separation, and distinction vanishing, and only the thing in itself obtaining. It is, indeed, all very mystical!

To conclude: The question "Does Schopenhauer maintain that will is the thing in itself?" is unanswerable, as posed. He maintains that will is the thing in itself in appearance, hence that will and thing in itself, on this conception, are identical; but he also maintains that will is not the thing in itself on the mystical conception. There is thus no self-contradiction in claiming that the will is and the will is not the thing in itself. Unfortunately, Schopenhauer does not explicitly say that he has two very different conceptions of the thing in itself, though, I submit, his late letters, late publications, and even a few passages in the first edition of *The World as Will and Representation* make the distinction fairly clear. He claims throughout that the essence of the world as representation is the affirmation of the will to life, and that with the denial of the will to life (hence with denial of the essence of the world as representation) the world as we typically know it vanishes.

Returning now to the philosophical level, where will is the thing in itself (or essence) of the world as appearance, it must be observed that will as so conceived lies outside the bounds of the principle of sufficient reason, hence not only outside time but also beyond objectity. For this reason alone, if for no other, the will we know in ourselves cannot be identified with will as thing in itself—even if we could rid this will in ourselves from time (which we cannot do) and know it only as object. For the will as thing in itself is never even object. The world, however, is the will become object, in which case will (as it were) gives up its nontemporal and nonobjective nature and "presents itself" to us. The will becomes object in three ways: as intuitive representations or normal perceptual objects (all of which are subject to time, space, and causality); as acts of will (all being in time); and as "pure" representations or Platonic Ideas (which are free from every aspect of the principle of sufficient reason except objectity). In this final instance, then, the will becomes simply object, albeit on different grades or levels. How this happens, and in fact whether it can happen, opens up the next chapter.

SIX

From Nature to the Ideas

Schopenhauer maintains that every area of his philosophy presupposes and is presupposed by every other area, such that, taken as a whole, the areas fully express the "single thought" that "the world is the self-knowledge of the will."[1] His philosophy consists then of a metaphysics (the essence of the world as appearance is will), an ethics (moral virtue consists of compassion, hence of recognizing "one's own will" in all animate creatures), and an aesthetics (will-free contemplation of things reveals will as Platonic Ideas). But Schopenhauer has not persuaded many commentators that his doctrine of Ideas really fits into his general philosophical system. One critic suggests that the Ideas could be excised altogether without losing or changing anything essential to Schopenhauer's philosophy as a whole.[2] Another doubts that there is any place for Ideas to "repose" between appearance and thing in itself, where allegedly they are intended to "repose."[3] Yet another finds it difficult to understand "how the Ideas are supposed to be related to everyday things."[4] Nearly every critic wonders how Schopenhauer can, if at all, explain the relation between the Ideas and will as thing in itself. Even those critics somewhat sympathetic to Schopenhauer's doctrine of Ideas believe one or another aspect of it to be terribly obscure; and, as indicated, some critics deem the entire doctrine superfluous and/or gratuitous.

What then are Ideas? And what role do they play in Schopenhauer's philosophy? Is that role, or set of roles, dispensable? Could Schopenhauer, in other words, have left the Ideas out of his general philosophy, with everything else remaining intact? This question must be answered in the negative. For if he had not introduced the Ideas, as he does in fact introduce them, he would have no way of clarifying on the philosophical level those changes in nature that science cannot adequately and fully explain.

Without the Ideas, that is to say, Schopenhauer could not put forth a philosophical account of those (allegedly) irreducible natural types and natural forces that figure indispensably in changes in nature. The doctrine of Ideas is first and foremost the philosophical interpretation of natural types and natural forces. The doctrine has additional functions, according to Schopenhauer, for instance, it casts light on aesthetic contemplation, on the genius, and on the objects of art, and it illuminates one form of liberation from the horrible world governed by the affirmation of the will to life, but it operates originally in metaphysics (the central topic of this treatise), where it serves as the clarificatory theory of natural types and natural forces. Consequently, if Schopenhauer were to dispense with the doctrine of Ideas, he would be abandoning the effort to provide a philosophical (or metaphysical) clarification of changes in nature; to put it another way, he would be stuck with mere science, which (as we have seen) leads up to and thus leaves unexplained, in a word, causality.[5]

Schopenhauer's definition of "Idea" is not very illuminating. He writes that "by *Idea* I understand every definite and fixed *grade of the objectification of the will,* insofar as it [the will] is thing in itself and is therefore foreign to plurality, which grades are certainly related to individual things as their eternal forms or their prototypes."[6] Just prior to this definition, Schopenhauer expresses concern with the fact that we encounter in normal experience an immense plurality of things, yet we have learned that will as thing in itself is not plural. "The thing in itself, as such [which, he says, has been shown to be will], is free from all forms of knowledge, even the most universal, namely, that of being object for the subject," consequently, it is not in time and space, thus it is not plural, which is to say that it is *one.*[7] "Yet," Schopenhauer adds, "it is not one as an individual or a concept is, but as something to which the condition of the possibility of plurality, that is, the *principium individuationis* [time and space], is foreign." Accordingly, "will" is a mass noun, not a count noun; it is like "sand" rather than "tree," for just as there are no sands though there are trees, so there is only will as thing in itself and not wills as things in themselves. Furthermore, just as sand is equally present in every bit of sand, so will as thing in itself is equally present in every thing in nature; or, as Schopenhauer puts it, "It is not a case of there being a smaller part of will in the stone and larger part in man, for the relation of part and whole belongs exclusively to space, and has no longer any meaning the moment we have departed from this form of intuition."[8] However, will is more clearly manifested, more clearly visible, in "man" than in a stone, and it is this fact, and it alone, that allows us to speak of different and higher grades of the objectification of the will, i.e., of different and higher Ideas. Schopenhauer thus writes:

> There is a higher degree of this objectification in the plant than in the stone, a higher degree in the animal than in the plant; indeed, the will's passage

into visibility, its objectification, has gradations as endless as those between the feeblest twilight and the brightest sunlight, the loudest tone and the softest echo.[9]

These gradations of the will's objectifications, the Ideas, the will's becoming object at different levels of clearness—ranging from the Idea of humanity to the Idea of stone, with innumerable Ideas in between—"do not directly concern the will itself," and "still less is it concerned with the plurality of appearance at these different grades, i.e., the multitude of individuals of each form or the particular manifestations of each force." Plurality is a matter only of space and time; and since space and time do not pertain to the will, plurality is a matter of indifference to will itself. As Schopenhauer puts it: "The will reveals itself just as completely and just as much in *one* oak as in millions." It might be said then that that which makes any particular oak an oak is its exemplification of the Idea of oak, but, Schopenhauer notes, no actual individual thing in nature exemplifies its Idea perfectly.[10] This observation raises problems about discerning Ideas, as we shall see later on, but for now the chief point to make is that an Idea is the philosophical counterpart of a natural species, that is, an Idea is the natural species seen from the standpoint of the will as thing in itself. It is otherwise the philosophical analogue of the "force" that gets "pluralized" in space and time, and that accounts for individuals of a certain natural type producing only individuals of the same type. This becomes clearer, I think, when Schopenhauer turns to a direct discussion of natural forces, which, in his judgment, are to be philosophically interpreted as Ideas no less than natural species are to be.

Every grade of will's objectification, Schopenhauer holds, is a force or power (*Kraft*), and for every explanation of a change (whether by a cause proper or a stimulus or a motive) appeal must be made to a force of some sort. In inanimate occurrences, such as a stone's rolling down a hillside, the relevant force is one of the most universal forces of nature, namely, gravity—that "thing" required for connecting the cause (e.g., an earth tremor) with the effect (the stone's motion). Gravity itself, however, is not a cause or an effect: It is simply the "original force" that forever remains atemporal, aspatial, and acausal (hence aplural) and that yet "objectifies" will at a definite grade, namely, at one of the very lowest grades present in all of matter. "The most universal forces of nature exhibit themselves as the lowest grade of the will's objectification," for, Schopenhauer says, "they appear in all matter without exception." Somewhat higher grades, such as electricity and magnetism, govern only certain areas of matter. "In themselves," Schopenhauer adds, "they [the many forces of nature] are immediate appearances of the will, just as is the conduct [*Thun*] of man; as such, they are groundless, just as is the character of man."[11]

This final remark gives us the essential clue for understanding Schopenhauer's conception of Ideas, at least as they are introduced at the very start, that is, in the context of causal and motivational explanation. As the philosophical analogue of science's force of nature, an Idea figures in the full understanding of a natural change just as the individual character of a human being figures in the understanding of that being's conduct; we cannot really or fully understand a natural change on the philosophical level without making appeal to an Idea, just as we cannot fully understand a human action on the philosophical level without making reference to the agent's character. In fact, as Schopenhauer puts it, "every person is to be regarded as an especially determined and characterized appearance of the will, and even to a certain extent as a special Idea."[12] But, as briefly noted above, Ideas range beyond natural forces operative in inanimate nature; they may also be found in the various species of living and animate nature, that is, in plants and animals. Sometimes Schopenhauer suggests that in some higher animals (perhaps in his beloved dog, Atma) a trace of individuality gets exhibited,[13] but usually he holds that the only individuality of an animal's behavior rests with its species (e.g., the dog) or possibly with its subspecies (e.g., the French poodle).[14] Accordingly, one will explain a particular dog's behavior by saying, for instance, that dogs of its kind do that sort of thing when motivated in this sort of way; and there is no reason to refer to this particular dog's "individual character," but only to its "species character." "On the other hand," Schopenhauer insists, "in the human species every individual has to be studied and fathomed by himself,"[15] and only then can the actions of an individual human being be explained. Hence, John Smith (his Idea or character) is to Mary Brown (her Idea or character) as, say, the cat (its Idea or species character) is to the dog (its Idea or species character).

To sum up, Schopenhauer introduces the Ideas, at least in *The World as Will and Representation*, for the very purpose that he introduces intelligible characters: to complete on the philosophical level that which is left incomplete on the scientific (or etiological) level of explanation.[16] Consequently, if the Ideas were removed from Schopenhauer's general philosophy (as some critics recommended they should), then—leaving aside everything else—there would be no philosophical account of the very many different kinds of changes in inanimate nature, of the great variety of behavior in different kinds of plants and animals, or (given that intelligible characters function in explanation of human conduct in the manner of Ideas) of the vastly different conduct of human beings. (Actually, Schopenhauer can no more do without the Ideas than he can do without intelligible characters.) On the score of explanation alone, then, Schopenhauer cannot "excise" the Ideas from his general philosophy. It is no accident therefore that I call this chapter "From Nature to the Ideas," for, in Schopenhauer's view, it is primarily from a consideration of nature (specifically, from a consideration of natural types and forces) that the philosophical notion of Ideas proves necessary and takes its start. But once Schopenhauer leaves his "philosophy of nature" behind and proceeds to other topics, he assigns to the Ideas roles and functions that are terribly difficult to understand in themselves and, more importantly, hard to reconcile with other aspects of his general philosophy.

The first problem, or rather set of problems, with the Ideas concerns their ontological status. Are they real? Do they exist or have being? Do they make up a level of reality (existence, being) different from both will as thing in itself and individual, intuitive representations? Do Ideas have an unconditioned being, that is, would they be or exist even if they were never objects of a knowing subject? Are Ideas encountered by a subject or are they, at least in part, fashioned by a subject? Unfortunately, Schopenhauer seldom provides direct answers to these questions, and sometimes his apparent answers seem to contradict each other. For these reasons commentators, understandably, hold very different views on the ontological status of Ideas in Schopenhauer's thought, and it is not at all easy to determine which view, if any, is correct.

But one thing is certain: Ideas are not real in the sense that intuitive (normal perceptual) representations, such as tables and chairs, are real. To begin with, Ideas are not *wirklich* or *wirkend*, that is, they are not themselves causally efficacious—no more than natural forces and human characters are—for they are not subject to the principle of sufficient reason and are therefore "groundless"; they do not by themselves cause sensations in animal bodies and they do not causally interact among themselves; time, space, and causality may never be attributed to them; hence, in short, Ideas are not real in the sense of being actual (*wirklich*). They may be *real* (*Realität* may be ascribed to them), but unlike intuitive representations subject to the principle of sufficient reason they are not *actual* (*Wirklichkeit* may not be ascribed to them).[17] On the other hand, Ideas are certainly not fantasies (such as the "objects" of the imagination or "objects" in dreams or hallucinations), and they are not abstract representations, or concepts, devised by human reason; thus Ideas are not unreal either, at least not in the sense that fantasies and concepts are.[18]

Ideas, as the philosophical analogues of natural forces and animate species, are real in the sense that individual human characters are real: They are the "third factors" operative in all particular appearances and occurrences of the intuitive world, thus the "factors" without which no natural change or human action can be adequately understood. Without appealing to the character of John Smith, his voluntary bodily movements (actions, "expressions of his will") cannot be motivationally explained or understood; and without appealing to the Idea of, say, the oak tree, its changes (growth, yielding of acorns, etc.) cannot be explained or understood either.

John Smith's physiognomy and bodily behavior express his character (will, "individual essence") and a particular oak tree's material structure and physical changes express the oak tree's Idea (or, simply the Oak Tree).[19] "Are Ideas real?" has on one score the same meaning as "Are human characters real?" And if the answer to the latter question is yes, then so is the answer to the former question—in the same sense and for the same reason. There is, however, an important difference between an Idea like the Oak Tree and a character like John Smith: An Idea is supposed to be an "eternal form,"[20] though a human character (or so one would surely think) originates and ceases. Despite this apparent disanalogy, which points to another sense in which Ideas are real and individuals are not, it remains true that Ideas and human characters are real in one of the same senses and for one of the same reasons: they are "third factors" required for causal and motivational explanations.

Even if we are agreed that, for Schopenhauer, Ideas in one sense are real in exactly the way that individual human characters are real—which might be called "explanatory reality"—we have still not determined whether Ideas, or for that matter human characters, are real in a sense that gains them a niche or level in Schopenhauer's ontological scheme. And that is precisely the question that most commentators wish to answer, or have answered. Perhaps the clearest (though not necessarily the correct) response to the question goes thus: For Schopenhauer, Ideas constitute a separate level or independent status between will as thing in itself and particular intuitive representations.[21] According to this interpretation, therefore, Schopenhauer advances a tripartite ontology, which consists of the will, the Ideas, and (say) perceptual particulars. Since the proponents of this interpretation all take Schopenhauer to hold that will is the thing in itself—or, as they often say, "the noumenon"—and since they believe the world of perceptual particulars or natural objects to be "the phenomenon," they attribute to Schopenhauer the belief that Ideas "exist" somewhere between "the noumenon" and "the phenomenon." Noting then that everything is either of the noumenon or of the phenomenon, these critics find no place for Ideas to occupy: Not being (exactly) noumenal and not being (assuredly) phenomenal, they have no homeland in Schopenhauer's ontology. Typically, speculation proceeds on how Schopenhauer could have committed such a blunder.

But, on this score at least, Schopenhauer has committed no blunder; his interpreters have. Once again they have viewed Schopenhauer through Kantian eyeglasses, which is to say that they have taken Schopenhauer to understand (in their language) the noumenal-phenomenal distinction in the way that Kant does, namely, as the split between the thing in itself and intuitive appearance (between *das Ding an sich* and *anschauliche Erscheinung*). Applying this understanding to Schopenhauer, he is said to hold that everything is either thing in itself or intuitive appearance; then, recognizing that Ideas fit into neither division, these critics conclude, with infallible logic, that Schopenhauer really has no place for Ideas. The argument would be perfectly sound if Schopenhauer did follow Kant tit for tat on the noumenal-phenomenal distinction—but he does not. He holds that both Ideas and intuitive appearances (that is, both "adequate" and "inadequate" objectities of the will) are phenomenal: For him, both are objects, both are representations, both are phenomena. The only difference is that Ideas are objects otherwise independent of the principle of sufficient reason, while intuitive appearances (or, better, intuitive particulars) are objects wholly dependent on that principle. Schopenhauer thus acknowledges objects (representations, phenomena) that Kant does not, namely, those called Platonic Ideas.

It is tempting to say of Schopenhauer therefore that he admits three things (or types of things) into his ontology, namely, will as thing in itself, the Ideas, and the ordinary objects of experience (what I called above intuitive or perceptual particulars). Then there arises, of course, the problem of how these three things are related to each other (which resembles the problem of how, in Plato's thought, the Form of the Good, the other Forms, and visible particulars relate). If one maintains that for Schopenhauer "reality" consists of only two kinds of things, say, the noumenon and phenomena or will and representations, the problem of relation arises still, though slightly differently. Regarding Schopenhauer, the whole discussion is misguided insofar as it presupposes that he believes "the world" to consist of types of things, whether two or three. (Even worse is the supposition that he believes there to be two, or even three, worlds.) What he does believe, and what he often explicitly asserts, is that there is nothing but will or that will is all that there is. Will as such, that is, will as thing in itself, is not a thing or an object or an entity; but it can take on objectification as Ideas and as intuitive particulars—both of which are will. It is not the case that there exists one thing called will and then other things called Ideas and finally still other things called intuitive particulars. (Schopenhauer does not put forth a "thing-ontology.") To amplify a bit: Will as such is no object at all; will as "adequate" objectification breaks up into various levels or grades called Ideas; and will as "inadequate" objectification is divided into the innumerable intuitive particulars. Or: When will's "ideational" face appears, the Ideas appear; and when will's "particularized" face appears—i.e., when the Ideas enter time, space, and causality—then intuitive particulars appear. Will as it is in itself never appears. Consequently, Schopenhauer's ontology does not consist of three things or types of things; consequently, no problem about how "three things" are related to each other can arise.

What I have just been claiming—basically, that will as thing in itself is no object, but when objectified "adequately" it shows itself as Ideas and when objectified "inadequately" it reveals itself as intuitive particulars—finds its clearest expression in *The World as Will and Representation,* volume 1, section 32. There Schopenhauer writes:

> Idea and thing in itself are not for us absolutely one and the same. On the contrary, for us the Idea is only the immediate, and therefore adequate, objectity [*Objektität*] of the thing in itself, which itself however is the *will*—the will insofar as it is not yet objectified, has not yet become representation.[22]

Not only is will as thing in itself free from the knowing forms of time, space, and causality, it is also free from "the first and most universal of all appearance, i.e., of all representation," namely, "that of being-object-for-a-subject."[23]

> On the other hand, the Platonic Idea is necessarily object, something known, a representation, and precisely, but only, in this respect is it different from the thing in itself. It has laid aside merely the subordinate forms of the appearance [namely, time, space, and causality] . . . but it has retained the first and most universal form, namely that of the representation in general, that of being object for a subject.[24]

When the Idea "enters" the subordinate forms of time, space, and causality (which derive from the individual knowing subject), it is multiplied by those forms into "particular and fleeting individuals, whose number in respect to the Idea is a matter of complete indifference." "Therefore," Schopenhauer adds, "the principle of sufficient reason is again the form into which the Idea enters, since the Idea comes into the knowledge of the subject as individual." For this reason "the particular thing . . . is only an indirect objectification of the thing in itself (which is the will)." Between the particular thing and will as thing in itself "the Idea still stands as the only direct objectity of the will, since it has not assumed any other form peculiar to knowledge as such, except that of the representation in general, i.e., that of being object for a subject." Not only is the Idea "the most *adequate objectity* possible of the will or of the thing in itself," it is even "the whole thing in itself, only under the form of the representation."[25] To summarize: Will as thing in itself is no object, no representation; it, as such, we cannot know. When it becomes only object (hence not temporal, spatial, and causal object), it is the Idea; that is to say, will as object alone is Idea, but then it is will as Idea and not simply will as thing in itself. When will is objectified (by the individual knowing subject) in time, space, and causality, it is multiplied into normal intuitive objects. Only in these two ways can it be said that will exists as object. And for these reasons it cannot be correctly said that Schopenhauer's theory of reality contains three things, or three sorts of things. Everything is will, albeit in different ways. To show this is the intent of the following sketch, though it fails to accommodate sensations (whether wanted, hence pleasures, or unwanted, hence pains, or "neutral," hence neither wanted nor unwanted) and acts of will (which are temporal, but neither spatial nor causal)—so it does not exhaust "Schopenhauer's ontology."

Schopenhauer's Ontology

Essence	Appearance (Representation)
Grades of will's (adequate) objectification, i.e., the Ideas	Instances of will's (inadequate) objectification, i.e., intuitive particulars
The real world (Objects proper)	*The actual world* (Transient objects)
Grade (or Idea) I—the human genius	100 geniuses
Grade (or Idea) II—the normal human being (consists of universal human traits, e.g., kindness, envy, etc.)	millions of individual people (all, or most, of whom have an individual character or quasi-Idea)
Grade (or Idea) III—the animal	millions of instances
Numerous sub-Ideas	dogs, cats, frogs, snakes, etc.
Grade (or Idea) IV—the plant	millions of instances
Numerous sub-Ideas	oak trees, sunflowers, etc.
Grade (or Idea) V—the inanimate thing	millions of instances
Numerous sub-Ideas	stones, clouds, water, etc.
Grade (or Idea) VI—natural forces	instances in nearly everything (with the very lowest instances in everything)
Numerous sub-Ideas (e.g., crystallization to gravity)	
(Objects of the "pure" subject; objects free from time, space, and causality; subject free from will)	(Objects of the "impure" subject; objects subject to time, space, and causality; subject governed by will)

(The letters W, I, L, L appear in the left margin aligned with Grades II through V.)

If, from quite a different perspective, we were to ascribe to Schopenhauer an "object ontology," meaning that only objects are real or that only objects make up "the world," then we would have to say that will as thing in itself does not belong to Schopenhauer's ontology. (Nor, of course, would the knowing subject, for it is never object.) We would find at most Ideas and intuitive particulars—Ideas from the philosophical (or metaphysical) standpoint and intuitive particulars from the scientific or "every-

day" standpoint. Rather than speak of two kinds of things—Ideas and intuitive particulars—we should speak of will's manifestation ("one thing")
viewed in two ways: When viewed "purely" (i.e., by the pure subject of
knowledge), Ideas are known; but when viewed "impurely" (i.e., by the
individual, will-governed subject of knowledge), intuitive particulars are
known. Or, to put it a bit differently, intuitive particulars are Ideas broken
up in accordance with the three subordinate forms of the principle of sufficient reason, that is, time, space, and causality.

If we were to retain our earlier distinction between "real" (*real*) and
"actual" (*wirklich*), and then were to admit to Schopenhauer's ontology
only those objects that are *real*, then "the world" would consist of nothing
but Ideas. And this is something that Schopenhauer very often proposes,
for example, when early in Book 2 (with Plato obviously in mind), he talks
as if the world as (particular) representation is or resembles a dream-
world.[26] He repeats much the same contention early in Book 4 (section
54) when he claims that

> it is not the individual that nature cares for, but only the species; and in
> all seriousness she urges the preservation of the species, since she provides
> for this so lavishly through the immense surplus of the seed and the great
> strength of the fructifying impulse. The individual, on the contrary, has no
> value for nature, and can have none, for infinite time, infinite space, and
> the infinite number of possible individuals therein are her kingdom.[27]

Nature will always let the individual perish; indeed, once the individual
has made its contribution to the preservation of its species, it is destined
to perish—all according to nature's plan (one might add). "In this way,"
Schopenhauer declares, "nature quite openly expresses the great truth
that only the Ideas, not individuals, have reality proper, in other words are
a complete objectity of the will."[28] This entails that "reality proper" (*eigent-
liche Realität*) may be ascribed only to objects that do not originate and
perish, and that is to the Ideas. Regarding human beings, "reality proper"
may be ascribed only to the Idea of humanity and not to the quasi-Idea or
character of an individual human being. Even though the character of an
individual person is, say, "explanatorily real" in the same sense as any Idea
in nature, it is not "real" in the sense of being eternal.

Now it may be that Ideas, in that they are nontransient (or even "eternal"), are the only objects having "reality proper." But since they are objects, and not will as thing in itself, or since they can at least become objects, then (given Schopenhauer's technical sense of "object") they have
to be objects for a knowing subject—no less than intuitive particulars are
objects only for a knowing subject. This is to say that Ideas cannot be objects in themselves, that they cannot have unconditioned or independent
being, that they cannot exist on their own, and then occasionally become

objects of a knowing subject—although it certainly seems that Plato ascribes these very qualities, summarized perhaps by unconditioned being, to the Ideas or Forms, and it certainly seems that Schopenhauer often follows suit. In other words, Schopenhauer frequently suggests that Ideas exist independently of any knowing subject (for example, when he accepts the definition of Ideas as patterns or prototypes existing in nature),[29] but he also holds that no object of knowledge exists independently of a knowing subject that "conditions" it. What he may believe then is this: Natural species and natural forces (patterns or prototypes in nature) exist unconditionally, that is, apart from being known, but their philosophical counterparts (i.e., the Ideas) exist only in relation to a knowing subject. Or perhaps this: When natural species and natural forces become objects of a knowing subject, they become subject-conditioned Ideas. But what kind of knowing subject is this? How can natural species and natural forces become objects of this knowing subject?

Schopenhauer has insisted all along (especially in Book 2 of *The World as Will and Representation*, and he now repeats in Book 3, that "originally and by its nature, knowledge is completely the servant of the will,"[30] in consequence of which both the knowing subject and known objects are individual (particular, single). The knowing subject as individual is embodied, which means that its knowledge passes through the body in virtue of sensation, thereby tying the subject to its will; known objects as individual are wholly subject to the principle of sufficient reason, which is to say that they appear in temporal, spatial, and causal connections. The individual knowing subject, being tied to its will, has an interest in its objects: It is concerned with, and only with, the relations that its objects have with each other, and ultimately with their utility for its will. Indeed, Schopenhauer states, "knowledge that serves the will really knows nothing more about objects than their relations," such that "if all these relations were eliminated, the objects also would have disappeared for knowledge, just because it did not recognize in them anything else."[31] In a sense, then, will-governed knowledge is knowledge only of objects as here, as now, as connected causally with certain other objects, and the like—all of which makes objects only sets of relations and therefore particular. Since will-governed knowledge encounters only objects as relations, and since "all relation has itself only a relative existence,"[32] all such objects can be said not to be as well as be. (This we have heard before in regard to Plato's thesis that visible, temporal things are not truly real, that only Ideas or Forms are truly real; and again Schopenhauer expresses full agreement with this thesis.)

For almost everyone, almost all the time, knowledge remains subordinate to will—as (one might say) it was originally intended—and its subordination amounts to the task of furthering will (and existence) in the individual and then, through procreation, in the individual's species. In a phrase, the individual human being is normally nothing but the affirmation of the will to life. On the possibility of exceptions to the normal case Schopenhauer makes a sharp distinction between human beings and animals. "With the animals," he notes, "this subjection of knowledge to the will can never be eliminated," and "with human beings, such elimination appears only as an exception."[33] But it can happen. As is so often the case, Schopenhauer finds evidence for a philosophical thesis by citing facts about physiology. He remarks that knowledge springs from will just as the head grows out of the trunk, hence in the two cases the former derives from and owes its existence to the latter; but, he adds, we notice that in the animal the head is much more closely connected to the trunk than it is in the human being, and in fact the human head "seems freely set on to the body, only carried by the body and not serving it."[34] And then this revealing observation: "This human superiority is exhibited in the highest degree by the Apollo Belvedere. The head of the god of the Muses, with eyes looking far afield, stands so freely on the shoulders that it seems to be wholly delivered from the body, and no longer subject to its cares."[35] In a way, then, human beings must become godlike if they are to discern the Ideas, or, in other words, if they are thereby to escape from slavery to the will.

Another way of stating the normal situation and then possible exceptions to it goes as follows. As a general rule, the subject of knowing and the subject of willing, in the human being, are "identical"—this being, Schopenhauer has said, the miracle *par excellence*. This means in the present context that in the human individual the subject of knowing is "chained" to the subject of willing, hence that if knowledge is to leave behind individual objects—objects subject to the subordinate forms of the principle of sufficient reason—and rise to discernment of the Ideas, then the subject of knowing must get free from the subject of willing.[36]

As long as the human being is individual, which means here, as long as in it the subject of knowing is "identical" with (and tied to) the subject of willing, its objects are individual (particular, single), and this is to say that they are known only in their relations to other objects and ultimately to the subject's will, and not as such. Such a subject does not and cannot know objects as Ideas. "Therefore," Schopenhauer says, "if the Ideas are to become objects of knowledge, this can happen only by abolishing individuality in the knowing subject."[37] Or, equally, "if it is possible for us to raise ourselves from knowledge of particular things to that of the Ideas, this can happen only by a change taking place in the subject," specifically, the change by which the subject is "no longer individual."[38] Schopenhauer adds that "such a change is analogous and correspondent to that great change of the whole nature [*Art*] of the object," whereby (he must mean) it loses its particularity and becomes (or, possibly, reveals) its Idea. The nature of the knowing subject "determines," as it were, the nature of the known object: When the former is individual, the latter is particular; and only if the subject loses its individuality and becomes, say, "pure" or "objective" does its object lose its particularity and become Idea; or, equally, only if the subject of knowing gets free from the subject of willing does the known object become Idea. The fundamental question is how, if at all, this mutual "change" in the subject and in the object can take place. Schopenhauer claims, of course, that it is a rare, exceptional occurrence, but he clearly holds that it can happen, indeed, that it does happen. But if anything is truly a miracle, it is not so much the "identity" of the knowing and willing subjects, but the knowing subject's getting free from the willing subject. Actually, this "getting free" cannot really be comprehended for the simple reason that freedom—which, after all, is what must occur—cannot be comprehended: We are able to comprehend matters only in terms of the principle of sufficient reason, and according to that principle everything that occurs is causally determined and thus unfree. Despite all of this, however, we are offered something of an account of how freedom as knowledge of Ideas takes place.

It is fundamentally a matter of "losing individuality" in the knowing subject. What exactly then has to be lost? What exactly is individuality in the knowing subject? Quite simply put, it is egoism. For the most part, Schopenhauer holds, human beings perceive objects in the world with the frame of mind that typifies the practical egoist's perceptional stance: Of what use can this object (or person) be to me? Is this object (or person) a likely benefit or a likely hindrance to me in the pursuit of my aims? Such a person views every thing (and every person) solely in terms of personal utility; his or her knowledge is wholly subjective, guided throughout by the powerful demands of the individual will; and what this person perceives is distorted or obscured by the perceiver's will-dominated mode of knowing. In short, individuality in the knowing subject is egoistic knowing; and to lose individuality is to eliminate egoistic knowing. It is, in Schopenhauer's judgment, a most extraordinary thing.

Nevertheless, there will occasionally occur a "transition from the common knowledge of particular things to knowledge of the Idea"—not a transition that slowly and gradually comes about, but one that "happens suddenly."[39] Schopenhauer describes this sudden (and, in a way, inexplicable) transition by saying that "knowledge tears itself from the service of the will, precisely by the fact that the subject ceases to be a merely individual one and is now a pure, will-free subject of knowledge, which no longer follows relations in accordance with the principle of sufficient reason, outside its connection with any other [object], and merges into it."[40] While acknowledging how astonishing his account must appear, Schopenhauer proceeds with a battery of statements and references that are indeed astonishing. He mentions "the power of the mind" that raises us above the ordinary way of considering things: He says "we no longer consider the where, the when, the why, and the whither of things, but only the *what*"; he remarks that "we *lose* ourselves entirely in this object"; that "we forget our individuality, our will, and continue to exist only as pure subject, as clear mirror of the object"; and that "we are no longer able to separate the intuiter from the intuition."[41] And perhaps most revealingly he adds:

> If, therefore, the object has to such an extent passed out of all relation to something outside it, and the subject has passed out of all relation to the will, what is thus known is no longer the individual thing as such, but the *Idea*, the eternal form, the immediate objectity of the will at this grade. Thus at the same time, the person who is involved in this intuition is no longer an individual, for the individual has lost himself in this intuition; he is *pure* will-less, painless, timeless *subject of knowledge.*[42]

In the normal course of events, the individual subject knows particular objects, but in "aesthetic contemplation" the pure subject knows pure objects (i.e., Ideas). (Or should we say that in the two cases the same objects are known, but known differently, first as particular and second as "pure"? More on this later.) Normally, knowledge is controlled by the principle of sufficient reason, but in contemplation knowledge gets free from that principle and thus from will. (Later I shall point out that this is not quite accurate: Contemplation gets free only from the subordinate forms of the principle of sufficient reason and the individual will.) Normally, the knowing subject is tied to the willing subject, but in contemplation the knowing subject gets loose from the willing subject. All of these expressions (and others) characterize the transition from "common knowledge" to knowledge of the Ideas.

Noteworthy is the correlativity operative here: There are Ideas only for the pure knowing subject, and there is the pure knowing subject only for Ideas. Pure knower and pure objects are correlative notions, hence it is not the case that either brings about the other; nor, of course, is it the case that either exists without the other. Pure knower and pure objects "arise" simultaneously, and correlatively. What this means, with regard to ontology, is that the Ideas have no existence independent of or apart from the pure knowing subject. No object, in Schopenhauer's thought, exists in and of itself, hence, because an Idea is an object, no Idea exists in and of itself. An Idea is as dependent on a knowing subject as much as a particular object in time, space, and causality is—the difference being that an Idea is dependent on the pure knowing subject and a particular object is dependent on the individual (perhaps "impure") knowing subject.

In the passage cited above, where Schopenhauer acknowledges that his account of the transition from knowledge of particular things to knowledge of the Ideas will seem astonishing or surprising (*Befremdendes*) to the reader, he adds that this astonishment must be suspended for a while, for it will "automatically vanish" after the reader has grasped "the whole thought to be imparted in this work."[43] This "whole thought," I take it, is the "single thought" that "the world is the self-knowledge of the will," and in fact this supposition is confirmed by subsequent remarks. In his effort to clarify "contemplation," Schopenhauer writes: "The pure subject of knowledge and its correlative, the Idea, have passed out of all these forms of the principle of sufficient reason [i.e., time, space, and causality]. Time, place, the individual that knows, and the individual that is known [in common knowledge], have no meaning for them."[44] The individual knowing subject loses its individuality and becomes the pure subject, and the known object loses its particularity and becomes the Idea; "the *world as representation* then stands out whole and pure, and the complete objectification of the will takes place, for only the Idea is the *adequate objectity* of the will." What takes place, further, is that in the Idea or, equally, in the adequate objectity of the will the object and subject, in effect, become one. Schopenhauer's actual statement goes thus:

> This [Idea or adequate objectity of the will] includes object and subject in like manner in itself [i.e., just as the individual representation does], since such are its only form; in it, however, both maintain entirely equal weight; and as the object is also here nothing but the representation of the subject, so the subject, since it passes completely into the intuited object [*Gegenstand*], also becomes this object itself, since the entire consciousness is nothing more than its most distinct image. This consciousness precisely, because one thinks of oneself thoroughly through the whole of the Ideas, or grades of the objectity of the will successively, constitutes properly the whole *world as representation*.[45]

One would suppose that an Idea is the object of the pure subject, not that it includes in itself both object and subject. But in the present passage (here in section 34) Schopenhauer claims otherwise. Indeed, after noting that particular things in time and space are nothing but Ideas multiplied by the principle of sufficient reason, he writes:

> As, when the Idea emerges, in it subject and object are no longer to be distinguished, because only when they reciprocally fill and penetrate each other completely does the Idea, the adequate objectity of the will, the proper [*eigentlich*] world as representation arise; so equally thereby the knowing and the known individual, as things in themselves, are also not different [*unterschieden*, separate].[46]

Well, is the Idea the object of the pure subject or does it comprise both the object and the pure subject?

What has happened here in section 34, in the discussion of Ideas, is the same as what happened in section 7, where it was said that the (particular) representation "contains and presupposes" both (individual) subject and (particular) object. I distinguished then between the world *of* representation (the world of particular objects "over against" the individual knowing subject) and the world *as* representation (the correlative world of individual subject and particular objects). In a parallel fashion one may now speak of the world *of* Ideas (in which the Ideas are objects of the pure subject) or of the world *as* Idea (in which the Idea comprises both pure subject and, say, pure objects). In the world *as* Idea, the pure subject and the pure object are aspects, or correlative poles, of the Idea; they "melt into one"; they are not separable or distinguishable, at least in the sense of existing independently of each other; they are "identical" (as Schopenhauer claims in his more dramatic moments). It is in connection with the world *as* Idea, rather than with the world *of* Ideas, that Schopenhauer proceeds to explicate the will's knowing itself.

After remarking, as cited above, that when the Idea emerges, the subject and object cannot be distinguished (or separated) "in it," Schopenhauer continues thus:

> In just the same way the knowing and the known individual, as things in themselves, are likewise not different [separable]. For if we look entirely away from that proper [*eigentlich*, true] *world as representation*, nothing remains except the *world as will.* The will is the in-itself of the Idea, which completely [*vollkommen*, perfectly] objectifies it; it is also the in-itself of the particular thing and of the individual that knows it, which [two together] objectify it incompletely [*unvollkommen*, imperfectly]. As will, outside the representation and all its forms, it is one and the same [will] in the contemplated object and in the individual, who soaring aloft in this contemplation becomes conscious of itself as pure subject; those two [the contemplated object and the pure subject] are therefore in themselves not different; for in themselves they are the will, which here knows itself, and only in the way and manner that this knowledge comes to it [the will], i.e., only in appearance, in virtue of its form, the principle of sufficient reason, is there plurality and difference.[47]

In themselves the Idea (the complete objectification of the will for the pure subject) and the intuitive representation (the particular thing for the individual subject) are not different; nor are the two aspects of the Idea and of the intuitive representation different in themselves; for in themselves all of these are will.[48] Everything in itself is will; hence whenever there is knowledge of an object by a subject, of any kind whatever, there occurs the will's knowing itself, that is to say, there occurs the world. For indeed: "The world is the self-knowledge of the will."

Schopenhauer then again underscores the correlativity of subject and object, of the knower and the known, and he reiterates his position that both poles of knowledge are "in themselves" one and the same will.

Without the object, the representation, I am not knowing subject, but mere blind will; and without me, as subject of knowing, the known thing is not object, but mere will, blind impulse [*bloßer Wille, blinder Drang*]. This will in itself, i.e., outside the representation, is one and the same with mine; only in the world as representation, whose form is always at least subject and object, do we separate from one another as knowing and known individual.[49]

With the origination of knowledge, the world as will becomes the world as representation; and with the elimination of knowledge, the world as representation disappears and only the world as will remains. Schopenhauer puts this twofold thesis thus:

> As soon as knowledge, the world as representation, is eliminated [*aufheben*], nothing at all remains over except mere will, blind impulse. That it should obtain objectity, become representation, supposes with one stroke both subject and object; but that this objectity is to be pure, complete, adequate objectity of the will supposes the object as Idea, free from the forms of the principle of sufficient reason, and the subject as pure subject of knowledge, free from individuality and servitude to the will.[50]

With this allusion to freedom from the will Schopenhauer ends his first, and most detailed, account of the transition of common knowledge to knowledge of the Ideas.[51]

Many, many questions might be raised about Schopenhauer's (admittedly "astonishing") account of knowledge of the Ideas, but in accord with the main concern of this chapter—the ontological status of Ideas—I intend to focus on this one: In discerning an Idea does one (the pure subject, as it were) become aware of a normal perceptual object in a special way or does one become aware of an object that differs entirely from the normal object? This issue leads directly into Julian Young's (and, to some extent, into D. W. Hamlyn's) unorthodox interpretation of Schopenhauer's conception of the Ideas, namely, that (in a phrase) Ideas, instead of belonging "to an ontological domain separate from the domains of ordinary perceptual objects," are in fact "ordinary perceptual objects" viewed in a special way.[52] In order to lead into the point at issue, a bit of elaboration is required.

Suppose (using one of Schopenhauer's examples) someone is observing moving clouds, which over a time take on different forms. These particular forms, it is said, are not essential to clouds: That at one moment one sees one form, and then a second later another, these are "indifferent to them."

> But that as elastic vapor they are pressed together, driven off, spread out, and torn apart from the force [*Stoß*] of the wind, this is their nature [*Natur*], this is the essence of the forces [*Wesen der Kräfte*] that are objectified in them, this is the Idea; only for the individual observer are there the figures in every case.[53]

One and the same Idea, the cloud, reveals itself in many different appearances; one and the same Idea "presents its nature to knowing individuals only piecemeal, one side after another."[54] In other words, what appears to the knowing individual is not the Idea of cloud, directly or immediately, but only a set of temporally, spatially, and causally determined sides (aspects, dimensions, facets) of the Idea of cloud. What the knowing individual sees is, in a way, the Idea; but how he sees it (in virtue of time, space, and causality) disperses it into multiple parts, or several figures, which "in each case exist [*sind*, are or are there] only for the individual observer."[55] What is there for itself, as it were, is simply the Idea of cloud—an objectification of will at a very low level.

It is similar, Schopenhauer maintains, with a brook that flows downward over some stones: The eddies, waves, and foam-forms, which it allows to be seen, are indifferent and inessential to the brook; "but that it follows gravity, and behaves as an inelastic, perfectly mobile, formless, and transparent fluid, this is its essence, this, *if known intuitively*, is the Idea; only for us, so long as we know as individuals, are there those formations."[56] And then a third example: "The ice on the window-pane is formed into crystals according to the laws of crystallization, which reveal the essence of the natural force there emerging, manifesting the Idea; but the trees and the flowers formed by the ice on the window-pane are inessential, and exist only for us." Therefore, in general, "only the *essential* in all these grades of the will's objectivation constitutes the *Idea*." How the Idea happens to unfold or develop, "drawn apart in the forms of the principle of sufficient reason into multiple and many-sided appearances, this is inessential to the Idea; it lies merely in the individual's mode of knowledge, and has reality [*Realität*] only for that individual."[57]

Accordingly, when Schopenhauer claims that only Ideas are the truly real objects, he means (in large part) that only the essential aspects of particular things (for instance, the elastic vapor of the cloud, the inelastic fluid of the water that follows gravity, the crystallization of ice) and not their accidental or incidental aspects (for instance, the particular forms the cloud takes, the individual waves of a brook, the particular tree-formations of ice on a window-pane) makes them what they are. Their accidental aspects or manifestations are determined by temporal, spatial, and causal relations, all of which derive from and have "reality" only for individual subjects of knowledge who always know things from individually different perspectives and thus piecemeal. Consequently, for the individual subject "an object" is simply a string of appearances, such as A and B and C through N, each one of which amounts to and exists only as a relation determined by time, space, and causality; in other words, such "an object" is exhaustively the string of appearances, A through N, with nothing accounting for the fact that it is this string of appearances, in this order, and not another. But something, Schopenhauer holds, must account for this fact, that is, something must provide an explanation for A's appearing, for its being followed by B, then by C, and so on through N—and that, it is maintained, is the essence or Idea "underlying" the whole string of appearances. Whatever this essence or Idea turns out to be—which, apparently, only many observations coupled with a flash of "intuitive insight" will tell—it will be that which differentiates one type of thing from another type, for instance, water from cyanide, animal from human being, or, more specifically, dog from cat.[58]

It is basically in virtue of his essential/inessential distinction that Schopenhauer denigrates the study of human history for the sake of coming to know the Idea of humanity. Following the remark that only what is essential to a natural object constitutes the Idea of the object, Schopenhauer writes:

> Now the same idea necessarily holds good of the unfolding of that Idea which is the most complete objectity of the will. Consequently, the history of the human race . . . is only the accidental form of the appearance of the Idea [of humanity]. All this does not belong to the Idea itself, in which alone lies the adequate objectity of the will, but only to the appearance. The appearance comes into the knowledge of the individual, and is just as foreign, inessential, and indifferent to the Idea itself as the figures they depict are to the clouds, the shape of its eddies and foam-forms to the brook, and the trees and flowers to the ice.[59]

What the human race is in essence, what it is in Idea, is constant, unchanging, unalterable (just as, one might add, an individual human character is). Only the individuals change, coming into existence and perishing, all acting a bit differently in virtue of different circumstances, but human nature—or rather the Idea of humanity—always was, is, and always will be the same. Consequently, in direct contradiction of those who preach human progress, Schopenhauer writes:

> In this world of appearance, true loss is as little possible as is true gain. The will alone is; it is the thing in itself, the source of all those appearances. Its self-knowledge and its affirmation or denial is then decided on, is the only event in itself.[60]

This is not to say, however, that human individuals and their actions are, say, dispensable to the Idea of humanity. Quite to the contrary: "No individual and no action can be without significance; in all and through all, the Idea of mankind unfolds itself more and more."[61]

The contemplator of Ideas, unlike the historian, the mathematician, and the scientist, discerns what is essential to individual things—whether natural objects or human beings. This "pure subject" attains a kind of knowledge that can only be called "*art*, the work of genius."[62] What is unique about artistic knowledge is its thoroughgoing "objectivity," and this in two ways: The contemplator "forgets" his or her own person and its relations to things, and he or she views an object vertically, whereby it is cut off from all relations and just "seen" for what it is "as such."[63] It is as if the object were lifted out of the (horizontal) course of time—for which reason, no doubt, Schopenhauer sometimes says that with contemplation "the wheel of Ixion stands still."[64] When the object is "lifted out" of time, it then no longer occupies space and it no longer stands in any causal relation: Its Idea appears, the essence of the object becomes object. But is this Idea, this "new" object, something different from the individual object or is it just the individual object viewed in that special way called contemplation?

Regarding this question, to which we have been leading up, Young entertains the suggestion that "the Ideas might just be ordinary objects . . . their universality having to do, not with their being non-natural *ones* resembled by the perceptual *many*, but rather with the selectiveness of attention paid to them by the observer."[65] Young concludes that this is in fact the correct interpretation. After quoting the passage in which Schopenhauer talks about water in the brook, he writes that "the important thing to notice is that perceiving an Idea (water) is a matter of perceiving an ordinary object (the brook) with one's attention focussed on the essential, and away from its inessential aspects."[66] Second, Young notes, "Schopenhauer does, sometimes, speak quite explicitly of the ordinary individual thing as the object of aesthetic contemplation," for example, where he says of art that "it plucks the object of its contemplation from the stream of the world's course, and holds it isolated before it. The particular thing, which in that stream was an infinitesimal part [*verschwindend kleiner Theil*], becomes for art a representative of the whole, an equivalent of the infinitely many in space and time."[67] Third, Young argues that the Ideas must be identified with "ordinary objects" because "there is nothing else they can be." The thing in itself is "one" and the Ideas are many (there is "a plurality of ideas"); "hence the Ideas must belong to the phenomenal world since, in terms of the Kantian structure of Schopenhauer's metaphysics, there is nowhere else for them to go." In other words, the Ideas are the second aspect of the world as representation, as, Young points out, the very title of Book 3 indicates. "So they must be identified with ordinary natural objects for those are the only kinds of objects there are in the phenomenal world."[68] Young concludes his account with this general statement: "Being conscious of, knowing, an Idea consists, not in acquaintance with some esoteric object, but in consciousness of an ordinary object with, however, one's attention focused upon the significant rather than the trivial in it."[69]

The chief merit of Young's interpretation is that it puts to rest several of the puzzles other commentators have found in Schopenhauer's doctrine of the Ideas: It tells us where Ideas exist, namely, "in the phenomenal world" rather than in some realm between the will and ordinary objects; it explains how Ideas and ordinary objects are related, namely, as the essential aspects of ordinary objects in contrast to their inessential aspects (or, alternatively, as what is significant in ordinary objects versus what is trivial); and, in general, it demystifies Ideas by bringing them into, say, the world of experience. Moreover, though only implicitly, Young's account accommodates Schopenhauer's contention that contemplation of an Idea amounts to viewing an object vertically rather than horizontally—which I take to be the meaning of plucking the object of contemplation from the stream of the world's course and holding it up in isolation.

It seems clear, however, that Ideas cannot be *identical* with ordinary (perceptual, natural) objects: Such objects are temporally, spatially, and causally connected (all being subject to the subordinate forms of the principle of sufficient reason) and Ideas are atemporal, aspatial, and acausal (all being subject only to the general form of the principle of sufficient reason, namely, that of being object for a subject). Basically, ordinary objects are in time and Ideas are not; hence the claim that they are identical is to misrepresent, by way of overstatement, Schopenhauer's position. They are also not identical in another sense: Ordinary objects include inessential or trivial aspects, as it were, while Ideas are only the essential or significant aspects of ordinary objects—or so at least Young himself holds; and this very fact makes ordinary objects and Ideas (strictly speaking) nonidentical. I suspect that Young would agree with this observation, but that he would persist in claiming that Ideas are the essential, observer-selected, universal aspects of ordinary perceptual objects, and indeed that they are ordinary objects with their inessential aspects disregarded and only their essential aspects regarded—and it is in this sense that "identity" is to be understood. In other words, the essence of an ordinary object is the Idea of that object. This proposition does, undoubtedly, represent Schopenhauer's view. But it raises a crucial question: Is the essence (the Idea) of an ordinary object *there* in the ordinary object and thus open to contemplation? In a moment I am going to argue that the answer is no (unless, of course, contemplation is interpreted so as to make the answer yes). Something beyond contemplation (as normally understood, or even understood as a special sort of paying attention to) is required for knowing an Idea.

As for the Ideas belonging to the "phenomenal world," there being "nowhere else for them to go," it may be pointed out again that the "phenomenal world" is twofold in Schopenhauer's thought (actually he does not use the term): On the one hand, it refers to the world of ordinary perceptual (or natural) objects, but, on the other hand, it refers to the world of any object, or indeed of any possible object, of a knowing subject, which thus allows Ideas to inhabit it. Schopenhauer acknowledges a sort of "phenomenal world" that Kant does not, namely, the phenomenal world as Idea, which, as he often puts it, is "the only real world." (It is the world of Apollo Belvedere, in other words, the world of the genius.) Phenomena, appearances, objects may be either perceptual representations or pure representations, i.e., either "ordinary objects" or Ideas; both, after all, are *Vorstellungen*, both are *Erscheinungen*, both are *Objektitäten* of the will (the first sort inadequately and the second sort adequately). Consequently, Ideas can belong to the "phenomenal world" or, equally, to the world as representation without being "ordinary objects."

Although I think that Young's interpretation is mistaken (partly because it is too Kantian),[70] I think that it points to a serious matter. Is pure contemplation of an ordinary object sufficient to bring forth the corresponding Idea? Suppose that I look at some object, without the slightest trace of willing it or without any regard for its possible use or hindrance to my will, hence further without any consideration of its temporal, spatial, and causal relationships; do I thereby attain the state of contemplating its Idea? The answer, on Young's account, it seems, ought to be yes; and the answer, according to one of Schopenhauer's accounts, is yes; but the real answer (I suggest) and the answer, according to Schopenhauer's account of the artistic (and other) genius, is no. The genius must be not only a "pure" (will-less, painless, objective, impersonal, disinterested) subject of knowledge, but also a highly imaginative one. He (and, in Schopenhauer's judgment, it is always *he*)[71] must possess pure objectivity and imagination (*Phantasie*),[72] and the latter for two reasons: First, the genius is a person who, as such, has only a limited knowledge of things, yet the Ideas extend beyond any person's knowledge (even unto eternity); hence he must, through imagination, reach out beyond personal experience and "construct" (*konstruiren*) Ideas, not every dimension of which has ever been experienced (or, I want to add, contemplated). The genius must somehow "create" the Idea or essence of the type of object that he, otherwise, views "objectively"; without this construction or creation the relevant Idea will not pass before his "clear eye of the world." Second, since "the actual objects are almost always only very imperfect copies of the Idea that manifests itself in them, . . . the man of genius requires imagination in order to see in things not what nature has actually formed, but what she endeavored to form, yet did not bring about because of the conflict of her forms with one another. . . ."[73] No actual thing in nature provides even the genius with a perfect copy of its kind's Idea (there is no perfect oak tree there in nature to be selectively discerned by even the most will-free observer), hence no contemplation of any perceptual object amounts to acquaintance with the Idea of that object's kind. Every actual thing in nature is "tainted" with "forms" or Ideas foreign to the "form" or Idea of its kind;

every natural object is a hodgepodge of "forms" or Ideas, hence none presents its Idea "clearly and distinctly." For that Idea to become a pure object of the genius's gaze, it must be "purified" of foreign elements, and that means that the genius's knowledge of an Idea requires (as in fact all knowledge does in a way) active creativity and not merely passive contemplation—and, further, not even selective attention. Finally, it should be said, the artistic genius must not only know Ideas—achieved through willless contemplation of things in conjunction with a high degree of imagination—he must be capable of remaining in such a state long enough to reproduce (through technical ability) the Idea in one or another form of art.[74]

The knowledge of the genius, that is, knowledge of Ideas, has to get its start from, but go beyond, ordinary experience. It starts with experience of objects, human beings, or actions as they occur in the nexus of time, space, and causality; and it goes beyond such experience through the willless contemplation of what is essential to those objects, coupled with imagination whereby the relevant Ideas are made "universal" objects. What the genius knows, in other words, is the type (say, loving-kindness) from the observation of a token or actual instance of that type (for example, the act of the Good Samaritan). This actual instance is "purified" from its place, its time, its causal antecedents and effects, and thereby raised up to the type, loving-kindness—where this raising up, through contemplation and imagination, delivers the pure Idea. From the single instance the genius becomes aware of the Idea, not unlike the way that the genius Cuvier "constructs" the entire animal from observing one bone or the way that a true *Menschenkenner* "recognizes" the unitary character of a person from observing one of the person's actions.[75] In short, the genius "sees" the One in the Single, the type in the token. Then, of course, the artist has the technical ability to reproduce what he or she "sees" in a work of art, which in turn allows us nongeniuses to catch a glimpse of the relevant Idea. Again, however, these Ideas do not exist in nature clearly and distinctly; they are in large part "constructs" of the pure knower (where "knowing" requires in part creating). As a consequence, Ideas are conditioned by the pure knower; and when this fact is recognized, the pure knower recognizes that "the true world," that is, the world as Idea, is dependent on him or her, which in turn produces the sense of being free from or nondependent on "this world." We have thus returned to the liberating effect of "knowing Ideas"—something the normal person never, or almost never, experiences.

In a literary tragedy, the author presents an individual human being who exhibits one of the essential forms of the Idea of humanity, for example, greed, envy, jealousy, compassion, or pride. (The author may even present a clear and distinct case of renunciation of the will to life, as, according to Schopenhauer, Goethe did with the character of Gretchen in *Faust.*)[76] The artist in this art form presents a paradigm case, an exemplar, a sub-Idea of the Idea of humanity in a human figure or human action, and for those who are capable of discerning Ideas at all the sub-Idea will be clearly experienced. (Incidentally, anyone capable of appreciating any art form has some capacity to discern Ideas, hence on this score many, many people will have some acquaintance with the world as Idea.) In actual fact or in human history no individual human being or human action will present us with as clear a case of, say, a human emotion or motive as a great tragedy does; in actual fact, a person will not display clearly and distinctly a single emotion or motive but, in almost every case, a mixture of emotions or motives. But in great art, according to Schopenhauer, the artist portrays an emotion or motive (or the like) both clearly (so that it can hardly be missed) and distinctly (so that it will not be confused with or mixed up with others).

In a painting, for example, the artist presents a particular image of a kind of thing that clearly and distinctly exhibits the kind, or at least this is what he or she tries to do; and when the attempt is successful, the painting will be called beautiful. In place of "a particular image of a kind," one might employ the expression, "a token of a type." The token is here, now, attached to the wall, and so on, but what it exhibits (the type or Idea, as Schopenhauer would have it) is not here, now, on the wall, which is to say that Ideas are not subject to time, space, and causality. Only in part, and never fully, in nature does a token of a type T fully exhibit type T—which is another way of saying that Ideas do not get fully (adequately, successfully) exhibited in nature.[77]

I want to conclude this chapter by considering what, according to Schopenhauer, the philosophical genius recognizes upon his or her unique viewing of nature. This consideration, which takes us back into Book 2, should help clarify several obscure aspects of the doctrine of Ideas, and it should help answer several of the questions that commentators typically raise about that doctrine, including the perhaps central question, "How can the intellect get free from the will?"

The world of nature is the gigantic battle that the various forces of nature wage against each other for the possession of matter. Matter is thus the territory fought over; the combatants are the forces of nature, no loser of which is ever completely annihilated (but only displaced for the moment) and no victor of which can ever cease struggling for the particular time and place it has won (and will inevitably lose); the rule of victory is the law of causality, by means of which one force of nature usurps a bit of matter just previously possessed by another force of nature and thereby appears; insofar as this battle called nature has "an ultimate aim," it is the production of an organism that knows what it and nature are and, in virtue of this knowledge, withdraws from the otherwise ceaseless strife, becoming then "the clear mirror of the world" ("the source of art") or even self-annihilator ("salvation from the world").[78]

From the standpoint of philosophy, strictly considered, all that has just been said can be expressed in terms of the Ideas and that which they "objectify," the will. Accordingly, the world of nature is the world as will, the various natural forces are the Ideas, the internecine battle is the struggle of Ideas to conquer each other, and the ultimate aim is (in art) the knowledge of the genius or then, possibly, the total elimination of will itself. Regarding the genius, the "pure subject of knowledge," in whom the intellect gets free from the will, this may be said: It is not the case that the intellect is an agent that overpowers the will; it is not the case that the genius brings about the intellect's freedom from the will; rather, it is the case that the intellect is that form of will whereby it knows itself and thereby may cease to will.[79] But why, one may ask, would the will allow one of its forms, namely, the intellect, to gain mastery over it?[80] The answer is forthcoming: Once the will found it necessary to create the intellect for the sake of preservation—which is precisely what has happened—it came to know what it is, namely, a war with itself carried out by the innumerable instances of its many objectifications (the Ideas). With this realization—the realization that it creates its own misery and suffering, that it can never reach satisfaction and peace—the will may then freely choose to cease willing.

SEVEN

From the World to Salvation

The task of philosophy, Schopenhauer holds, is to provide an interpretation of the world of experience whereby—so far as this is possible—the many different sorts of people, the various kinds of human conduct, and the several types of natural states and occurrences become fully and clearly understandable. The vast majority of people and their conduct, along with all of nature, are to be understood in terms of what Schopenhauer calls the affirmation of the will to life, which is of course the chief topic of discussion in Books 1 and 2 of *The World as Will and Representation*. For human beings, affirmation of the will engenders knowledge only of particular things (though, in virtue of reason, human beings can put these things into classes and thus devise concepts), hence of things subject to the principle of sufficient reason; it allows (or indeed necessitates) perception of things distinguished from each other by means of the *principium individuationis*; it makes all objects for the (individual) knowing subject potential motives, and thereby makes the human subject and human conduct unfree; it arouses in the human subject, at least now and again, a sense of the futility, vanity, transitoriness of life along with an intense fear of death. To put the matter in slightly different terms, the world in accord with the affirmation of the will is essentially a world of suffering—not only the suffering that one perceives in, and perhaps inflicts on, others (including animals), but also the suffering that one experiences in oneself. That life devoted to affirmation of the will is essentially suffering constitutes the keynote to Schopenhauer's doctrine of pessimism. It is, in his judgment, the only *Weltanschauung* consonant with the affirmation of the will to life; it is the only thesis correspondent to normal human (and animal) life.

Despite all of this, we find in the world of experience people whose conduct and "states of mind" (my term) set them apart from the normal run of human beings. These exceptional, truly extraordinary people fall into three main classes: the aesthetic contemplator (or even the genius), the morally virtuous individual (even the moral saint), and the ascetic (or even the mystic).[1] What sort of philosophical interpretation will elucidate and render intelligible these rare human beings with their abnormal conduct and "states of mind"? Schopenhauer's general answer is that they exemplify—in some, but different, senses or ways—the denial of the will to life, and he depicts the various aspects that this denial takes in Books 3 and 4 of *The World as Will and Representation*. There is simply no way, Schopenhauer holds, to elucidate philosophically the existence of the genius, the saint, and the ascetic (or the mystic) except by attributing to them the denial of the will—in one or another of the forms that this denial can take. It is in terms of the denial of the will that Schopenhauer supplements his doctrine of pessimism with a doctrine of salvation (*Erlösung*). This dark, obscure, and somewhat unsettling doctrine is the chief topic of the present chapter.

Denial of the will to life takes place in one fashion in aesthetic contemplation. Since affirmation of the will to life presupposes the individual subject facing particular objects (which figure as potential motives), and since the aesthetic contemplator abandons individuality and thus comes to know "general objects," i.e., Ideas (which do not function as motives), aesthetic contemplation entails denial of the *individual* will.[2] Yet, quite clearly, will of some sort remains in the picture, for here, it is said, the will knows itself; and, most assuredly, knowledge or representation, with subject and object, also remains. In aesthetic contemplation, then, what is denied is individual or subjective willing on the part of the subject, whereby the subject becomes a "pure" or objective knower and its objects become "pure" too, hence Ideas or adequate objectities of the will. If everything of will disappeared entirely, then there would be no knowledge of Ideas or objectities of the will, and by no means could it be said that here, in aesthetic contemplation, the will knows itself. The sort of will or willing that remains is admittedly difficult to understand (elsewhere I have called it "objective willing"),[3] but clearly what is renounced in aesthetic contemplation is individual or subjective or even egoistic willing—and not all willing, hence (strictly speaking) not full denial or elimination of the will.

Something rather similar takes place upon the advent of the morally virtuous person whose incentive to action is compassion or pity (*Mitleid*). The pitying agent denies or renounces the will to life as belonging exclusively to himself or herself (he or she abandons egoism, which is the normal incentive for human beings) and "identifies" with the will to life in other animate (and suffering) creatures. For the pitying agent any known suffering is taken on as his or her suffering, hence he or she works toward eliminating it wherever it occurs. This agent therefore renounces only the will to life in himself or herself, that is, this agent renounces the selfish will, and does so only in the sense of regarding any suffering on a par with his or her suffering. Again, then, this agent adopts what might be called the "objective" or "impartial" will to life; but he or she continues to affirm life as such. Consequently, with compassion or pity it is not the case that suffering, life, and will—all of which intermingle—are denied or eliminated; instead, they are fully acknowledged, taken on, or accepted for what they are, and then opposed.

Despite the difference between compassion or pity and full denial of the will to life, the two have, Schopenhauer claims, a common source. He writes that "from the same source from which all goodness, affection [*Liebe*], virtue, and nobility of character [*Edelmuth*] spring, there ultimately arises also what I call denial of the will to life."[4] That common source of moral virtue and denial of the will to life is the penetration of the *principium individuationis* (the principle of individuation), or the "seeing through" the veil of Maya, whereby the distinction between one's own individuality and that of others is abolished. (As noted earlier, and as repeated in effect here, knowledge limited to the difference and separation of one's own individuality and that of others is the source of egoism, which, Schopenhauer holds, can lead to hatred and sheer wickedness.)[5] The crucial role played by knowledge with regard to both moral virtue and full denial of the will to life comes to the fore. Schopenhauer accordingly claims: "Now, if seeing through the *principium individuationis*, if this direct knowledge of the identity of the will in all its appearance, is present in a high degree of distinctness [*Deutlichkeit*, clarity] it will at once show an even further influence on the will."[6] The person involved here does not know anything that exists individually and separately, including his own person in contrast to other persons and animals (which is the knowledge associated with egoism); and he does not know only the "identity of the will" in all persons and animals (which is the knowledge associated with moral virtue). Instead: "He knows the whole, comprehends its inner nature [*das Wesen desselben*], and finds it involved in a constant passing away, a vain striving, an inward conflict, and a continual suffering. Wherever he looks, he sees suffering humanity and the suffering animal world, and a world that passes away."[7] This knowledge of "the whole," Schopenhauer holds, is bound to have an influence on his will beyond that which leads to moral virtue. For how could anyone wish to participate in such a world? "Now how could he, with such knowledge of the world, affirm this very life through constant acts of will, and precisely in this way bind himself more and more firmly to it, press himself to it more and more closely?" Unlike that knowledge wedded to the *principium individuationis*, to distinction and particularity, to egoism; and even unlike that knowledge of the one will in all persons and animals, which awakens moral virtue, knowledge of the whole, of the inner nature of things in themselves [*das Wesen der Dinge an sich*] . . . becomes the *quieter* of all and every willing. The will now turns away from life; it shudders at the pleasures in which it recognizes the affirmation of life. Man attains to the state of voluntary [*freiwillig*] renunciation, resignation, true composure, and complete will-lessness.[8]

In most people this state of renunciation lasts little longer than the state of aesthetic contemplation (one "backslides," as it were); the will reasserts itself, and most people find themselves again in its clutches. Freedom from the will is then lost, and enslavement to it recurs. But there is, Schopenhauer notes, an exception: the ascetic. In the next paragraph an effort is made—not with full success, it must be said—to provide a philosophical elucidation of this rare human being.

Comparing life to "a circular path of red-hot coals having a few cool places, a path that we have to run over incessantly," Schopenhauer contrasts the normal person to the ascetic thus: The normal person takes consolation in the few cool places and strives to reach them; "but the man who sees through the *principium individuationis*, and recognizes the essence of things in themselves, and thus the whole [*das Ganze*], is no longer susceptible of such consolation; he sees himself in all places simultaneously, and withdraws." In other words: "His will turns about [*Sein Wille wendet sich*]; it no longer affirms its essence, mirrored in appearance, but denies it."[9] This denial of the will or, equally, this withdrawal from the world makes itself known in "the phenomenon" (*das Phänomen*) that Schopenhauer calls "the transition from virtue to *asceticism* [*Askesis*]."

> In other words, it is no longer enough for him [the ascetic] to love others like himself, and to do as much for them as for himself, but there arises in him an aversion [*Abscheu*] to the essence whose expression is his own appearance, to the will to life, to the kernel and essence of that world recognized as full of misery. He therefore renounces precisely this essence, which appears in him and is expressed already by his body, and his action now gives the lie to his appearance, and comes into open contradiction with it. Essentially nothing but appearance of the will, he ceases to will anything, guards himself against attaching his will to anything, seeks to establish in himself the greatest indifference to all things.[10]

Nothing is important to the ascetic; unlike the moral saint he or she makes no effort to relieve the suffering of those about him or her. Complete indifference (*Gleichgültigkeit*) is the state reached by the ascetic.

The action (*Thun*) of the ascetic that comes into open contradiction with his appearance, that is, with the body, is especially evident, not so much with his indifference to others, but with the denial of the sexual impulse.

> His body, healthy and strong, expresses the sexual impulse through the geni-

tals, but he denies the will and gives the lie to the body; he wills no sexual satisfaction under any condition. Voluntary [*freiwillig*], complete chastity is the first step in asceticism or the denial of the will to life.[11]

It is as if, Schopenhauer suggests, the ascetic were to think, "With the cessation of my body [i.e., with death], the will, whose appearance is my body, will cease; and I shall do nothing to perpetuate it." If this policy were universally adopted, if, in other words, the human species were to die out, then, Schopenhauer speculates, the animal kingdom would also become extinct. He bases this speculation on the intimate interconnection of all appearances of the will, supposing that if the highest manifestation of the will (the human being) were to cease, then so would all lower manifestations (or at least all lower manifestations dependent on the sexual impulse).[12]

One highly significant point that Schopenhauer makes about the true ascetic's denial of the will to life is its voluntariness: The first step of this denial, as noted above, is "voluntary, complete chastity," but the denial is also shown by "voluntary and intentional poverty"[13] and, beyond this, by (clearly voluntary) mortification of the body through fasting, self-castigation, and self-torture, so that death is then "cheerfully accepted as a longed-for deliverance [*Erlösung*]."[14] In fact, when Schopenhauer comes to define "asceticism"—"in the narrower sense"—he emphasizs its voluntary or intentional nature:

> By the expression asceticism [*Askesis*] . . . I understand in the narrower sense this intentional breaking of the will [*diese vorsätzliche Brechung des Willens*] by refusal of the agreeable and search for the disagreeable, the self-chosen, penitent way of life and self-chastisement, for the continuing mortification of the will.[15]

Schopenhauer acknowledges, however, that fully voluntary or intentional denial of the will is extremely rare, being ascribable only to the person who carries it out solely in virtue of knowing, and not personally feeling, the suffering of the world as a whole. For the most part, and in the wider sense of "asceticism," denial of the will, he holds, occurs in those persons who do not simply know but who rather personally experience, or feel, great suffering; in other words, "in most cases the will must be broken by the greatest personal suffering before its self-denial comes about."[16] This Schopenhauer calls the "second path" to denial of the will;[17] and in this connection he speaks of "the purifying flame of suffering,"[18] citing the person of Gretchen in Goethe's *Faust* as "a perfect specimen of the second path."[19]

Denial of the will is, in every case, "occasioned" by suffering: On the "first path" (exemplified by the true ascetic) mere knowledge of the whole (animal and human) world as one of suffering "occasions" the denial; on the "second path" (exemplified by the person, like Gretchen, whose will has been crushed by fate) personally felt suffering "occasions" the denial. In both cases, according to Schopenhauer's philosophical account, the individuals involved recognize "the contradiction of the will to life with itself,"[20] although they may not have the slightest idea that this is what is actually happening and although they may have the most bizarre conception of what the world is.[21] In both cases, moreover, denial of the will must be understood as an instance, indeed, the only instance (Schopenhauer holds), in which freedom enters appearance. It has already been pointed out that the true ascetic, the denier of the will on the "first path," voluntarily or intentionally denies the will; it may now be pointed out, perhaps contrary to what one would think, the individual of the "second path" also freely denies the will. Noting that personally felt suffering is not sufficient for adopting the "second path," since many sufferers persist in affirming the will even in the face of immediate death and hopelessness, Schopenhauer remarks:

> In general, the denial of the will by no means results from suffering with the necessity of effect from cause; on the contrary, the will remains free. For here is just the one and only point where its freedom enters directly into the appearance; hence the astonishment so strongly expressed by Asmus [Matthias Claudius] about the "transcendental change." For every case of suffering, a will can be conceived which surpasses it in intensity, and is unconquered by it.[22]

Consequently, there can be no causal explanation of the denial of the will, that is, no explanation of the form, "Whenever suffering—whether merely known or personally felt—occurs, denial of the will is causally produced." No, every case of denial of the will is a case of freedom; it is a case of the will's freely denying itself! But is this not a manifest self-contradiction? It is one thing to acknowledge the rare phenomenon of ascetic "withdrawal from the world," but it is quite another thing to explicate this phenomenon in terms of Schopenhauer's philosophy—a philosophy that makes the will the will to life and that precludes, or so it certainly seems, any will to death (as it were). And how could denial of the will possibly be regarded as uncaused and thus free? How, further, are we to understand the will's freedom entering directly into the appearance?

Every commentator on Schopenhauer's philosophy finds the account of the denial of the will—although "to a certain extent . . . the most important point of our whole discussion"[23]—extremely difficult to make sensible, at least within the general framework of that philosophy. I am no exception; for although I believe that denial of the will makes fairly good sense when understood as denial of the individual or subjective will and thus as the adoption of a general or objective will (which occurs in genuine scholarship, in moral virtue, and in aesthetic contemplation),[24] I believe that denial of the will in the ascetic realm tends to defy comprehension.[25] In a way, of course, Schopenhauer fully admits, or even insists, that the ascetic's mode of life cannot be understood, which is to say, quite literally, that it cannot be brought to understanding in accord with the principle of sufficient reason; and the reason for this, he holds, is simply that the ascetic's mode of life exhibits freedom (from the world as representation) and therefore independence of the principle of sufficient reason (and the world as representation). But how this freedom enters appearance, how anything in appearance can be uncaused and thus free—this seems to contradict everything Schopenhauer has said about appearance.

In order to render denial of the will as comprehensible as the nature of the case allows, I want to point out a number of things. First, the will cannot deny itself apart from knowledge, indeed, it cannot do so apart from a special sort of knowledge of which only human beings are capable (if it were otherwise, animals could deny the will). Second, denial of the will is not, literally speaking, something that an individual person, a particular phenomenon, can execute "at will" (despite the talk of the truly voluntary ascetic); rather, it is the will that denies the will, though "in" or "through" an individual person. Third, denial of the will can apparently never reach the stage of complete extinction (though Schopenhauer waffles on this issue); for even the most extreme ascetic remains embodied, and in his or her body a trace of will, however faint, persists. Fourth, to the extent that denial of the will can reach, it reaches freedom from the world of suffering and therefore freedom from the world in which the many manifestations of will struggle against and, as individuals, destroy each other. And fifth (which really only amplifies the first point, above), the intellect or knowing subject and the will or willing subject in a human being, though different, are so closely tied to each other (and even said to be "identical"—the great miracle or mystery) that knowledge can be the "quieter of the will."[26]

After distinguishing sharply between denial of the will and suicide in section 69 of *The World as Will and Representation,* volume 1,[27] Schopenhauer opens section 70 by entertaining the proposition that his discussion of the denial of the will, which allegedly takes place freely, stands in logical conflict with his earlier account of necessity, which (among other things) makes all actions merely reactions of the human character to motives and thus unfree.[28] In other words, the possible objection goes, if every action is motivated and thus unfree, then the ascetic's action of denying the will is motivated and also unfree; hence freedom cannot be ascribed to the ascetic's action, to what was called earlier his doing or conduct (*Thun*). One way to escape this difficulty would be to claim that the ascetic's denial of the will is not an action, that is, that it is not a reaction of his character to a motive; instead, it is a cessation of action and, therewith, an elimination of the individual character. In fact, this possible response is strongly suggested by the characterization of the ascetic's denial of the will as resignation (*Resignation*) or withdrawal (*Versagung*), and it is explicitly claimed in an important letter.[29] But even so, denial of the will is still a phenomenon, it still enters into appearance, it is, in some sense, an appearance; hence, one would think, it must still be caused, even if not actually motivated. Consequently, the problem of reconciling the allegedly free denial of the will with the alleged necessity of all appearances remains acute. And Schopenhauer obviously recognizes this, as the following passage reveals:

> In truth, real freedom [*eigentliche Freiheit*], i.e., independence of the principle of sufficient reason, belongs only to the will as thing in itself, not to its appearance, whose essential form is everywhere the principle of sufficient reason, the element of necessity. The only case where that freedom can become immediately visible in appearance is the one where it makes an end to what appears, and because the mere appearance, insofar as it is a link in the chain of causes, namely, the living body, still continues to endure in time, which contains only appearances, the will, manifesting itself through this appearance, then stands in contradiction with it, since it denies what it [the appearance] expresses.[30]

The crucial point is that freedom of the will as thing in itself becomes visible (or, as it were, "makes an appearance in appearance") in only one case, namely, where, though manifested in the living body (particularly, in the genitals), it denies and "stands in contradiction" with the living body's (i.e., with the genitals') normal and natural appearance or expression (i.e., the sexual impulse). Accordingly, Schopenhauer then repeats the remark about the genitals' appearing "in health," though "no sexual satisfaction is willed."[31] It is evident that in this presentation Schopenhauer employs the term "appearance" to refer to two things: first, to the living body, which can be perceived; and second, to the normal expression or "appearance" of the living body, that is, to the sexual impulse. Both are appearances of the will (just as everything perceivable or visible is an appearance of the will); but with the ascetic, devoted to chastity, the living body's normal or natural "appearance" is suppressed and therefore does not "appear," though the living body itself remains in full "appearance." For this reason, it may be said that the ascetic "gives the lie to the body," in other words, he or she is a body (an appearance) but he or she denies the body's normal expression (which does not appear). In such a case, Schopenhauer holds, freedom of the will as thing in itself "becomes immediately visible in appearance," for will in the ascetic "contradicts" the body.[32] This has to mean that freedom of the will as thing in itself "becomes visible" through the fact that it appears as body (as genitals) but it does not appear or get expressed as the body (the genitals) normally appears. So, in a way, it is the nonappearance of the sexual impulse that, in "contradicting" the appearing body, constitutes the will's "becoming visible." Consequently, too, in full accord with Schopenhauer's general position, it is the negative proposition that the body's natural "appearance" *does not appear* that informs the positive proposition that freedom of the will as thing in itself *does appear.*

But how, exactly, is denial of the will possible? Does the will (in the truly voluntary ascetic and in those personally suffering individuals who allegedly "freely" deny the will) turn around on and negate itself? In a way, Schopenhauer holds, this is precisely what does happen; but it does not happen "directly," that is to say, it is not the case that the will ceases to affirm life "all by itself" and apart from everything else. That, Schopenhauer recognizes, would be impossible, for "by itself" the will does nothing but will; and what it wills is its own continuation, in the human individual and/or in the propagation of the individual's offspring. Only in virtue of some intermediary that is not, or is not simply, a matter of will can the will deny itself or, what is the same, cease to will. This intermediary is a form of knowledge, but it is not the normal or natural form of knowledge, which, in the service of the will itself, knows only particular objects as potential motives; it is then a form of knowledge whereby individual motives lose their power over the will or, in the person, lose their impact on the person's character. Schopenhauer leads into this intricate account by first saying a bit more about the ascetic's body:

> The whole body is the visible expression of the will to life, yet the motives corresponding to this will no longer act [*wirken*]; indeed the dissolution of the body [*Auflösung des Leibes*], the end of the individual, and thus the greatest suppression of the natural will [*größte Hemmung des natürlichen Willens*] is complete and wished-for.[33]

This state of affairs generates what Schopenhauer calls a "*real* contradiction"—a contradiction in the world of appearance between (1) "the necessity of the will's determinations through motives according to the character" and (2) "the possibility of the whole suppression of the will, whereby motives become powerless." This "*real* contradiction," Schopenhauer adds, "arises from the direct encroachment of the freedom of the will in itself, knowing no necessity, on the necessity of its appearance."[34]

If freedom of the will as thing in itself is to appear, it must appear in someone whose (individual) will or character is free from determination by motives; thus something must occur whereby motives lose their power over this will or character, and this "something" cannot be a motivated act of the person involved. A person is capable only of willing and knowing, and since willing (or at least direct willing) has been ruled out, knowing must provide the "something" by which freedom appears—yet it cannot be normal knowing, that is, knowing of particular things, which offers only motives. It must be therefore a special form of knowing. And this is precisely what Schopenhauer claims in his treatment of the *"real contradiction"*:

> The key to the reconciliation of these contradictions lies . . . in the fact that the state [*Zustand*, condition] in which the character is withdrawn from the power of motives does not proceed [*ausgehen*] directly from the will, but from a changed form of knowledge [*eine veränderte Erkenntniß-weise*]. Thus, so long as the knowledge is only that which is involved [*befangen*, ensnared] in the *principium individuationis*, and which absolutely follows the principle of sufficient reason, the power of the motives is irresistible. But when the *principium individuationis* is seen through, when the Ideas, and indeed the essence of things in themselves, are immediately recognized as the same will in all, and out of this recognition a universal quieter of willing proceeds, then the individual motives becomes ineffective, because the form of knowledge corresponding to them withdraws by a completely different one that obscures them.[35]

Schopenhauer then adds, in line with his doctrine of the unalterability of the human character, that the character of a person whose knowledge is that of the whole (rather than that of particular things) does not partially change; instead, it is eliminated or "set aside" (*aufheben*), hence the talk in Christianity of the *"new birth"* (*Wiedergeburt*) and, regarding the knowledge from which it proceeds, the *"effect of grace"* (*Gnadenwirkung*).[36]

Fully acknowledging the strangeness of freedom's entrance into appearance, Schopenhauer cites, with full approval, Malebranche's remark, *La liberté est un mystère*.[37] It is this mystery, he holds, that the Christian mystics refer to in theological terms; in philosophical terms, it is "the sole immediate expression of *freedom of the will*." Very little can be said by way of elucidating freedom of the will in appearance, other than that which has already been said, namely, that with the truly free being, the ascetic, the body appears but the normal "expression" of the body, the sexual impulse, does not appear. That this does occur, however rarely, is an undeniable fact, according to Schopenhauer, and that it amounts to freedom in appearance is the only reasonable philosophical interpretation. To these few comments on freedom's entrance into appearance, Schopenhauer adds two more. First, "It occurs only when the will, arriving at the knowledge of its essence in itself, receives from this [knowledge] a quieter [*Quietiv*], and just because of that is released from the effect of *motives* which [effect] lies in the province of a different kind of knowledge, whose objects are only appearances." Notice that it is the will that arrives at a knowledge of its essence in itself, so here again "the will knows itself." This knowledge (or actually self-knowledge) is apparently necessary, but not sufficient, for the quieter to operate or, equally, for one to gain release from the effect of (individual) motives. In other words, one could come to know that the world is the will in conflict with itself, or that the world as a whole is essentially suffering without necessarily turning away from the world, hence without necessarily denying the will in oneself. In any case, I suggest, Schopenhauer wants to retain a "causal gap" between knowledge of the world as a whole (knowledge of the world as essentially suffering) and denial of the will (withdrawal from the world): He wants to insure thereby that denial of the will is free. Second, he writes, "The possibility of the freedom that thus manifests itself is man's greatest prerogative, which is forever wanting in the animal, because the reflectiveness [*Besonnenheit*] of the faculty of reason, enabling him to survey the whole of life independently of the impression of the moment, is the condition therefor." The animal, like the stone, "acts" under necessity; the human being, in virtue of reflectiveness, has the possibility of freedom. Therefore: "*Necessity is the kingdom of nature: freedom is the kingdom of grace.*"[38]

Schopenhauer concludes this discussion of freedom's entrance into appearance with further reference to knowledge and grace. Self-elimination of the will, he says first, proceeds from knowledge; but since knowledge is wholly independent of "free choice" (*Willkür*), "that denial of willing, that entrance into freedom," cannot be forced by intention (*Vorsatz*). (This curious claim means, I suggest, that no phenomenal, human being can—in light of the requisite knowledge—plan and deliberately bring about denial of the will.) Denial of the will proceeds rather from "the innermost relation of knowing and willing in man; hence it comes suddenly, as if flying in from without." When, if ever, it comes about, *it* comes about; one does not bring it about in a calculative, deliberative manner. And it is not the case either that the requisite knowledge causally produces denial of the will, for that, apparently, would presuppose (what is false) that the knowing and the willing subjects are causally connected. The knowledge in question resembles, in theological terms, the offering of grace; but, for denial of the will, grace must be accepted "in" or "through" the person to whom it is offered, hence here Schopenhauer speaks of the *Aufnahme der Gnade*; "so too the effect of the quieter is still an act of freedom of the will" (*Freiheitsakt des Willens*).[39] Schopenhauer suggests that every human being, in virtue of the capacity of surveying "the whole" (all of life as essentially suffering), is offered liberation from this world of suffering, hence from this world in which the *principium individuationis* reigns,[40] but almost no human being accepts, or freely takes on, the proferred liberation. It is as if the will might deny itself in every human being, whereby liberation would come about, but almost every human being opposes this offer of grace or liberation by continuing to will the life of individuality, subjectivity, and (in a word) egoism. If we ask, quite simply, "Why do they not accept grace?" the answer has to be, "because they do not will to" or "because they prefer the allurements of life." But then in defiance of all reason (one might say), they perpetuate their own suffering, illusion, and enslavement to the insatiable will.

In the final section of Book 4, section 71, Schopenhauer draws to a close "the whole development of that one thought [*jenes eine Gedanken*], the imparting of which was my goal," by considering an objection to his discussion of the complete denial of the will to life.[41] The objection—which, he notes, cannot be resolved, but belongs to the very nature of the case—is that this denial, with all that it involves, "appears to us as a transition into empty *nothingness*."[42] Apparently, though not explicitly said, this amounts to the objection (*Vorwurf*) that the end of the liberation process, negation of the world, and freedom from suffering is, paradoxically, an entrance into nothingness; hence one would wonder what sort of liberation, freedom, or salvation that can be. Does one become free only by the complete cessation of the world and of oneself? What sort of freedom would that be? And why would it be desirable? The senselessness of such a supposition would be unavoidable, Schopenhauer suggests, if this nothingness were absolute, that is, if it were *nihil negativum*; but, he reminds us, "the concept of nothingness is essentially relative, and always refers to a definite something that it negates," which is to say that it is only *nihil privatum.* In short, nothingness is always and necessarily nothingness of something positive, and thus never nothingness *simpliciter* or nothingness "pure and simple." Indeed, "no absolute nothingness, no really proper *nihil negativum*, is even conceivable."[43]

As a consequence, the nothingness in question has to be a nothingness of "the world of representation," which, Schopenhauer claims, has been shown to be "the objectity [*objektität*] of the will, as its mirror," and since "we ourselves are also this will and this world" there will be a nothingness of ourselves as well.[44] With the denial of the will to life, hence with liberation from the world and salvation from suffering, a nothingness ensues, but it is the nothingness of the world subject to the principle of sufficient reason, thus of the world of time, space, and causality. Schopenhauer then writes:

> Denial, abolition [*Aufhebung*, elimination], turning of the will is also abolition and disappearance of the world, its [i.e., the will's] mirror. If we no longer look into this mirror, we ask in vain in what direction it has turned, and then, because it no longer has any where and when, we complain that it has gotten lost in nothingness.[45]

Once the world as representation disappears, concepts ("the material of philosophy") and their signs, namely, words, disappear, that is, they no longer have any application. We cannot conceptualize or say anything about what remains; we cannot give any philosophical account of what is left over. Having drawn this logical entailment of his general position about what can be and what cannot be said, Schopenhauer continues with an extremely important (and puzzling) passage, which I quote in full:

> A contrary standpoint, if it were possible for us, would allow the signs [the words] to be changed, and [it would] show what exists for us as nothingness and that nothingness as what exists. But as long as we ourselves are the will to life, this latter [this nothingness as what exists] can be known and designated by us only negatively, because the old saying of Empedocles, that like can be known only by like, deprives us precisely here of all knowledge, just as, conversely, on it ultimately rests the possibility of all our actual knowledge, i.e., the world as representation, or the objectity of the will. For the world is the self-knowledge of the will.[46]

For the denier of the will to life, that which had existed prior to the denial (the "conversion") is nothingness and this nothingness is that which had existed; for him or her, "existence" and "nothingness" are coextensive terms. (He or she "recognizes" the *Nichtigkeit*—sometimes called the "vanity"—of all existence as determined by temporal, spatial, and causal dimensions.) For those of us still wedded to affirmation of the will, including those still involved in philosophy (conceptualization, talking and speaking), this "existence = nothingness," can be "known" (*erkennen*) and "designated" (*bezeichnen*) "only negatively," only as (say) "*not* the world as representation," "*not* the complex of particular appearances," or "*not* the objectity, or mirror, of the will." Only so long as we are will can we know the manifestation of the will, that is, the world as representation; for indeed it is "the self-knowledge of the will," whereby we will know the world as will, or, strictly speaking, as the will's become object. That self-knowledge, which is in effect "the will's knowing the will" (as just said), constitutes the world as representation, the world for us. But with the denial of the will, all of this knowing ceases and the world slips into (relative) nothingness.

Schopenhauer is acknowledging at this point the mystical state of consciousness (if even the word "consciousness" may be used), which philosophy can characterize only negatively, that is, as denial of the will to life and abolition of the world. In the language of the mystics, this state goes by the names of "ecstasy, rapture, illumination, union with God, and so on" (*Ekstase, Entrückung, Erleuchtung, Vereinigung mit Gott, u.s.w.*)—all of which lack philosophical content. Moreover, the mystic's state of "consciousness" cannot be called knowledge at all, "since it no longer has the form of subject and object"; and "it is accessible only to one's own experience that cannot be further communicated."[47] In full accord with what has been argued throughout the main work—that the world's inner nature or essence is will, and that all appearances in the world make up the objectity of the will—it must be concluded, Schopenhauer notes, that with the denial of the will, the world as representation vanishes, hence the dramatic phrase:

"No will: no representation, no world."[48] It apparently follows that as long as there is a world, there is will, and that, conversely, if there were to be complete denial of the will, there would be no world. Since, obviously, the world remains, it must be the case that no human being has ever reached the stage of complete denial of the will; or, assuming that complete denial has been reached by some human being, it must be the case that his or her complete denial somehow failed to "bring about" the elimination of the world. Several (friendly) critics of Schopenhauer's final position—that with complete asceticism in any human being the world should disappear, but it has not—brought up the clearly evident difficulty.

In response to this "difficulty," Schopenhauer could seek several—at least three—routes of escape. First, he could admit (perhaps reluctantly) that no human being has ever reached the stage of complete denial of the will, so this fact explains why the world has not vanished. Since every human being is embodied, and since the body is a manifestation of the will, no human being can completely deny the will; for indeed the body is "the objectity of the will." Even with the most sexually abstinent ascetic, the body with healthy genitals remains in existence—thus genitals "objectify" the will—even though this person does not permit the body to express itself in the normal manner, that is, in the sexual impulse. As mentioned earlier, this account requires a distinction—not typically recognized by Schopenhauer—between two sorts of manifestations of the will: the human body by itself (merely as a perceivable object, subject only to time, space, and causality) and the human body as the counterpart to the individual will (thus as the sexual impulse, among other things). Second, Schopenhauer could argue that, as the difficulty presupposes that complete denial of the will in one single individual should "bring about" the abolition of the whole world as representation, it depends on a presumed knowledge of how far the roots of individuality go into the will as a whole. In a letter he writes:

> Concerning the question—why, in virtue of the metaphysical unity of the will, the saint does not eliminate the world?—it is to be said first that this unity is a metaphysical one and second that we come closer to answering the question when we come to know "how deep the roots of individuality go into the thing in itself"—a problem that I have raised, but left alone as transcendent and therefore irresolvable."[49]

Schopenhauer's third response to the difficulty is divided into two parts: The first claims that the formulation of the problem involves an amphiboly (specifically, the application of terms to the will as thing in itself, which terms truly apply only to appearance or representation); and the second suggests that whether the world remains or disappears varies with the individual person's affirmation or denial of the will. This third response can be found in Schopenhauer's final letter, in which he replies to two military cadets who had formulated the difficulty in a syllogism (apparently arguing that, given the presence of will in all things and the full denial of the will in a moral saint, or extreme ascetic, the whole world vanishes). Schopenhauer's letter (in part) goes thus:

> Your syllogism [*Schluß*] is formally correct, also the premises are true, and yet the statement of the conclusion is false. This comes about therefore because an amphiboly of the concept occurs. The will is taken as individual in appearance; but then next as thing in itself. In the latter regard however the object is transcendent, i.e., goes out beyond all possibility of our understanding, because beyond experience the forms of our intellect [namely] space, time, and causality, are no longer applicable. These forms you retain, however, since you apply the predicates of whole and part, number and unity, cause and consequence, to the will as thing in itself. For example, you conceive of it in terms of our form of intuition space, consequently quantatively, when you say, "since the will in every individual is *whole*, with its negation in this individual the whole world must be eliminated." But if you want to comprehend the matter so purely quantitatively, then you [*sie*; but should be *Sie*] should have above begun with and said, "no longer can the one and indivisible will be whole in every one of the innumerable individuals." For this is a spatial impossibility. Likewise your question also really pertains to causality, which the eliminated will exercises on the world of appearance. Equally, it [your argument] takes time into consideration, when it says, "*after* the entrance of a negation of the will must etc."
>
> This whole amphiboly originates in the fact that your question has been raised at the border of the accessible and inaccessible of our knowledge, transcendents, and then it throws the concepts over and back to this border.
>
> For my part, I avoid all transcendence and always speak only of that which lets itself be confirmed in appearance; [I] show therefore the will in its affirmation in addition to it in these lingering appearances, the world, as its consequence—thus [in addition to] the will in its negation; but here I can conclude nothing about the consequences except negatively and there they are for us—nothing.
>
> Now whether the will-affirming individuals and the, as an exception, [will-]negating [individual] present themselves in time as *before* or *after* one another, makes no difference, no more than whether they must arise in space *beside* one another; all of this occurs merely in appearance and in virtue of its forms. . . .
>
> . . . One can also reply to your objection [thus]: If in the person who negates the will the world disappears, so in virtue of another who affirms it [the will] it [the world] is again produced. The truth is: for the one who wills it, it is always there; for the one who wills it not, it is not [there].[50]

The world is there (*sie ist da*) for those persons who will it to be there, for those who affirm the will to life; but the world is not there (*sie ist nicht da*) for those who do not will it to be there, for those who do not affirm, but rather deny, the will to life. This is Schopenhauer's final world on the matter. He died on September 21, 1860, twenty days after writing this letter.

We return now to the concluding section of the main work, section 71. After declaring that the state of the denier of the will cannot be called knowledge,[51] Schopenhauer proceeds to claim, in effect, that with this state "only knowledge remains; the will has vanished."[52] But how can this be? Schopenhauer must mean that with the denier of the will subject-object knowledge ceases, but some sort of knowledge comes about. It must be a knowledge whereby the will knows itself as a whole, whereby it finds itself in everything, and then *freely* denies itself. Although we, who are still wedded to the will, cannot personally experience this knowledge and free denial of the will, we have to acknowledge its existence. And although we view the resultant nothingness with abhorrence—which simply means that we will life so much—we nevertheless look upon the state of the denier of the will with a sense of longing (*Sehnsucht*). Schopenhauer puts the matter thus:

> When we turn our view away from our own need and enslavement to those who have overcome the world, in whom the will, having reached complete self-knowledge, has found itself again in everything and then freely denied itself, and who then merely wait to see the last trace of the will vanish with the body that is animated by that trace; then—instead of the restless stress and exertion, instead of the constant transition from desire to apprehension and from joy to suffering, instead of the never-satisfied and never-dying hope that constitutes the willing person's life-dream—we see that peace that is higher than all reason, that total ocean-like calmness of the spirit, that deep serenity, unshakable confidence and satisfaction, whose mere reflection in the countenance, as depicted by Raphael and Corregio, is a complete and certain gospel. Only knowledge remains; the will has vanished.[53]

We can hardly avoid looking upon the state of the denier of the will, as just described, "with deep and painful longing," for in contrast to our own recognized state as one of "incurable suffering and endless misery," it appears to us, not as a nothingness to abhor and fear, but as a nothingness of (as it were) bliss. For this reason contemplation of the life and conduct of the saints, and only it, "can enduringly console us," who, failing to attain the state of the saints, continue to exist in our state of suffering and misery. For us, of course, in whom the will is still affirmed, the world of the saints is regarded as "only empty nothingness"; indeed

> what remains after the complete abolition of the will is, for all who are still full of the will, assuredly nothing. But also conversely, to those in whom the will has turned and denied itself, this very real world of ours with all its suns and galaxies [*Milchstraßen*, milky ways] is—nothing.[54]

On this note Schopenhauer ends, except for the appendix on Kant, *The World as Will and Representation*.

Perhaps the greatest difficulty with Schopenhauer's account of the most extreme denier of the will (whether called moral saint, ascetic, or mystic) derives from the fact that this rare individual retains a body while (allegedly) losing will. Since the body is a manifestation, or objectity, of the individual will, since the body and the individual are "identical," since, in sum, there can be no body without the will, complete loss (denial, negation, renunciation, elimination) of the will is impossible for any living, breathing, embodied human being. This is something that Schopenhauer seems to acknowledge when he speaks of the possible "backsliding" of the ascetic:

> For as the body is the will itself only in the form of objectity, or as appearance in the world as representation, that whole will to life exists potentially so long as the body lives, and is always striving to reach actuality and to burn afresh with all its intensity.[55]

This means, as indicated a few lines later, that the most saintly persons are faced with "the constant struggle with the will to life," and that "on earth no one can have lasting peace." Consequently, Schopenhauer suggests here, denial of the will is never complete or, perhaps more accurately, it is never final—for any living, embodied human being. There remains the possibility that the "converts," especially those brought to denial of the will by personally felt suffering, will return to the "old state" of affirming the will once that suffering has disappeared.[56]

On the other hand, Schopenhauer sometimes suggests that denial of the will does reach completion and finality, for example, in the mystic to whom resignation may be ascribed.[57] Yet mystics retain a body, hence they retain a will—though they are literally defined as "will-less." To escape this apparent self-contradiction, Schopenhauer has to rely, once again, on a distinction between two sorts of manifestations or appearances of the will: simply the living body itself and the normal, natural impulses of the body. Accordingly, with the mystic the body persists, but the impulses of the body cease. Alternatively, the will (simply as the visible, living body) remains, but the will (as willing the natural impulses) ceases. This amounts, it seems, to a distinction between the will and willing, whereby the will remains but willing ceases (*der Wille bleibt, aber das Wollen hört auf*). As spurious as this distinction seems, it will simply have to be acknowledged—if there truly exist mystics and therewith complete and final salvation.

Mystics attain a state not only of will-lessness but a state in which all knowledge proper—that is, all subject-object knowledge—disappears, and (as it were) absorption into the One (which knows no distinctions, hence no subject-object distinction) ensues.[58] Does this mean that in the end

Schopenhauer recognizes the world as it is in itself apart from or "beyond" the world as will? Does it mean that in acknowledging the existence of mystics Schopenhauer acknowledges the (philosophically unknowable) thing in itself? Young answers these questions affirmatively, arguing that "the possibility of salvation *demands* that the metaphysical account of the world as Will should not be an account of the world in itself."⁵⁹ The world as will, he points out, is "a world *inalienably* permeated by suffering and evil"; hence if we identify the world as will and the world in itself, "suffering would be *absolutely* inescapable and salvation impossible."⁶⁰ Relying on Schopenhauer's remark that nothingness is only a relative, not an absolute, concept, Young claims that "only relative to 'our knowledge' can it be said that there is nothing beyond the will," which does not entail, Young adds, that there is absolutely nothing beyond the will; for beyond it is the thing in itself, the possibility of which Schopenhauer acknowledges, most clearly, in acknowledging the salvation (from suffering) attained by the mystic.⁶¹

Earlier, in chapter 5, I cited some of Schopenhauer's late letters in which he claims to speak of the thing in itself only in relation to appearance, and this suggests that the world as will is the world in itself—there being no possible separation of the two. This could simply mean, however, that Schopenhauer refuses to *speak* of the thing in itself apart from appearance, for any such speaking would go beyond the realm of philosophy and become "transcendent"; it does not necessarily mean, as Young would point out, that Schopenhauer denies the thing in itself apart from appearance. And he should not deny it, Young holds, if he admits the possibility of salvation, the possibility of freedom from the world as will (with its essential elements of suffering and evil). So, is Young's suggestion correct? More to the point, is he correct in arguing that the possibility (or even actuality) of salvation *demands* the nonidentity of the world as will and the world as it is in itself? (Actually, with the mystical state, the world has vanished, hence at this point one should not use the phrase, "the world in itself" or "the *world* as it is in itself." But this is a minor point, which I shall ignore.)

In chapter 5 it was suggested that Schopenhauer may have, probably unwittingly, two conceptions of the thing in itself: the philosophical, according to which will is the thing in itself or, equally, will is the essence of (the world as) appearance; and the mystical, according to which the thing in itself lies beyond will, hence beyond the world and even beyond (we can now add) all suffering, all comprehension, all thought. (These two conceptions may reflect what Gardiner calls the two concepts of mysticism, as reported in endnote 58.) But, to repeat, is it true, as Young apparently holds, that the possibility of complete salvation *demands* that, in effect, we ascribe to Schopenhauer only the second, the mystical, conception of the thing in itself? Not necessarily. For one could argue as follows. In the mystical "state," the will as thing in itself (not the thing in itself apart from will) "becomes one with" the will as thing in itself, so that "subject" and "object" coalesce and nothing (no "object") remains over that might motivate any will (by the "subject"). All the elements that make for willing have been eliminated by melting into one: All division, separation, individuality, and distinction have been annulled, hence all willing and all suffering cease. There is suffering only if there is willing, there is willing only if there is motivation (on the part of a human being), and there is motivation only if there are individual objects for the individual subject; but with the mystic's penetration of the principle of individuation, with the elimination of the world subject to the principle of sufficient reason, all individuality disappears, all motivation ceases, hence no willing and no suffering occur. All of this comes about simply because the will as thing in itself has become one with itself, not because the thing in itself has gotten free from will. In short, salvation or total absence of suffering does not necessitate a distinction between the world as will (as, I would add, the thing in itself) and *the* thing in itself—even though Schopenhauer may sometimes allow for a (negative) conception of the thing in itself in addition to a conception of the thing in itself as beyond will. It is not necessary, however, that he makes such an allowance in order to accommodate the cessation of suffering. For, as just argued, suffering will cease upon the will's "knowing" the will and, in light of this "knowledge," ceasing to will. It should be noted that I am only contesting Young's argument for distinguishing will from the thing in itself; I am not claiming that the distinction itself is absent from Schopenhauer's thought.

CONCLUSION

The main aim of this conclusion is to clarify "the single thought"—the world is the self-knowledge of the will—on the level of the individual, and then to trace out some of its more significant implications. This requires that we return, as it were, to the beginning of things philosophical.

The first, undeniable truth of philosophy, Schopenhauer holds, is that "the world is my representation." But this truth, though certain, is "one-sided," by which is meant that it is "occasioned by some arbitrary abstraction." It has to be supplemented by "a truth that is not so immediately certain," hence

> only deeper investigation, more difficult abstraction, the separation of what is different, and the combination of what is identical can lead us to this truth. This truth, which must be very serious and grave if not terrible to everyone, is that a man also can say and must say: "The world is my will."[1]

Not only is the world my representation (which states the central tenet of Schopenhauer's version of idealism), it is also my will (which expresses the core of his metaphysics of will). On the latter score, one should note, the world is not a foreign or alien will, not a will imposing itself on me, not a will to which I am subservient; rather, the world is *my* will.

If we are to understand what the world is, we must not say, or at least not simply say, that it is representation and will but that it is *my* representation and *my* will. In accord with the single thought, this means that the world is the self-knowledge of my will; and this means in turn that only what I know and what I will reveals to me what I, as will, am. In other words, I cannot know what I am apart from knowing, or noting, the objects of my knowledge and the objects of my will. This thesis, which, among other things, rejects the (Cartesian) notion of a unified, self-contained "self" available to consciousness, finds expression in the following passage:

> Every individual, on the one hand, is the subject of knowing, i.e., the complementary condition of the possibility of the whole objective world, and, on the other, a particular appearance of the will, of that will that objectifies itself in every thing. But this two-sidedness of our essence [*Wesen*] does not rest in a unity existing for itself; otherwise we would be able to be conscious of ourselves *in ourselves and independently of the objects of knowing and willing*. Now this we simply cannot do, but as soon as we try to enter into ourselves and want to become aware of ourselves by directing our knowledge inwards, we lose ourselves in a bottomless void; we find ourselves like a hollow glass globe, from the emptiness of which a voice speaks. But the cause of this voice is not to be found in the globe, and since we want to comprehend ourselves so [i.e., in this way], we grasp with a shudder nothing but a wavering and unstable phantom [*bestandloses Gespenst*].[2]

In the first part of this passage Schopenhauer suggests that I, as an individual, am the subject of knowing and "a particular appearance of the will," hence knower and body; and this is of course something that Schopenhauer does maintain. But later in the passage, and elsewhere, Schopenhauer holds that I am the subject of knowing and the subject of willing (where the latter is perhaps "a particular instance of the will") as well as a body. In short: On the subjective side, I am two subjects, one of knowing and one of willing (or, as sometimes suggested, one subject that both knows and wills); and on the objective side, I am a body. Schopenhauer's most significant contention is that I cannot become conscious of myself as subject of knowing and as subject of willing "*independently of the objects of knowing and willing.*" As a matter of fact, self-consciousness reveals me to be a composite (not a unity, and not an underlying unity) of knowing and willing certain objects, and it is only by awareness of known and willed objects that I become conscious of myself as knower and willer. Both knowing and willing are essentially tied to what is known and willed; and both what I know and what I will, and they alone, reveal to me what I am cognitively and volitionally.

One aspect of what has just been reviewed concerns then self-revelation; and the other aspect concerns, perhaps surprisingly, responsibility, according to which what I am volitionally makes the world be what it is for knowledge. In other words, to claim that "the world is my will" is to claim, in part, that the world is my responsibility or simply that I am responsible for the (my) world.[3] This responsibility takes different dimensions, and it extends to the very existence of the (my) world. Consider first the individual things that I encounter in the world: They appear to me in their relations to each other and ultimately to me in their relations to my will; they thus appear to me as potential motives, none being for me totally devoid of "value." If a given thing appears "good" to me, this is due to its accord with my will; and if it appears "bad" to me, this is due to its disaccord with my will. Referring to *good* Schopenhauer writes:

> This concept is essentially relative, and denotes the *suitableness of an object to any definite effort* [*Bestrebung*, striving] *of the will.* Therefore everything agreeable to the will in any one of its manifestations, and fulfilling the will's purpose, is thought of through the concept *good*, however different in other respects such things may be. We therefore speak of good food, good roads, good weather, good weapons, good auguries, etc.; in short, we call everything good that is just as we want it to be. Hence a thing can be good to one person, and the very opposite to another. . . . The concept of the opposite, so long as we are speaking of beings without knowledge, is expressed by the word *bad* [*schlecht*], more rarely and abstractly by the word *evil* [*Uebel*], which therefore denotes everything that is not agreeable to the striving [*Streben*] of the will in each case.[4]

Nothing, on this view, is good or bad in itself; everything is either good or bad depending on its agreeableness or disagreeableness to the individual person's will. Conversely, but equivalently, it is one's will that accounts for the value (whether positive or negative) of things in the world; and insofar as the world consists of things of (positive or negative) value—which it does for everyone caught up in the affirmation of the will—the world is the responsibility of one's will.

Even the value of the world as a whole is determined by one's will (or character), as Schopenhauer indicates in comparing the world of the egoist with the world of "the good person":

> The egoist feels himself surrounded by strange and hostile appearances, and all his hope rests on his own well-being. The good person lives in a world of friendly appearances; the well-being of any of these is his own well-being. Therefore, although the knowledge of the lot of man generally does not make his disposition a cheerful [*fröhlich*, happy] one, the enduring knowledge of his own essence in all living things nevertheless gives him a certain equilibrium and even serenity of disposition [*Heiterkeit der Stimmung*]. For the participation extended over innumerable appearances cannot cause such anxiety as that which is concentrated on *one* appearance. The accidents that befall the totality of individuals equalize themselves, while those that encounter the individual induce fortune and misfortune [*Glück und Unglück*].[5]

The well-being of the good person is heightened and extended by the well-being of other persons and even of other nonhuman beings, which entails no doubt that he or she is capable of *Mitfreude*, that is, the taking of joy in any living being's joy.[6] Hence his or her "world" stretches far beyond the confines of his or her individual position, which is quite unlike the "world" of the egoist. Moreover, the good person inhabits "a world of friendly appearances" (in which he, as it were, feels "at home"), while the egoist inhabits a world of "strange and hostile appearances" (in which he constantly feels threatened and apprehensive). One might criticize Schopenhauer's account here (arguing, for example, that the good person's capacity for *Mitfreude* must be conjoined with his or her capacity for *Mitleid*, thus often yielding suffering), but the main point holds: The world of the good person differs greatly from the world of the egoist, and that difference depends on and derives from their very different wills (or characters).

Similar differences occur elsewhere. If I have renounced the individual will and thereby become the pure (or impersonal) subject of knowing, the world appears to me as a gradation of Ideas—the contemplation of which engenders peace of mind. But if I affirm the individual will and thereby remain the impure (or personal) subject of knowing, the world appears as a network of particular objects whose changing states are subject to the principle of sufficient reason—the knowledge of which (like the knowledge of the egoist) breeds fear and anxiety. In this latter case I as egoist know arising and perishing appearances, each of which arises in the matter previously occupied by another appearance, and each of which perishes by being replaced by another. And then the world is a pretty frightful place, governed, as it were, by Hobbes' saying, *bellum omnium contra omnes* (a war of all against all)—this too being a consequence and responsibility of my will. Finally: For the complete denier of the will, the entire world (at least as normally known) ceases to exist altogether, along with its petty pleasures and terrible pains—all in virtue of this denier's cessation of willing. To sum up: Just as I find out what sort of person I am by attending to the world as it appears to me, so the world appears to me as it does (or even if it does) depending on the sort of person I am.

"The world is my will" will be "serious and grave" to everyone who fully recognizes its true meaning, namely, that the (value) nature of the world depends on the nature of one's will; and it will be "terrible" (*furchtbar*) to everyone who recognizes that one is responsible for the world's being, say, terrible, filled with strife, a "vale of tears," a place of incessant suffering and misery. On this score, Schopenhauer suggests that "the world as such" (if such a concept were legitimate) is value-neutral, that only one's will makes it either terrible or endurable (even "friendly"). Consequently, when Schopenhauer claims that life is essentially suffering, that nonexistence would be preferable to existence, that existence is a sin for which death is the appropriate desert, and so on, he must mean to report the nature of the world from the standpoint of the egoist; for these claims do not reflect the standpoint of "the good person," the aesthetic contemplator, the saint, or the mystic. "The world" for each of them takes on the quality corresponding to their (different) qualities, hence each of them can and must say, "the world is my will."[7]

"The world is my will" may be assigned a second meaning, namely, what the world is in essence is precisely what I am in essence—will, will to life. This does not mean that the essence of the world and the essence of myself are two things sharing the same inner quality—as, for example, two things before me share the quality of "appleness," and yet differ in other respects such as size, color, location, taste, and so on, in which case it might be said of them that they belong to the same kind. It means rather that the essence of the world and the essence of myself is the very same will, which is not to be understood as a kind of thing distinguished from other kinds of things. The will that is the essence of the world is indistinguishable from the will that is my essence. Distinguishability has its place only in the world as representation (appearance), not in the world as will (reality); hence (Schopenhauer holds) once it is determined that my essence is will, it is determined that the world's essence is the "same" will. Any particularity or individuality belonging to me, and that distinguishes me from other particular things, is marked solely by will's appearing during a specific period of time, at a certain place, and standing in a definite set of causal relations, hence by will's appearing as this particular body that I am. Only the various appearances or manifestations of the will may be distinguished from each other; only the world as representation may be divided into parts; the will itself or the world as will is immune to all distinction and all divisibility.

As indicated earlier, "will" (*der Wille*) for Schopenhauer is a mass noun, not a count noun; it is more analogous to "water" than to "drop (of water)," more like "the sky" than "star." (Mass nouns take no plural, but count nouns do.) For the most part, one should translate (or at least understand) *der Wille* as will, not as *the* will in order to acknowledge the fact that it is a mass noun. Consequently, to say that I am *a* will is to say, strictly speaking, that I am will appearing here and now, in a certain set of causal relations; it is not to say that I am one will, with the suggestion that you are another will, and so on—as if all individual wills, taken together, constituted *the* will. (By much the same token, each Idea is simply will "objectified" in a certain way, and not in another way; yet every Idea is will "objectified" at a different grade or level of distinctness, with the different grades or levels making the sole distinction between one Idea and another.) Although all analogies threaten misunderstanding, consider this one. Suppose, *pace* Thales, that all is water (not, note, *the* water). There will then be nevertheless water here and now and water there and then, but there will never be anything except water. So it is, similarly, with Schopenhauer's notion of will—but only similarly, for water is representational and will (as thing in itself) is not. Yet, further, we might conceive of all reality as the spatially and temporally infinite mass of water—rather like a stormy sea—whose particular waves and upsurges can be discerned individually before they sink back into the indiscernible mass of water and, as individuals, die.

This line of thought illustrates the general metaphysical impulse that, in a phrase, all is one, which serves as the basis of Schopenhauer's metaphysical explication of moral virtue ("this art thou," i.e., every other living being is oneself over again). That all is one (meaning specifically now that all individual things are at bottom one and the same will) lies at the heart of Schopenhauer's chief argument for (a sort of) immortality. That argument commences with the premise that all things subject to time come into being and then cease. Such things go by the name of individuals, and they encompass, of course, human individuals. Human beings are individuals in virtue of the body, which makes them subject to both space and time as well as to causality; but also human beings are, on the one hand, the subject of knowing and, on the other hand, will. And neither of these latter two features is subject to space or time or causality; hence, most significantly, neither begins or ends. The whole story goes thus:

> We certainly see the individual originate and perish; but the individual is only appearance, [it] is there only for knowledge involved in the principle of sufficient reason, in the *principium individuationis*. Naturally, for this knowledge, it [the individual] receives its life as a gift, rises out of nothing, and then suffers through death the loss of this gift, and returns to nothing. But we want to consider life just philosophically, i.e., according to its Ideas, and there we find that neither the will, the thing in itself in all appearances, nor the subject of knowing, the spectator of all appearances, is in any way affected by birth and death. Birth and death belong only to the appearance of the will, and therefore to life. . . .[8]

Anything that lives begins and ends: "Birth and death belong equally to life, and hold the balance as mutual conditions of each other."[9] One should not then think of life *and* death; one should think of life as birth-and-death. For, as the Indian mythologies have it, "generation and death are essential correlatives, which reciprocally neutralize and annul [*aufheben*] each other."[10] To be a (living) human being is to be an individual that has been born and that is about to die; but it is also to be the subject of knowing and will, neither of which is born or dies. Schopenhauer puts forth therefore no doctrine of personal (or individual) immortality, which would have "the individual consciousness bound to the individual body" last forever,[11] but he does put forth a doctrine of nonpersonal (or nonindividual) immortality, according to which will and "the subject of knowledge which is ultimately in a certain regard the will itself or its manifestation"[12] are atemporal. Schopenhauer enunciates the same doctrine by holding that nature itself, unlike its various aspects, neither begins nor ends.[13] The upshot of this doctrine is that although I, as appearance, begin and end, I, as essence (i.e., as will and subject of knowledge), neither begin nor end.

No human being, as an individual, can escape death, but (Schopenhauer holds) some human beings can escape or master the "natural" fear of death—and this in two distinct ways.[14] Such mastery on the first route derives from the abstract, philosophical knowledge (gained through the "faculty of reason") that death comes only to the individual appearance of will and not to will itself, in other words, that death from the standpoint of will itself (to which it does not apply) is an illusion and nothing to be concerned with. Schopenhauer even provides a characterization of the person who has attained the requisite philosophical knowledge:

> A man who had assimilated firmly into his way of thinking the truths so far advanced [chiefly that he, as thing in itself, is the will that appears in the whole of nature], but at the same time had not come to know, through his own experience or through a deeper insight, that constant suffering is essential to all life; who found satisfaction in life and took perfect delight in it; who desired, in calm deliberation, that the course of his life as he had hitherto experienced it should be of endless duration or of ever new recurrence; and whose courage to face life [*Lebensmuth*] was so great that, in return for life's enjoyments, he would willingly and gladly put up with all the hardships and miseries to which it is subject; such a man would stand "with firm, strong bones on the well-grounded, enduring death" [from Goethe], and would have nothing to fear. Armed with the knowledge we confer on him, he would look with indifference at death hastening toward him on the wings of time, regarding it as a false illusion, an impotent specter, frightening to the weak but having no power over him who knows that he himself is that will of which the whole world is the objectification or copy, to which therefore life and also the present—the only real form of the appearance of the will—always remain certain. Therefore no endless past or future in which he did not exist can frighten him, for he regards these as an empty mirage and web of Maya, thus he would no more fear death than the sun would the night.[15]

After alluding to the *Bhagavad-Gita* (where Krishna persuades the reluctant Arjuna, who foresees the death of thousands of warriors, to give the signal for battle), to Goethe's *Prometheus* (the apparent point being that just as Prometheus and his created race of human beings will not do homage to Zeus and his race of gods, so they will not pay any heed to death), and to the philosophies of Bruno and Spinoza (which urge us to view things *sub specie aeternitatis*), Schopenhauer concludes:

> Finally, many men would surely [*wohl*] occupy the standpoint here set forth, if their knowledge kept pace with their willing, i.e., if they were in a position, free from every illusion [*Wahn*], to become clearly and distinctly themselves

[*sich selbst klar und deutlich zu werden*]. For this is for knowledge the standpoint of the complete *affirmation of the will to life*.[16]

In the person conceived here the will affirms itself, unimpeded by the abstract knowledge that its own essence is fully and distinctly given as representation in its objectity (*Objektität*), i.e., in the world and life. While earlier life was willed without knowledge and as a blind impulse, now "this so recognized life" is willed by the person with conscious and reflective knowledge.[17] An example of the person who with full knowledge affirms the will to life would apparently be the artistic genius, who remains wedded to life so as to convey to humankind his insight into it. In any case, Schopenhauer shows the possibility of a person who, as it were, affirms "life and the world," while knowing full well that its essential nature and his or her own essential nature are one and the same will that neither originates nor perishes. Consequently, this person has no fear of death, which is always in the future, and no concern about what has happened, which is always in the past; indeed, this person knows that the future and the past exist only in concepts, and that only the present is real.[18]

The second way of escaping the fear of death is, as we know, the denial of the will to life, which, Schopenhauer says here,[19] derives, not from abstract, but from "living knowledge expressing itself in deed and conduct alone." This escape from the fear of death may be attributed to, say, the ascetic, who renounces the will owing either to the insight that life is essentially suffering or to personally felt suffering. Through conduct the ascetic shows that the individual is mere appearance, hence that the disappearance of the individual is no matter of concern. As this line of thought has been considered in the previous chapter, it need not be repeated here.

Despite what we have been led to think, Schopenhauer allows for a sense in which every individual, human and otherwise, is immortal. It may be explained as follows. In the world of individuals the principle of sufficient reason reigns supreme, hence—contrary to what was said above—no individual "rises out of nothing" and none "returns to nothing"; rather, every individual rises out of some of the individuals preceding it and originates, at least in part, from some of the individuals succeeding it; in short, every individual is tied up with other individuals, all in accord with the principle of sufficient reason, specifically, with the principle of causality. One can even say that every individual exists in all the (prior) individuals that generate it, and every individual exists in all of the individuals that it helps to generate. No individual is dispensable to the whole of nature, indeed, the whole of nature is nothing but all individuals, which *as* individuals rise up and then sink down—as the sea is nothing but the individually discernible waves, undulations, upsurges, depressions, and so on that constitute it.

And not only that: "Every thing is entirely in nature, and she is entirely in every thing."[20] If, then, nature is endless, so is every individual instance of nature; for no individual ceases from the standpoint of its causality, just as every individual "already exists" in the individuals that generate it.[21] Every (existing) individual can say therefore "I have existed from all time and I shall exist for all time; I am 'in' every thing that brought me about and I shall be 'in' every thing that I help bring about; I, even as an individual, am beginningless and endless—in a sense."

The idea that every individual exists in all the individuals that generate it grounds, I suggest, Schopenhauer's firm conviction that certain people (often women) possess the gift of "seeing" a given individual in individuals existing long before the given individual actually originates. Those people are clairvoyant somnambulists, about whom Schopenhauer says that "they can even predict that which does not yet exist but still lies hidden in the womb of the future and only in the course of time comes to be realized by means of innumerable intermediate causes that come together by chance."[22] Accordingly, "it must be possible for an event to be known just as well before it has happened as after" (for "time is not a determination of the real essence [*Wesen*] of things" and "in respect thereof, before and after are without meaning").[23] Moreover: "Animal magnetism, sympathetic cures, magic, second sight, dreaming the real, spirit seeing, and visions of all kinds are kindred phenomena, branches of one stem. They afford certain and irrefutable proof of a nexus of beings [*Wesen*] that rests on an order of things entirely different from *nature*."[24] Schopenhauer believes that "clairvoyance [*Hellsehn*] is a confirmation of the Kantian doctrine of the ideality of space, time, and causality" and that "magic is also a confirmation of my doctrine and of the sole reality [*Realität*] of the *will* as the kernel of all things."[25]

Every individual, though in itself ephemeral, is everlasting, Schopenhauer suggests, in the sense of being tied up with other individuals, which are in turn tied up with still other individuals, such that the whole infinite nexus of individuals—being the manifestation of the "one" will—guarantees the infinity of every single individual. It follows, first, that if any one individual were different (thus were not what it is, and thus were not at all), then the whole world as representation (and the world as will) would be different (thus, finally, not at all); and conversely, given the world as it is, every individual must be exactly as it is. It follows, second, that if just one individual in the world as representation—whether a person, a thing, or an event—is judged ineradicably evil ("It can never be justified"), then the world as representation as a whole is judged evil ("The whole is unjustified"). This conclusion, which Schopenhauer accepts, is captured in the slogan of pessimism, "Nonexistence is preferable to existence."[26] Whether one makes this judgment or not reveals, and derives from, one's will (or character)—so again on this score the "nature" of the world depends on the "nature" of one's will.[27]

POSTSCRIPT

In this study I have attempted to portray Schopenhauer, the metaphysician of will, as in my earlier study I attempted to portray Schopenhauer, the moral philosopher of the human character. When conjoined the two works provide English-speaking readers with a reasonably complete picture of Schopenhauer, the philosopher of will (omitting only his political theory, his aesthetics proper, and his popular essays). For readers of German there are of course many, many studies available, the most recent being a monumental volume by Rudolf Malter, called *Arthur Schopenhauer: Transzendentalphilosophie und Metaphysik des Willens* (Stuttgart-Bad Cannstatt: Frommann-Holzboog, 1991).[28]

My chief aim in this study has been to examine and explicate Schopenhauer's entryways into metaphysics, for which reason I have dealt almost exclusively with volume 1 of *The World as Will and Representation* (often as it appeared in the first edition). But I have also tried to clarify many theses found in the heart of Schopenhauer's metaphysics, relying heavily on the guideline that world-understanding proceeds from self-understanding, or that the character of the world parallels in many ways the character of the human individual. I have said a fair amount about Schopenhauer's relation to Kant, but very little about his relation to Fichte, Schelling, Hegel, and other contemporaries.[29] Many times I have been tempted to make reference to Nietzsche, Freud, and Wittgenstein (who are often said, e.g., by Magee, to have been influenced by Schopenhauer), but also to Edmund Husserl and Jean-Paul Sartre (who are seldom, if ever, mentioned in connection with Schopenhauer), but for the most part I have resisted that temptation.[30] Nor have I speculated on how Schopenhauer's metaphysics and his method of philosophizing bear on current intellectual trends, but I shall mention here two points: Schopenhauer would oppose those current investigators, both philosophical and scientific, who hope to clarify the nature of human beings by examining the nature of nonhuman and even nonliving entities; and he would challenge the supposition that the human mind is capable of grasping and conceptualizing in language all of "reality." On the first score, Schopenhauer would argue that self-understanding, or even understanding of understanding, must guide world-understanding, that is, that "human studies" must direct "nonhuman studies"; and on the second score, he would insist on the possibility, or even the certainty (given the actual existence of moral saints, ascetics, and, above all, mystics), that "reality" extends beyond the range of human comprehension, in other words, that the puny human intellect cannot pretend to fathom all that is.

In my judgment, Schopenhauer stands both historically and doctrinally at the crossroads between "modern philosophy" (say, Descartes through Kant) and its aftermath (or, if one pleases, "postmodern thought," from, say, Nietzsche through Michel Foucault). In philosophy proper, Schopenhauer annihilated every form of metaphysics not thoroughly "grounded" in experience; he introduced into intellectual, cultural, and literary circles the terrible, awesome power of reasonless will along with the often uncontrollable sexual drive; he acknowledged and tried to explain, instead of trying to explain away, vastly different sorts of persons, from the diabolical villain to the morally pure saint, from the practical egoist to the mystic, from the money-grubbing professor of philosophy to the true scholar; he suggested a metaphysical framework of moral virtue that owes virtually nothing to reason or intellect (and which, I think, has not even yet today been adequately considered); he advances a theory of responsibility that, interestingly, has been emulated in recent years, but not been acknowledged as originally Schopenhauer's, namely, the view that disconnects avoidability from responsibility; in short, Schopenhauer, to a considerable extent, ended one long reign of philosophical thought and commenced a new one—for which reason, incidentally, one can regard him as a Kantian and an implacable foe of Kant, as a rationalist and an irrationalist, a moralist and an amoralist, indeed as a metaphysician and an antimetaphysician. Consequently, and by no means surprisingly, Schopenhauer is charged—perhaps above all other famous philosophers—with inconsistency. If the charge is valid, and it may be at least in part, it is also explainable in part; and here we encounter one of Schopenhauer's greatest weaknesses—despite his conviction that he was a philosophical genius, he failed to see just how novel, how unique, how utterly radical his philosophy was, and just how far it broke away from his avowed mentor Kant. As I have said several times, Schopenhauer persisted in formulating his conception of the world in terminology, namely, Kant's, that often distorts that very conception. Possibly something similar is the fate of every great philosopher: He or she is a philosopher (and not, say, a poet or mystic or mad person) only in virtue of continuing a long tradition of linguistic and conceptual usage, and he or she is great only in virtue of breaking free from that tradition; hence the philosophy that eventuates is tied linguistically and conceptually to the past and forges ahead into very new and untilled grounds. (Witness Nietzsche and Martin Heidegger, just to mention two others caught in the same predicament.)

In some cases, with a sympathetic will and a bit of imagination, a commentator can rescue his or her subject from the quandary of (apparent) inconsistency. And this of course I have made an attempt to do rather often: I have claimed that Schopenhauer is not (necessarily) inconsistent in regarding "perceptual objects" as both causal sources of sensation and mental constructs out of sensations (chapter 2); that he is not precluded from putting forth a metaphysical scheme within a broadly Kantian framework (chapter 5); that he does not contradict his notion of the world as appearance in positing the existence of the Ideas (chapter 6); that he does not have a single, but inconsistent, conception of the thing in itself (mainly chapter 5); that his account of salvation or freedom from the world is neither incoherent nor inconsistent with other main features of his philosophy (chapter 7); and so on. In very many cases, I have claimed, when Schopenhauer appears to get himself involved in intractable difficulties, it is because he or his critic employs Kantian terminology.

Schopenhauer, I have argued in general, advances a philosophical system centered on a single (unitary) thought, namely, that the world is the self-knowledge of the will—so that in a few rare human individuals the will may then cease, thereby liberating itself from the world of suffering and engendering "a peace that passeth understanding." The world of suffering in its manifold dimensions is the manifestation of will in the individual, hence if that world is to be surpassed the individual will (the egoistic will) must be eliminated; it is eliminated in part by the aesthetic contemplator, more so by the moral saint, and still further by the ascetic and the mystic.[31] That this elimination is possible Schopenhauer takes to be the one bright spot in his otherwise bleak philosophical scheme—a scheme depicting in the main the "world" of the human individual devoted to affirmation of his or her own will, without the slightest regard for beauty, moral virtue, and (for lack of a better term) union with the All. In Schopenhauer's view, even if one does not actually travel these "paths of salvation," the mere recognition of their existence provides, or can provide, one with a high degree of consolation. Salvation may be called the "telos of human life," or even the highest good (*summum bonum*), understood as that without which human life would be devoid of any redeeming feature. In virtue of, but solely in virtue of, the genuine possibility of salvation, human life admits of worth or value—ranging from appreciation of beauty, to compassion for all living things, to finally acceptance of (personal) death.

ABBREVIATIONS

In citing Schopenhauer's works in the notes, short titles have been used. Works have been identified by the following abbreviations:

WWR *The World as Will and Representation,* 2 vols., trans. E. F. J. Payne (New York: Dover Publications, 1966). The first edition (1818, dated 1819) contained only volume 1; the second (1844) changed and added several passages in volume 1 and added all of volume 2; the third edition (1859) enlarged the work still further. Where deemed helpful, references to volume 1 are given by page and section number, e.g., WWR, 1, 25 (§ 7) and to volume 2 by page and chapter number, e.g., WWR, 2, 202 (Ch. 19).

FR *On the Fourfold Root of the Principle of Sufficient Reason,* trans. E. F. J. Payne (La Salle, Illinois: Open Court, 1974). Translation is of the second, greatly enlarged edition of 1847; the first edition appeared in 1813. For references to the dissertation, I have had to use volume 3 of *Arthur Schopenhauers sämtliche Werke,* ed. Paul Deußen (München: R. Piper, 1912). References are given by paragraph number.

WN *On the Will in Nature,* trans. E. F. J. Payne; ed. David E. Cartwright (New York: Berg, 1992). First edition, 1836; second, 1854.

FW *Essay on the Freedom of the Will,* trans. Konstantin Kolenda (Indianapolis: Bobbs-Merrill, 1960). First published, with BM, as *The Two Basic Problems of Ethics* in 1841; second edition appeared in 1860.

BM *On the Basis of Morality,* trans. E. F. J. Payne (Indianapolis: Bobbs-Merrill, 1965).

PP　　*Parerga and Paralipomena,* 2 vols., trans. E. F. J. Payne (Oxford: Clarendon Press, 1974). First published in 1851.

GB　　*Arthur Schopenhauer: Gesammelte Briefe,* ed. Arthur Hübscher (Bonn: Bouvier Verlag Herbert Grundmann, 1978). References are given to letter number and date and addressee. Translations are mine.

HN　　*Arthur Schopenhauer: Der handschriftliche Nachlaß,* 5 vols., ed. Arthur Hübscher (Frankfurt am Main: Waldemar Kramer, 1966), hence the use of "HN." References are given to the volume and paragraph numbers in the English translation: *Arthur Schopenhauer: Manuscript Remains in Four Volumes,* trans. E. F. J. Payne (Oxford/New York/Hamburg: Berg, 1988).

The German texts chiefly relied on are *Arthur Schopenhauer: Zürcher Ausgabe,* 10 volumes, ed. Arthur Hübscher, with Angelika Hübscher (Zurich: Diogenes, 1977).

In several places I have altered the translations cited above, not usually because I judged them incorrect and mine accurate, but because the altered translations are more literal and often help make a point I am urging. It may also be noted that I use Schopenhauer's spelling of German words, not the current spelling (hence, for example, I use *Erkenntniß* rather than *Erkenntnis*).

NOTES

INTRODUCTION

1. GB, #38.

2. Two sources may be cited: a bibliography compiled by David E. Cartwright and Eric von der Luft, in *Schopenhauer: New Essays in Honor of His 200th Birthday*, ed. Eric von der Luft (Lewiston, NY: Edwin Mellen Press, 1988); and the many notes in Arthur Hübscher *Arthur Schopenhauer: Denker gegen den Strom: Schopenhauer: Gestern-Heute-Morgen* (Bonn: Bouvier Verlag Herbert Grundmann, 1973). The latter has been translated into English by Joachim T. Baer and David E. Cartwright under the title, *The Philosophy of Schopenhauer in Its Intellectual Context: Thinker Against the Tide* (Lewiston, NY: Edwin Mellen Press, 1989).

3. WWR, I, xii.

4. WWR, I, xii. Schopenhauer says essentially the same thing at least twice in his early notes; see HN, I par. 572 (1816) and HN, I, par. 688 (1817). In a comment appended to the former paragraph, he writes: "My system is not architectonic, but an organic whole, in other words it does not rest on one main principle, or on a few, on to which the others are built, but each part is necessarily the condition for the whole just as the whole is for each part." In the latter paragraph there is this remark: "*My philosophy* differs from all others in that the connection of its parts is not an *architectonic* one, in which one part always carries the other, though not the latter the former, and in which the foundation-stone carries all the parts. On the contrary, the connection of its parts is an *organic* one, where the whole maintains and necessarily makes every part, and conversely every part also maintains and makes the whole and all the other parts. Therefore, for a consideration of my philosophy, there cannot be an essential starting-point, but only an arbitrary one."

5. HN, I, par. 92.

6. HN, I, par. 92n.

7. WWR, I, xiii.

8. WWR, I, xiii.

9. Rudolf Malter has made the first edition available in *Faksimilenachdruck der 1. Auflage der Welt als Wille und Vorstellung mit einen Beiheft zur Einführung in das Werk* (Frankfurt: Insel, 1987). Malter's *Beiheft*, "Ein neues philosophisches System—neu im ganzen Sinn des Worts," has been very valuable to me in writing this book.

10. WWR, I, xiii.

11. WWR, I, xiii–xiv.

12. One should keep in mind that the English translation of FR, translated by E. F. J. Payne, is based on the second edition of 1847, and that in many places it differs radically from the dissertation of 1813.

13. WWR, I, xiv.

14. See Malter, *Beiheft*, p. 22.

15. WWR, I, xv. See also WWR, II, 144 (Ch. 15): "Goethe once said to me that, when he read a page of Kant, he felt as if he were entering a bright room."

16. See, for example, GB, #175 (letter to Charles Lock Eastlake, dated 1841); GB, #307 (letter to Dr. Paul Battel, 18 August 1853); and GB, #346 (letter to Julius Frauenstädt, 6 November 1854).

17. WWR, I, 417.

18. WWR, I, 421.

19. WWR, I, 422.

20. WWR, I, 422.

21. WWR, I, 422.

22. WWR, I, 423.

23. WWR, I, 424.

24. WWR, I, 424–425.

25. All important references to the dissertation of 1813 will cite the paragraph (§) number. For a discussion of the second edition of FR, with occasional remarks on the dissertation, see F. C. White's book, *On Schopenhauer's Fourfold Root of the Principle of Sufficient Reason* (Leiden: E. J. Brill, 1992).

26. WWR, I, 102 (§ 18).

27. This overview is only provisional and superficial: It will be corrected and dealt with in detail later in the book.

28. HN, IV, par. 36.

29. For a discussion of the ideas relevant to this final note—suffering, pessimism, eternal justice, and original sin—see Part 3 of Atwell, *Schopenhauer: The Human Character* (Philadelphia: Temple University Press, 1990).

CHAPTER 1: THE SINGLE THOUGHT

1. In several places Schopenhauer does use *der einzige Gedanke* (the single thought), *der eine Gedanke* (the one thought), and *mein Hauptgedanke* (my main thought), and he frequently states what may be considered the single thought; but he never puts the two together in an explicit fashion, that is, he never says, "See, here is the single thought, and it goes thus and so."

2. WWR, I, vii.

3. WWR, I, vii.

4. See *Arthur Schopenhauer: Gespräche* (Stuttgart-Bad Cannstatt: Friedrich Fro-

mann Verlag Günther Holzboog KG, 1971), p. 368, where Jessie Taylor (the Mme. Karl Hillebrand, who translated into English *On the Fourfold Root of the Principle of Sufficient Reason and On the Will in Nature* [London: George Bell and Sons, 1891]) reportedly said to Schopenhauer that she found his main work too long, only to hear in response: "Not one word too many!"

5. WWR, I, 162 (§ 29).

6. WWR, I, 162 (§ 29). Payne here translates *Gedanke* by "idea," as he also does in at least six additional places, WWR, I, 272 (§ 53), 407 (§ 70), and 408 (§ 71), and WWR, II, 297 (Ch. 23, twice), 498 (Ch. 41). Not surprisingly, then, the reader of the translation is likely to miss Schopenhauer's fairly frequent uses of "the single thought."

7. WWR, I, 162. Schopenhauer then adds: "So here we see that the philosophy of Thales, concerned with the macrocosm, and that of Socrates, concerned with the microcosm, coincide, since the object of both proves to be the same."

8. Arthur Hübscher, *Schopenhauer: Biographie eines Weltbildes* (Stuttgart: Reclam Verlag, 1967), p. 64.

9. See GB, #396, where Schopenhauer writes: "If I say 'the moon has two sides, of which we see the one, never the other,' is that dualism?—Appearance and thing in itself—Will and representation—just as little" (letter to Julius Frauenstädt, 14 August 1856).

10. Julian Young, *Willing and Unwilling: a Study in the Philosophy of Arthur Schopenhauer* (Dordrecht: Martinus Nijhoff, 1987), p. ix; see also all of chapter 3.

11. See, for example, WWR, I, 103 (§ 19), 110 (§ 21), and 112 (§ 23).

12. See P. F. Strawson, *Skepticism and Naturalism: Some Varieties* (New York: Columbia University Press, 1985), p. 46. I thank David Welker for this reference.

13. See chapter 1 ("Descartes' Myth") of Gilbert Ryle, *The Concept of Mind* (New York: Barnes & Noble, 1949), where Ryle argues that, for Descartes, human minds have for the most part precisely those "properties" that human bodies do not have: not in space, not subject to mechanical explanation, not public, and so on.

14. This phrase is not used in the first edition of WWR, but it occurs in WWR, II, 320 (Ch. 25); see also PP, II, 236. In the penultimate section of WN called "Reference to Ethics," Schopenhauer speaks of both "the single thought" and "the aseity of the will." He claims there that his philosophical system is the "development of a single thought" (*Entfaltung eines einzigen Gedankens*) and that freedom and responsibility cannot be thought "without the presupposition of the aseity of the will" [*ohne die Voraussetzung der Aseität des Willens*] (p. 140).

15. See WN, 36, 140–141.

16. WWR, I, 150 (§ 27).

17. See Mark Cyzyk, "Conscience, Sympathy, and Love: Ethical Strategies toward Confirmation of Metaphysical Assertions in Schopenhauer," *Dialogue* (October 1989): 24. On the following page Cyzyk attributes to Schopenhauer "an idealistic monism."

18. See especially WWR, I, 170–174 (§ 31).

19. At WWR, I, 272 (§ 53) Schopenhauer writes that "besides the will there is nothing," but on that very page this claim is considerably qualified.

20. HN, I, par. 662.

21. Christopher Janaway, *Self and World in Schopenhauer's Philosophy* (Oxford: Clarendon Press, 1989), p. 5; see also p. 358.

22. Ibid., pp. 7–8.

23. Actually, Janaway seems to be portraying self-consciousness rather than explicating "the world is the self-knowledge of the will." That, in some sense, the two amount to the same thing may be true, but to demonstrate that truth would require a long, and complicated, story.

24. Rudolf Malter, *Der eine Gedanke: Hinführung zur Philosophie Arthur Schopenhauers* (Darmstadt: Wissenschaftliche Buchgesellschaft, 1988), p. 32.

25. See, for example, WWR, I, 275: "The will, considered purely in itself, is devoid of knowledge, and is only a blind, irresistible urge"; and WWR, I, 5: "That which knows all things and is known by none is the *subject.*"

26. WWR, I, 272 (§ 53).

27. Malter, *Der eine Gedanke,* p. 32.

28. FR, § 42 (which, in the dissertation, is § 43).

29. See Janaway, *Self and World in Schopenhauer's Philosophy,* p. 301: "A self that both wills and apprehends the world cannot be, in its own conception of itself, something composite. . . . Schopenhauer is fond of saying that willing subject and knowing subject 'flow together into the consciousness of one I,' and earlier I criticized him for saying of this that it constitutes 'the miracle *par excellence.*' My complaint . . . was largely that he had no right to assert the identity of willing subject and knowing subject in view of his attempts to convince us of the utter distinctness of the two subjects in question. Nevertheless, *what* he describes here as a miracle is undoubtedly a truth."

30. WWR, I, 102 (§ 18).

31. HN, I, par. 278.

32. WWR, I, 275 (§ 54).

33. See WWR, II, 293 (Ch. 23), 499 (Ch. 41).

34. WN, 75.

35. PP, II, 46.

36. See especially WWR, II, 291 (Ch. 22).

37. D. W. Hamlyn, *Schopenhauer* (London: Routledge & Kegan Paul, 1980), pp. 85, 96.

38. HN, I, par 278. Schopenhauer claims here that "the world as appearance is the knowledge of its self which is imparted to this will; in it the will knows what it wills." Then he adds: "Insofar as this knowledge comes about, it destroys the will; it wills then no more, because what it wills contradicts itself and it now knows what it wills. The identity of the subject of knowing with that of willing appears also here as a miracle. For can the will ever know? can the will do anything other than will? On the other hand, can knowledge guide the will, it which is just simply the guide, the world-creator?" All in all, it seems pretty clear that Schopenhauer struggled with the relationship between the subject of knowing and the subject of willing— distinct but conjoined in the human being—from his earliest to his latest writings.

39. HN, I, par. 159. It is not possible "for us to be conscious of ourselves *in ourselves and independently of the objects of knowing and willing*" (WWR, I, 278n.).

40. This is to say that the character of a person is empirical, that one gets to

know it only by observing what one does in various situations; see, for instance, FW, p. 50.

41. WWR, I, 275 (§ 54).

42. Schopenhauer speaks of the world as "the mirror of the will" in many places; see WWR, I, 165 (§ 29), 266 (§ 52), 274 (§ 54), 275 (§ 54), 302 (§ 55), 351 (§ 63), 365 (§ 65), and 410 (§ 71). This is not to be confused or conflated with "the mirror of the world," which is the "pure subject of knowledge"; see WWR, I, 152 (§ 27), 178 (§ 34), 186 (§ 36), 287–288 (§ 55), and 390 (§ 68).

43. WWR, I, 354 (§ 63).

44. WWR, I, 410 (§ 71).

45. WWR, I, 411.

46. WWR, I, 411.

47. Malter, *Der eine Gedanke*, p. 29.

48. Crucial to this interpretation is section 27 of WWR, I, especially pp. 144–147. Much that I say here derives from Terri Graves Taylor's excellent paper, "Platonic Ideas, Aesthetic Experience, and the Resolution of Schopenhauer's 'Great Contradiction,'" *International Studies in Philosophy* (1987): 43–53. Incidentally, that the will can be teleological (have aims) and yet be blind (be nonconscious) is revealed, above all, in the plant kingdom.

49. GB, #175 (letter to Charles Lock Eastlake, 1841). This letter is in English.

50. GB, #200 (letter to Johann August Becker, 3 August 1844). In WN, as noted above, Schopenhauer does speak of the will's becoming conscious of itself (75), and he notes that his "philosophical system," as stated in the preface of his main work, is "the unfolding of a single thought" (140). It may also be observed that in volume 2 of WWR (Ch. 41), Schopenhauer at least once mentions "my fundamental thought" (498), which there seems to be that although the phenomenon and the thing in itself "meet" in self-consciousness, they are "absolutely incommensurable" (WWR, II, 497).

51. Many, many paragraphs in HN, III (1818–1830) deal with the primacy of the will over the understanding, and several are concerned with macrocosm and microcosm.

CHAPTER 2: FROM PERCEPTUAL
KNOWLEDGE TO METAPHYSICAL INQUIRY

1. WWR, I, 3 (§ 1).

2. Payne uses "perceptual" to translate *anschaulich* and "perception" to translate *Anschauung*, and I usually follow suit, occasionally adding "intuitive" for the former German term and "intuition" for the latter. Translators of Kant typically use "intuitive" and "intuition" for the respective German words, *anschaulich* and *Anschauung*.

3. See WWR, I, 18 (§ 5): "What is this world of perception besides being my representation?" And WWR, I, 98 (§ 17): "We ask whether this world is nothing more than representation."

4. Schopenhauer insists that on the path of representation one can never discern the thing in itself; in other words, no examination of the world as represen-

tation, no matter how probing, can reveal to us the nature or essence of the world as will. See WWR, I, 99 (§ 17); WWR, II, 195 (Ch. 18); FR, 120; and PP, I, 93.

5. WWR, I, 3.

6. See, for example, WWR, I, 20 (§ 6): "The mere changes sustained [*erleiden*] from without by the sense-organs through the impression specifically appropriate to them can themselves be called representations, insofar as such impressions stimulate neither pain nor pleasure, i.e. have no immediate significance for the will, and yet are perceived, i.e., exist only for *knowledge*."

7. Perhaps the first critic to attribute correlativism to Schopenhauer was Johannes Volkelt, in his book *Arthur Schopenhauer: Seine Persönlichkeit, seine Lehre, sein Glaube* (4th ed.; Stuttgart: Fromann, 1910), pp. 89–101.

8. See WWR, I, 424; also FR, 50–51: "In India idealism is the doctrine even of popular religion, not merely in Brahmanism, but also of Buddhism; only in Europe is it paradoxical in consequence of the essentially and inevitably realistic fundamental view of Judaism." (This was not in the dissertation of 1813.)

9. Janaway, *Self and World in Schopenhauer's Philosophy*, p. 147. He then adds: "The truth about Schopenhauer's attitude is probably that, following Kant's lead and resting to some extent on Kant's authority, he feels himself entitled to present idealism as the legitimate (if not the properly recognized) heir of the modern European tradition in philosophy." Hamlyn, in *Schopenhauer*, p. 66, writes: "We have to turn to the first of the supplementary essays of the second volume for more elucidation and argument [for transcendental idealism]. It is perhaps interesting and significant that it was not until these essays that Schopenhauer felt the need to engage in substantial argument for his position; in the first volume he seems to have thought that he could largely take it for granted." Young, in *Willing and Unwilling*, p. 3, writes: "Idealism is the first thing one confronts in the main work: 'The world is my representation' are its opening words. But very soon one is liable to become worried by the paucity of argumentation for this (these days) not uncontroversial doctrine. In Schopenhauer's day, however, the view *was* uncontroversial: Schopenhauer's attitude towards idealism as, simply, an unquestionable result of 'the philosophy of modern times' (WR, II, p. 3 [WWR, II, 3]) is explained by the fact that in the first decades of the nineteenth century no one was prepared to question it. Whatever their differences, the one thing the German Idealists all had in common was—idealism."

10. WWR, II, 3, 4 (Ch. 1). In PP, I, 4, Schopenhauer even claims that Descartes's proposition *dubito, cogito, ergo sum* is "the equivalent of that from which I started, namely: 'The world is my representation.'" Then he adds: "The only difference is that his proposition stresses the immediateness of the subject, whereas mine stresses the mediateness of the object. Both propositions express the same thing from two points of view." In the essay in which this passage occurs, "Sketch of a History of the Doctrine of the Ideal and the Real," Schopenhauer tries very hard to establish his connection to, say, modern philosophy from Descartes through Kant—and to dissociate himself from Hegel, Schelling, and Fichte.

11. WWR, I, 3 (§ 1).

12. See Hamlyn, *Schopenhauer*, pp. 66–72.

13. WWR, II, 3 (Ch. 1).

14. WWR, II, 14 (Ch. 1).

15. For Kant, whose terminology Schopenhauer adopts, a proposition is analytic when its denial is self-contradictory, and a proposition is a priori when it is knowable independent of empirical experience. Hence to say, for example, that "[there is] no object without subject" is analytic a priori is to say that to be an object is to be an object-for-a-subject, that is, that the notion of for-a-subject is contained in or entailed by the notion of object; so merely to understand "an object" is to understand it as "for-a-subject," no empirical or observational experience being required.

16. That the proposition, "All perceptual objects are temporally, spatially, and causally determined (by the subject)" is synthetic is shown by the fact that the denial of this proposition is not self-contradictory; and that it is nevertheless knowable a priori, and not empirically, is shown by the fact that time, space, and causality derive from the subject, and not from perceptual objects themselves. This latter thesis Schopenhauer takes Kant to have established, hence he sees no need to repeat Kant's argument.

17. WWR, I, 15 (§ 5).

18. Janaway, *Self and World in Schopenhauer's Philosophy*, p. 134.

19. Ibid., p. 136.

20. Ibid., p. 133 ("though not always," p. 132).

21. See WWR, II, 191 (Ch. 18): "What is *representation?* A very complicated *physiological* occurrence in an animal's brain, whose result is the consciousness of a *picture* at that very spot."

22. WWR, I, 19 (§ 6).

23. WWR, I, 11 (§ 4), 13 (§ 5), 19 (§ 6).

24. WWR, I, 11.

25. WWR, I, 11–12.

26. WWR, I, 25 (§ 7).

27. See WWR, I, 20 (§ 6).

28. WWR, I, 12 (§ 4).

29. WWR, I, 12.

30. The total account turns out to be faulty; see, for example, Hamlyn, *Schopenhauer*, especially pp. 18–21, 54–63. But for our concern—how Schopenhauer proceeds from perception to metaphysics—this does not matter, beyond what I say just below.

31. BM, 64.

32. WWR, II, 195 (Ch. 18).

33. PP, II, 18.

34. WWR, I, 444.

35. WWR, I, 4. Payne calls this "the phantom of a dream."

36. FR, 121.

37. FR, 57, 58.

38. FR, 53; also FR, 55, 56.

39. FR, 63.

40. WWR, I, 12 (§ 4).

41. This passage, from "On Vision and Colors," is translated by Payne in FR, 240; see also FR, 85.

42. FR, 114.

43. Notice here that there is no suggestion of the understanding's finding (or positing) a cause of sensations; it simply constructs, fashions, or creates a perceptual object out of sensations. In his overzealous effort to eliminate all of Kant's "categories of the understanding" except for causality (see especially WWR, I, 448), Schopenhauer has to construe causality—the sole function of the understanding—beyond the bounds of reasonableness. Nowhere is this more evident than in his attempt to explicate the understanding's creation of perceptual objects solely in terms of causality.

44. Patrick Gardiner, *Schopenhauer* (Baltimore: Penguin Books, 1963), p. 108.

45. Janaway, *Self and World in Schopenhauer's Philosophy*, pp. 159–160.

46. Ibid., p. 160.

47. See ibid., p. 159: "If we assume that it is not a real option to say that our sensations are not in fact caused at all (but that we merely come to treat the object 'constructed' on the occasion of having the sensation as if it were the cause of the sensation), then Schopenhauer is in great difficulty." I am not so certain that sensations do have to be caused, but apparently the bodily changes lying at their basis do. Maurice Mandelbaum states that "Our sense organs receive stimuli (from whence Schopenhauer never says), and the organ *reacts* to them"; see his essay "The Physiological Orientation of Schopenhauer's Epistemology," in *Schopenhauer: His Philosophical Achievement*, ed. Michael Fox (Totowa, NJ: Barnes & Noble, 1980), p. 56.

48. FR, 254. (This is from "On Vision and Colors.")

49. FR, 118.

50. FR, 118–119.

51. FR, 119.

52. See my *Schopenhauer: The Human Character*, especially Part 1, where some of these ideas are treated more fully.

53. Hamlyn, *Schopenhauer*, p. 82.

54. Ibid., p. 94.

55. Young does not speak of the connection between natural forces and metaphysics until he takes up the issue of nature; see *Willing and Unwilling*, pp. 40–43. In his discussion of perception (pp. 18–22) nothing is said about natural forces or metaphysics (though, understandably, for his concern differs from mine).

56. WWR, I, 5.

57. WWR, I, 25; see also WWR, I, 34 (both in § 7).

58. WWR, I, 13 (§ 5); see also WWR, I, 25–26. "Of Fichte" was not in the first edition of WWR.

59. WWR, I, 14.

60. WWR, I, 26.

61. WWR, I, 32.

62. WWR, I, 14.

63. WWR, I, 14 (§ 5). The German goes thus: *das S e y n der anschaulichen Objekte [ist] eben ihr W i r k e n.* Consequently, a perceptual or intuitive object is a set of "doings" exercised on other objects, including the animal body, which set is localized in time and space by the understanding. The object is not distinct from this set of "doings," hence it is not literally the cause of this set; equally, I suggest, a human agent is a set of "doings" (actions), who does not literally cause that set.

Empirically, everything is what it does—nothing more, nothing less. But for anything to do anything, it must have, as it were, "an inner nature," which is a natural force in the case of a perceptual object and an underlying character in the case of a human agent, whereby causality operates in the former case and motivation operates in the latter.

64. WWR, I, 25–26.

65. See WWR, I, 452 (Appendix), and FR, 52.

CHAPTER 3: FROM SCIENCE TO METAPHYSICS

1. WWR, I, 95 (§ 17). Here "form" translates the German term *Form*; elsewhere it translates both *Gestalt* (e.g., WWR, I, 95; see passage cited in endnote 3 in this chapter) and *Gestaltung* (e.g., WWR, I, 8). I do not think that this practice causes any confusion, but often I shall indicate which German term "form" translates. Note too, as evident just below, that "content" translates both *Gehalt* and *Inhalt*, which again I think is appropriate.

2. On concepts, see sections 9–12 (WWR, I, 39–58); also WWR, I, 474, where Schopenhauer claims that "concepts [*Begriffe*] obtain all meaning [*Bedeutung*], all content [*Inhalt*], only from their reference to perceptual representations, from which they have been abstracted, drawn off, in other words, formed by the dropping of everything inessential." All concepts, Schopenhauer usually holds, are empirical, that is, abstractions from percepts or intuitions; and none is a priori, that is, inherent in the perceiving mind "prior" to perception or intuition. To be sure, causality and its essential partners, time and space, belong a priori to the perceiving mind, but, Schopenhauer seems to hold, they are not concepts, but only functions or modes of perceptual knowledge. Alternatively, for Schopenhauer, all concepts are made (not "given"), and they are made by the faculty of the human reason, which derives them by way of abstraction from percepts. Hence nonhuman animals have no concepts, but they certainly do perceive objects—a fact cited for proving that the use of concepts is not necessary for perception. That Schopenhauer's account of concepts is inadequate has been urged by several critics: Hamlyn, *Schopenhauer*, pp. 20–25, 56–60, 60–63; Young, *Willing and Unwilling*, pp. 18–25; Rudolf Malter, "Abstraktion Begriffsanalyse, und Urteilskraft in Schopenhauers Erkenntnislehre," in *Schopenhauer: New Essays in Honor of His 200th Birthday*, ed. Eric von der Luft, pp. 257–272; and White, *On Schopenhauer's Fourfold Root of the Principle of Sufficient Reason*, chapter 6. (Malter holds that the source of difficulties in Schopenhauer's theory of knowledge rests with his account of concepts, not with the fact that he believes intuition [Anschauung], in contrast to conceptualization, to be basic knowledge, but with the fact that he believes intuition to involve no concepts, and he believes this because he acknowledges concepts only as empirical concepts.) Schopenhauer's failure to acknowledge nonempirical or a priori concepts in perception probably follows in part from his insistence that philosophy itself rests on percepts and not concepts (contrary to what even Kant, but especially Hegel and Schelling, had maintained); but, as Malter points out, there is no reason why perception could not retain its primacy in knowledge and yet necessitate the employment of nonempirical concepts. Actually, I suspect that—rightly or wrongly—Schopenhauer denies the use of concepts in perception chiefly be-

cause he believes that philosophy, like art and unlike science, has the task of portraying what is intuited or perceived, not what is conceived. It might be added,
however, that according to Schopenhauer we can have no empirical, "but only an
abstract concept," of matter as such. See WWR, I, 213. In the end, one has to conclude, I think, that Schopenhauer never was clear on concepts.

3. WWR, I, 95.

4. Around 1830, Schopenhauer attempts to save Kant's doctrine of the thing
in itself "without leaving the domain of the representation." He proposes that the
material aspect of perception, i.e., sensation, comes to a person from without,
often against the person's will, and thus that it must indicate something existing independently of the person. After considerable discussion Schopenhauer concludes that the argument does not succeed: "*But in the end the truth is that we can
never go on the path of the representation beyond the representation.* The representation is
a whole complete in itself and does not have in its own resources any thread leading to the essence of the thing in itself, an essence that is *toto genere* different from
it. In and by itself the sensation as such is even less able to lead beyond the sensation." The reason for this is simply that sensation is subjective, that is, that it
belongs to the subject, depends on the subject, exists only in relation to the subject, hence, in short, it belongs to the world as representation. See HN, III, par.
302. A somewhat similar conclusion is arrived at still later, in HN, IV (1830–1852),
par. 166.

5. WWR, I, 95.

6. See WWR, I, 16–18 (§ 5), where Schopenhauer raises this very question. He
holds, I suggest, that if the world were nothing but representation, then it would
be a dream world—and life itself would be a "long dream." Moreover, considered
from the standpoint of the world as thing in itself, the world as representation, i.e.,
the world as perceptual representation (in contrast to the world as Idea), seems to
us like a dream. On these matters, see Janaway, *Self and World in Schopenhauer's
Philosophy*, pp. 167–171.

7. WWR, I, 95 (§ 17).

8. WWR, I, 95–96.

9. Schopenhauer distinguishes the What of the appearance from its Why or,
equally, the content of the appearance from its form very often; see, e.g., WWR, I,
121–122 (§ 24).

10. WWR, I, 96.

11. See also WWR, I, 121–123, 141 (§ 27).

12. The question "What is the world besides representation?" has now been
construed such that no answer in terms of something concomitant to or alongside
representation is possible. We cannot now reply that the world, besides being representation, is also will (conation, volitional, action, etc.), if we mean that representation and will simply complement each other and thereby make up the two aspects
of the world. In such a case, incidentally, the world as representation and the world
as will might be correlational, such that the one is dependent on the other and the
other is dependent on the one: no representation without will but also no will
without representation. But with the new construal of the question, whatever the
world is besides representation (let it be will), it cannot be relative to or dependent on representation, though representation must be relative to and dependent

on it. Moreover, it must not be relative to or dependent on anything else, which is presumably the very meaning of "thing in itself" or, if one allows, "aseity." In short, Schopenhauer's original question of metaphysics, as its meaning develops, is not simply seeking something other than representation, but something lying at the very ultimate basis of representation, hence something that has beyond it no further basis. The whole idea of the absolute nondependence of the will (or, possibly, of the thing in itself) gets modified considerably in Schopenhauer's later thought, as I argue in chapter 5. And all to the better.

13. WWR, I, 96 (§ 17); also pp. 141 and 184. Morphology encompasses, of course, taxonomy (the science of classifying living structures, say).

14. WWR, I, 97. Schopenhauer therefore suggests that these "forms" (kinds, types, classes, species, genera, etc.) need an interpretation, indeed, a metaphysical clarification.

15. WWR, I, 97. See also WWR, I, 138 (§ 26): "Malebranche is right; every natural cause is only an occasional cause." This means that the natural force is not, strictly speaking, a cause of its own manifestation; the cause of that manifestation is only a preceding state of matter to which, as it were, the natural force is susceptible. The same holds for the intelligible character of a human agent regarding his or her manifestations, i.e., his or her actions, the cause of which is a motive. Strictly speaking, neither one's intelligible character nor one oneself *causes* one's actions.

16. WWR, I, 97; also WWR, II, 287 (Ch. 22) and Ch. 4 of that volume ("On Knowledge a Priori").

17. WWR, I, 98. See also HN, I, par. 435, where this comparison is first stated (1815).

18. WWR, I, 98. See original of this statement in HN, I, par. 335, which, significantly, carries the title, *De vanitate scientiarum* (On the Vanity of the Sciences). The paragraph begins thus: "All *science* is not accidentally (i.e., according to its present state) but essentially (i.e., always and eternally) *unsatisfactory [ungenügend]*. For even if physics were to reach perfection, i.e., even if I knew how to explain every phenomenon from another, the whole series of phenomena would remain unexplained, i.e., the phenomenon as a whole [*das Phänomen überhaupt*] would remain a riddle." This was written in 1814.

19. WWR, I, 98.

20. As indicated in endnote 12, above, by "more than" or "other than" or "besides," Schopenhauer does not mean simply "in addition to" or "alongside"; he means apparently the "content" or "meaning" of representation, in fact, its essence or inner nature, which allegedly had no reference to or dependence on anything further (and that is supposed to be the thing in itself). As remarked in that endnote, however, Schopenhauer's view on this matter changes later on.

21. WWR, I, 99.

22. Since the term "relation" (*Verhältniß*) has meaning only within the domain governed by the principle of sufficient reason, there cannot be a *relation* between the world as representation and the world as thing in itself. Consider this passage, written in 1815: "What are things other than that they are our representations? What are they independently of this, what are they *in themselves*?—Simply that which we recognize in ourselves as will. This is the kernel of all things, this is it 'that holds the world together in its innermost being.'—The relation of the will to rep-

resentation, however, is *toto genere* different from the relations of representations to each other, i.e., [it] is not in accordance with the principle of sufficient reason. Therefore only metaphorically can it be called a relation. Here lies the one great mystery of the objectity of the will" (HN, I, par. 521). This paragraph makes clear that it is not the case that the world as will is one thing and the world as representation is another, at least not in the sense that the former is the *Grund* (ground or cause) of the latter; thus, it is not the case that the representation is the consequence or effect of the will. Instead, the representation is the objectity of the will, the will become object or the will as object. Otherwise put, the world as representation is the mirror of the will, it is that in which the will is manifested and apparent: The world is the self-knowledge of the will. (The phrase that Schopenhauer quotes appears in *Faust*, Part 1, lines 82–83: *was die Welt/Im Innersten zusammenhält.* . . .)

23. See BM, 4 and GB, #255 (26 September 1851, letter to Julius Frauenstädt).

24. See WWR, I, 140 (§ 27).

25. WWR, I, 123–124 (§ 24); on the latter page, which was not in the first edition, Schopenhauer notes that "magnetism has been derived from electricity."

26. See WWR, I, 143 (§ 27) for a typical statement of this position. There he claims that "it is indeed a mistake of natural science for it to try to refer the higher grades of the will's objectity to lower ones," that "Kant is right when he says that it is absurd to hope for the Newton of a blade of grass" (meaning that a blade of grass cannot be regarded merely as a phenomenon of physical and chemical forces, for it reveals a characteristic Idea of its own), that to believe that the will is revealed only in inorganic nature and not in higher levels "would be a complete denial of the *forma substantialis,* and a degrading of it to a mere *forma accidentalis.*" Added in a later edition is this: "Aristotle's *forma substantialis* denotes exactly what I call the grade [*Grad,* level, degree, stage] of the will's objectification in a thing." Nevertheless, "in all Ideas, i.e., in all the forces of inorganic and in all the forms [*Gestalten*] of organic nature, it is *one and the same will* that reveals itself, i.e., enters the form [*Form*] of the representation, enters *objectity.*" One might then suppose that the will is the one ultimate force and the Ideas are the multiple individual forces of nature. (More about this supposition in chapter 6.)

27. WWR, I, 80 (§ 15).

28. FR, 68 (§ 20). This passage does not appear in the dissertation of 1813.

29. WWR, I, 80.

30. WWR, I, 80.

31. The term "chemical properties" was not in the first edition; see *Faksimiledruck*, p. 120.

32. WWR, I, 80–81.

33. The full passage in German (taken from the Diogenes edition, I/1) goes thus: *So z.B. ist die Schwere eine qualitas occulta: denn sie läßt sich wegdenken, geht also nicht aus der Form des Erkennens als ein Nothwendiges hervor: dies hingegen* [on the contrary] *ist der Fall mit dem Gesetze der Trägheit, als welches aus dem der Kausalität folgt: daher eine Zurückführung auf dasselbe eine vollkommen genügende Erklärung ist* (p. 122).

34. See FR, 64; there it is also said that now and again someone expresses doubt about the universality of gravity (which is perfectly sensible), but no one can express doubt about the universality of inertia or of matter (for that would be to

doubt the principle of sufficient reason of becoming, i.e., the law of causality itself).

35. See FR, 66.

36. See FR, 64.

37. WWR, I, 123 (§ 24).

38. WWR, I, 99.

39. Passages supporting this argument include: HN, I, par. 373 (1815); HN, I, par. 425 in the additional note called "Rectification of the whole essay" (1815 or later); and BM, 18 on causality, inertia, and so on.

40. WWR, I, 81. See also WWR, I, 73; FW, 48; and FR, 67.

41. WWR, I, 81.

42. See WWR, I, 140 (§ 27); also GB, #373 (24 November 1855, letter to Julius Frauenstädt), where Schopenhauer writes: "Have forgotten to remind you that you are wrong in saying that a philosophy, like mine, that proceeds from experience must undergo modifications with further advances in natural knowledge. Then it would be physics! not metaphysics. Never and never more can my philosophy undergo any sort of modification, even if oxygen were to dissolve and the unicorn discovered. It [my philosophy] proceeds from experience, but in the widest sense; hovers high above all detail and micrology."

43. FR, 53.

44. FR, 53.

45. There are two aims here, to show the beginninglessness of causes and effects and to deny that a body is ever a cause. Schopenhauer also notes that "the cause" might be called either the individual new factor or the entire set of factors.

46. A clear statement of this contention occurs in BM, 98. See also HN, I, par. 153 (1814): "External impressions [*Einwirkungen*] do not alter and form the character, but only disclose it. They are to the mind [*Geist*] what chemical reagents are to matter; only from their reaction to these is its nature [*Beschaffenheit*, constitution] known." And HN, I, par. 159 (also 1814) was this: "Life is to the human being, i.e., to the will, precisely what chemical reagents are to the body [*Körper*]; only with these does it reveal what it is, and it is only to the extent that it reveals itself." Interestingly, at this point Schopenhauer adds that "life is the *intelligible character's* becoming known," that "life is only the mirror into which we look not so that it may reflect something, but so that we may recognize ourselves in it, may see *what* it reflects," and finally that "life is the proof sheet in which the errors made in setting the type becomes known." So, again, as indicated here, "the world is the self-knowledge of the will." And part of this emphasizes the assertion, "the world is *my* will."

47. FR, 54.

48. If we add matter to the second account, then it involves five factors—at least in certain cases.

49. He first uses the term *qualitas occulta* in 1815, so far as I can tell; see HN, I, par. 373. In FR it occurs, I think, only in the second edition, not in the dissertation of 1813.

50. See, e.g., FR, 67–68.

51. Young, *Willing and Unwilling*, pp. 41–42.

52. See WWR, I, 136–137 (§ 26); in the first edition, this sentence has "twenty

years" (not three thousand) and "a tree" (not a plant); see also HN, I, par. 413 and 435 (1815).

53. Something very much like this is explicitly stated in HN, I, par. 523 (1816).

54. See WWR, I, (§ 24–27).

55. WWR, I, 505.

56. FR, 42.

57. If this conclusion did follow, we would have one reason for accepting one version of the cosmological argument for the existence of God.

58. See Kant's remark in *Prolegomena to Any Future Metaphysics* (Academy edition volume 4, 354); "The sensory world is nothing but a chain of appearances connected according to universal laws; it has therefore no subsistence [*Bestehen*] by itself; it is not really [*eigentlich*] the thing in itself, therefore [it] refers necessarily to that which contains the ground [*Grund*] of this appearance, to beings that cannot be known merely as appearance but rather as things in themselves." Notice that, like Schopenhauer, Kant switches from "appearances" (plural), which form a chain according to universal law, to "appearance" (singular), which is the chain.

59. See WWR, I, 119 (§ 24), where Schopenhauer echoes the sentiment quoted in the previous note from Kant: "Now, however, if the objects appearing in these forms [of time, space, and causality] are not to be empty phantoms, but are to have a meaning, then they must point to something, must be the expression of something, which would not again be, like themselves, object, representation, something existing merely relatively, namely, for a subject, but rather something that existed without such dependence on something that standing over against it as its essential condition with its forms, i.e., would be *no representation* but a *thing in itself.*"

60. WWR, I, 417.

61. WWR, I, 418. This discussion does not appear in the first edition of WWR.

62. Oddly, Schopenhauer suggests here that he has no objections to all of this, but as we well know, he actually rejects the allegedly Kantian idea that the thing in itself, or the unknown x, "effects" qualities. This rejection is precisely what Schopenhauer has in mind when he says that Kant did not "deduce" or "derive" the thing in itself in the right way; see, e.g., WWR, I, 422, 502.

63. For example: WWR, II, (Ch. 2) ("On the Doctrine of Knowledge of Perception or Knowledge of the Understanding"); *On the Will in Nature*, particularly the last few pages of the chapter called "Physical Astronomy"; and *Parerga and Paralipomena*, volume 1, the chapter entitled "Sketch of a History of the Doctrine of the Ideal and the Real."

64. In his early notes Schopenhauer does, however, say this: "Descartes has demonstrated the subjectivity of the secondary qualities of perceptible objects, but Kant has also demonstrated that of the primary qualities" (HN, I, par. 716). One would think that Locke, not Descartes, is meant.

65. WWR, I, 99.

66. Young has stressed this point; see his *Willing and Unwilling*, p. 42.

67. WWR, I, 419.

68. WWR, I, 171–172 (§ 31).

69. WWR, I, 419.

70. HN, I, par. 210; see also WWR, I, 169.
71. HN, I, par. 228.
72. HN, I, par. 191.
73. HN, I, par. 305.
74. HN, I, par. 305 note.
75. HN, I, par. 359. In effect, the same thing is said in HN, I, par. 321.
76. See Malter, *Der eine Gedanke*, pp. 4–12, whose account I follow, for the most part, though I emphasize time and temporality a bit more than he does.
77. HN, I, par. 79.
78. HN, I, par. 89.
79. See, especially, HN, I, par. 35, but also HN, I, par. 66.
80. HN, I, par. 86.

CHAPTER 4: FROM THE BODY TO THE WILL

1. In fairly recent times the body figures prominently in the philosophical theories of Jean-Paul Sartre (*Being and Nothingness: An Essay on Phenomenological Ontology,* 1943) and of Maurice Merleau-Ponty (*Phenomenology of Perception,* 1945).
2. WWR, I, 99 (§ 18).
3. WWR, I, 99.
4. See FR, 121–122: "Only *indirectly* is it [the body] known objectively and hence as object, since, like all other objects, it presents itself in the understanding or in the brain (which is the same thing) as the recognized cause of the subjectively given effect [i.e., the sensation], and precisely in this way presents itself *objectively.* This can happen only by the body's parts acting each on its own senses, thus by the eye seeing the body, the hand touching it, and so on, and on these data the brain or understanding spatially constructs it, like other objects, according to its shape and condition." This passage does not appear, at least in these words, in the dissertation.
5. See again FR, 121; also HN, I, par. 524 (written in 1816).
6. WWR, I, 99–100.
7. In the first sentence Payne translates *ihm* by "to him" and "for him," instead of "to it" and "for it," and in the second sentence he, of course, has "he" for *er.* This conceals the fact that in the first sentence reference is made to a neutral noun (*das rein erkennende Subjekt,* the purely knowing subject) while in the second sentence reference is made to a masculine noun (*der Forscher,* the investigator); since the dative case for both is *ihm,* the change of reference is not easily noticed. But, as I observe in the text just following, this is an important matter; for the body and its movements or actions are foreign to the purely knowing subject, though they are intimately tied up with the (embodied) investigator. Thus "he would see his conduct" (*er sähe sein Handeln*) should read—if the subject remained the purely knowing subject instead of the investigator—"it would see the body's conduct" (and not even "it would see *its* body's conduct").
8. WWR, I, 100.
9. WWR, I, 100. When Schopenhauer uses the word "identity" (or "identical" or "one and the same thing"), he often means *inseparable from* or *unthinkable apart*

from; hence here he does not intend to say that "the subject of knowledge" and "the body" are everywhere interchangeable terms, but only that there can be in reality no subject of knowledge independent of the body. In a phrase, the subject of knowledge must be somewhere in space and time, i.e., it must be embodied. Consequently, the notion of the purely knowing subject, that "winged cherub without a body," is an abstract, one-sided conception of what alone truly exists as knowing subject, namely, the embodied or "individual" subject of knowledge. Equally, "the world is representation" is an abstract, one-sided conception of what truly exists as world. In sum, both the purely knowing subject and the world as representation, though not exactly fictions, are one-sided notions of, respectively, the knowing subject and the world.

10. WWR, I, 100.

11. WWR, I, 100–101.

12. WWR, I, 125 (§ 24).

13. WWR I, 101–102.

14. For the view that arguments by analogy are not valid at all, see Monroe Beardsley, *Thinking Straight*, 4th ed. (Englewood Cliffs, NJ: Prentice Hall, 1975), pp. 13–15.

15. WWR, I, 99–100.

16. WWR, I, 100.

17. WWR, I, 100.

18. WWR, I, 101.

19. Similar statements occur in HN, I, par. 292, 524, 534, and 650. Arousal of the will is called irritability, while sensation in the absence of such arousal is called mere sensibility. See also WWR, II, 250 (Ch. 20): "The will objectifies itself directly in irritability, not in sensibility."

20. See FR, 64.

21. For the two senses of "moves," see Jennifer Hornsby, *Actions* (London: Routledge & Kegan Paul, 1980), pp. 1–15.

22. What has been summarized here can be found in many places in Schopenhauer's writings, for example, WWR, I, 115–119 (§ 23) and FW, 27–64.

23. See my *Schopenhauer: The Human Character*, especially, pp. 33–65.

24. Since we are no longer concerned with a strict argument by analogy, we can gloss over the issue of what sort of representation one's own body is (or at least I shall assume we can). All we really need to suppose here is that one's own body is a "body" in causal connection with other "bodies," hence that it can move them and that they can move (and otherwise affect) it. In being aware of these things, one is aware of one's own body as representation, albeit as unique representation.

25. WWR, I, 104 (§ 19).

26. WWR, I, 104. To say that theoretical egoism can never be refuted by proofs is to say that it can never be proved that any body other than my own manifests a will. In a sense, of course, it cannot be proved that my own body manifests a will, but it needs no proof: This is a fact of which everyone is "immediately aware"—in virtue of pains and pleasures based on sensations and of voluntary bodily movements.

27. WWR, I, 14 (§ 5).

28. Exactly why would adoption of theoretical egoism be "mad"? Why would a serious proponent of this doctrine be found only in a madhouse, and thus in need of a cure? Such an individual would be maintaining this: "The world is *my* representation" and "The world is *my* will." Or, equally, this: "The world is a construction of my understanding" and "Will belongs only to me." Is this not the very position that Schopenhauer puts forth? Is it not the position, according to Schopenhauer, of everyone, except for the nonegoist? I touch on these matters later in this chapter and in the conclusion. For other discussions, see Gardiner, *Schopenhauer*, p. 265; Hamlyn, *Schopenhauer*, p. 64; and Janaway, *Self and World in Schopenhauer's Philosophy*, pp. 149–150, 325–326.

29. WWR, I, 104.

30. What I am calling the evil person differs from the malicious person in this way: The evil person is a pure practical egoist, who in pursuit of his own ends will do anything so long as it (in his judgment) does not detract from his overall well-being, while the malicious person aims at hurting others as much as he can even when doing so threatens his own well-being. Although egoism *as such* is not evil, it is the dispositional readiness to do evil whenever doing so is judged to be personally advantageous; maliciousness, on the other hand, is *as such* evil, for it is the disposition to cause harm to others apart from considerations of personal advantage. For Schopenhauer, there are three basic moral (i.e., practical) incentives: egoism, malice, and compassion. See especially BM, 145. (The ascetic exemplifies yet a further incentive, namely, self-harm or, in today's language, masochism [see WWR, II, 607, note 6].) In *Schopenhauer: The Human Character* I discuss these and related matters in some detail, especially in Part 2, "Ethics and Virtue."

31. Consider WWR, II, 175 (Ch. 17): "The necessary *credo* of all righteous and good men" is "I believe in a system of metaphysics." In saying this Schopenhauer supposes that every system of metaphysics holds that all individually different things are at bottom one thing. So if one flatly denies that all animate beings are somehow "one" or somehow "identical," then one undercuts the possibility of that identity that lies at the heart of compassion, and one thereby precludes the possibility of, first, metaphysics, and, second, ethics. There is thus good reason to speak of "Schopenhauer's ethical metaphysics" (as David Cartwright has told me).

32. WWR, I, 125 (§ 24).

33. HN, I, par. 548.

34. HN, I, par. 621.

35. By "representation analysis," I mean what Malter calls *Vorstellungsanalyse*; and by "representation interpretation," I mean what he calls *Vorstellungsdeutung*. See Malter, *Der eine Gedanke*, p. 15. Relevant too is Rüdiger Safranski's *Schopenhauer and the Wild Years of Philosophy*, trans. Ewald Osers (London: Weidenfeld and Nicolson, 1989); on p. 205 Safranski calls Schopenhauer "a hermeneutical philosopher."

36. WWR, I, 126 (§ 24).

37. WWR, I, 139 (§ 27).

38. WWR, I, 125.

39. WWR, I, 109 (§ 21).

40. WWR, I, 109.

41. WWR, I, 110.

42. See WWR, I (§ 15, 16).

43. See, for example, WWR, I, 26 (§ 7).

44. See WWR, I, 105. That "will" *must* be used occurs in a passage not in the first edition.

45. See WWR, I, 162–165 (§ 29). Schopenhauer says very little about reflection anywhere in his writings. And when he does discuss it a bit in WN, 93–97 he has it function in a way different from its "application" in WWR: In WN it connects outer knowledge of causality with inner knowledge of will, thus avoiding the error of thinking that movements divide into two separate types, those by causes in nature and those by will (or, presumably, motives) in oneself. He claims, further, that "wherever there is causality there is will" (p. 96), hence all movements by will—though outer movements are known to us as causal.

46. HN, I, par. 529.

47. WWR, I, 110 (§ 22).

48. WWR, I, 110.

49. WWR, I, 111.

50. WWR, I, 111.

51. GB, #372 (3 November 1855, letter to Julius Frauenstädt).

52. GB, #391 (6 June 1956, letter to Julius Frauenstädt).

53. See BM, 63, where Schopenhauer actually says that "we are never entitled to set up a genus that is given to us only in a single species," and that "to talk of rational beings apart from man is as if we attempted to talk of *heavy beings* apart from bodies."

54. See HN, III, par. 144.

55. See WWR, I, 105 (§ 19): "If I say . . . that the force which attracts a stone to the earth is of its nature, in itself, and apart from all representation, will, then no one will attach to this proposition the absurd meaning that the stone moves itself according to a known motive, because it is thus that the will appears in man." A stone never moves in virtue of *Willkür,* that is, voluntarily in conjunction with a known motive.

56. Demonstration of empirical support for holding that the world is will is the project of WN.

CHAPTER 5: FROM THE WILL TO THE THING IN ITSELF

1. For example, WWR, I, 110 (§ 21), 120 (§ 24), but also in many other places.

2. See WWR, I, 170 (§ 31).

3. Among the many passages where this is said, see WWR, I, 99 (§ 17), 112 (§ 23).

4. In an early note (HN, I, par. 521, written in 1816) Schopenhauer writes: "The relation of the will to representation is . . . *toto genere* different from all relations of representations to each other, i.e., it is not in accord with the principle of sufficient reason. It can therefore be called a relation only metaphorically. Here lies the one great mystery of the objectivity of the will." In a much later note (HN, IV, par. 4, written in 1832) Schopenhauer suggests that the world as representa-

tion is the world as will become object subject to the principle of sufficient reason, just as a bodily movement is the "objectity" of an act of will. But this alleged parallel does not hold perfectly, for the world as will (understood as the thing in itself) is wholly free from the principle of sufficient reason, while an act of will is subject to one aspect of this principle, namely, time.

5. In what follows I rely heavily on Julian Young's book, *Willing and Unwilling*; G. Steven Neeley's paper, "A Re-Examination of Schopenhauer's Analysis of Bodily Agency: The Ego as Microcosm" presented at a session of the North American Division of the Schopenhauer Society in April 1990, and Moira Nicholls' article, "Schopenhauer, Young and the Will," *Schopenhauer-Jahrbuch*, 72 (1991), 143–157.

6. Frederick Copleston, *Arthur Schopenhauer: Philosopher of Pessimism* (London: Burns, Oates and Washbourne, 1947), p. 64.

7. Ibid., p. 65.

8. See WWR, I, 109 (§ 21).

9. Gardiner, *Schopenhauer*, p. 172.

10. See WWR, I, 71 (§ 15).

11. See WWR, I, 469, 474, 476–477.

12. Janaway, *Self and World in Schopenhauer's Philosophy*, pp. 192–193.

13. HN, I, par. 406; for the claim that philosophy is more like art than science, see also HN, I, pars. 220, 221, 256, 301, 328, 336 and so on. Philosophy is like science, however, in that it presents its findings in abstract language; it arrives at those findings through intuition rather than through an analysis of concepts, and in this way it resembles art.

14. Schopenhauer's frequent references to the "teleology of nature" and to the victory of one Idea over another (see next chapter) strongly suggest that he is not limiting himself to what literally falls within experience. On these matters, see Young, *Willing and Unwilling*, pp. 64–77.

15. Young has a good, though possibly exaggerated, discussion of this matter; see his *Willing and Unwilling*, pp. 22–25.

16. WWR, II, 160 (Ch. 17).

17. WWR, II, 164. I add the brackets to this passage because it is not possible to determine with certainty what "that" refers to, but "nature" or, equally, "the given appearance of things" seems a safe bet.

18. WWR, II, 182 (Ch. 17).

19. WWR, II, 183.

20. WWR, II, 183.

21. WWR, II, 184.

22. In WN, 110, however, Schopenhauer writes that "we are plunged into a sea of riddles and incomprehensibilities and have no thorough and direct knowledge and understanding of either things or ourselves." This statement occurs after a discussion of magnetizing, curing by charms, and the power of will over inanimate objects.

23. WWR, II, 184.

24. WWR, II, 185. For questions that cannot be answered, see WWR, II (Ch. 50) including "From what has this will sprung, which is free to affirm itself, the appearance of this being the world, or to deny itself, the appearance of which we do

not know?" and "Whence comes the great discord which permeates this world?" and "How deeply in the being in itself of the world do the roots of individuality go?" and "What would I be if I were not the will to life?" and so on.

25. Schopenhauer cites this sentence in GB, #278 (22 July 1852, letter to Adam von Doß).

26. WWR, II, 185.

27. Payne translates the title of this chapter "On the Possibility of Knowing the Thing in Itself."

28. WWR, II, 194 (Ch. 18).

29. WWR, II, 198.

30. GB, #202 (21 Sept. 1944, letter to Johann August Becker). The expression "No will, no representation, no world" comes from WWR, I, 411. By "the 3 sophists" Schopenhauer means Hegel, Fichte, and Schelling.

31. GB, #279 (6 August 1852, letter to Julius Frauenstädt). The cloud-cuckooland derives from Aristophanes' *The Clouds*; the term *pon stō* derives from Archimedes' boast, "Give me a lever long enough and a foothold, and I will move the world."

32. In his comments on Schopenhauer's correspondence, Hübscher includes this remark by Frauenstädt; see GB, p. 570.

33. GB, #280 (21 August 1953, letter to Julius Frauenstädt). Hegel is supposed to have pronounced *Idee* as *Uedäh*.

34. See Young, *Willing and Unwilling*, especially pp. 28–35.

35. For this suggestion, see Moira Nicholls, "Schopenhauer, Young and the Will," cited in note 5 of this chapter.

36. See WWR, I, 428; Young cites it, with the brackets, in *Willing and Unwilling*, p. 33. This passage, as noted in the main text, does not appear in the first edition of WWR.

37. Here again I alter Payne's translation of the title.

38. If acts of will were not experienced at least in time, if they were not known in at least one dimension belonging to outer appearances, then there would be no basis for taking inner experience as the key for interpreting or understanding outer appearances. What is experienced internally must have at least one facet in common with what is known or represented externally, for otherwise no "transference" from inner experience to outer things could proceed.

39. WWR, II, 194 (Ch. 18).

40. WWR, II, 194.

41. WWR, II, 195.

42. See Young, *Willing and Unwilling*, p. 29.

43. WWR, II, 195.

44. WWR, II, 196.

45. WWR, II, 196.

46. WWR, II, 197.

47. WWR, II, 197.

48. WWR, II, 197.

49. WWR, II, 197.

50. WWR, II, 198.

51. WWR, II, 198.

CHAPTER 6: FROM NATURE TO THE IDEAS

1. As noted in chapter 1, if the "single thought" is to encompass Books 3 and 4 of *The World as Will and Representation,* and not just Books 1 and 2, there must be added the words "so that denial of the will to life may occur."

2. See Bryan Magee, *The Philosophy of Schopenhauer* (Oxford: Clarendon Press, 1983), p. 239: "I am not convinced that the Platonic Ideas—adduced primarily to explain the existence of genera and species—are necessary to Schopenhauer's philosophy at all. A careful shave with Occam's razor could, I suspect, succeed in removing these without trace."

3. See Janaway, *Self and World in Schopenhauer's Philosophy,* p. 277: "In Kantian terms, the Ideas are . . . required to repose somewhere between appearance and thing-in-itself, and it is deeply uncertain whether there is any such location for them to occupy."

4. See Gardiner, *Schopenhauer,* p. 207.

5. Schopenhauer writes that "that which always endows a cause with efficacy" is "a force of nature." And he claims that in etiology "it is seen as an original force, i.e., a *qualitas occulta,*" while in philosophy "it is known as immediate objectity of the will," i.e., Idea. See WWR, I, 131 (§ 26), where the claim that Ideas are natural forces, viewed philosophically, is most clearly put forth.

6. WWR, I, 130.

7. WWR, I, 128 (§ 25). One should note well that will as thing in itself is never known, it is never an object of a knowing subject.

8. WWR, I, 128. See also HN, I, par. 604. In Hamlyn's sentence, "What makes it necessary to refer to grades [of the objectification of the will] is that some phenomena seem to manifest the will more than others" (*Schopenhauer,* p. 104), the word "clearly" should be inserted between "more" and "than."

9. WWR, I, 128.

10. See WWR, I, 129, where Schopenhauer refers to the "innumerable individuals" as "the unattained patterns" of Ideas, of the different grades of the objectification of the will.

11. WWR, I, 130. Later on Schopenhauer makes clear that the lowest grades appear in all higher grades, as, for instance, the Idea of gravity appears in the Idea of humanity, such that, altogether, they form a pyramid, and the Idea of humanity cannot be clearly manifested alone, "torn apart" from all lower Ideas; see WWR, I, 153.

12. WWR, I, 132. A good deal later Schopenhauer writes that "each person exhibits to a certain extent an Idea that is wholly characteristic of him" (WWR, I, 224).

13. See BM, 151.

14. See WWR, I, 131.

15. WWR, I, 131.

16. Apparently wanting to emphasize their basis in will, Schopenhauer often calls both Ideas and (intelligible) characters "acts of will"; see WWR, I, 155–156 (§ 28).

17. Usually, but not consistently, Schopenhauer reserves the German adjective *real* for Ideas and applies the adjective *wirklich* only to intuitive particulars.

18. On the difference between concepts and Ideas, see WWR, I, (§ 49), where it is said, among other things, that: "The *Idea* is the unity that has fallen into plurality by virtue of the temporal and spatial form of our intuitive apprehension. The *concept*, on the other hand, is the unity once more produced out of plurality by means of abstraction through our faculty of reason; the latter can be described as *unitas post rem*, and the former as *unitas ante rem*" (234–235).

19. See, again, WWR, I, 131 (§ 26).

20. Schopenhauer speaks of Ideas as "the eternal forms of things" (WWR, I, 129).

21. Among those who adopt this view are Gardiner, *Schopenhauer*, pp. 190, 206; Magee, *The Philosophy of Schopenhauer*, p. 239; and Janaway, *Self and World in Schopenhauer's Philosophy*, pp. 277–279; but not Hamlyn, *Schopenhauer*, pp. 104–107 or Young, *Willing and Unwilling*, pp. 92–93.

22. WWR, I, 174.

23. WWR, I, 175.

24. WWR, I, 175.

25. WWR, I, 175.

26. WWR, I, 99 (§ 17); also 170–174 (§ 31).

27. WWR, I, 276.

28. WWR, I, 276. See also HN, I, par. 345 (written in 1814): "Everything except the (Platonic) Ideas, except the objects of art, is absolutely nothing but relation, nothing but an empty and unsubstantial existence. That which exists in any place and at any time is finite, and that which is finite does not really exist at all." Also HN, I, par. 518 (1815): "Whoever perceives and knows in the individual thing only this [the appearance of the Idea in time and space] and not its (Platonic) Idea, is still involved in knowledge according to the principle of sufficient reason, and this is never an adequate knowledge of the will. For such a person knows the given actual thing only insofar as it exists *here, now, and under these circumstances.* . . . Such a person has known something which exists and yet at the same time does not exist; for time is precisely that by virtue of which opposite determinations are attributed to a thing. Therefore every appearance in time is again always *non-existent*. The existence of all individual things, even of ourselves as individuals, also of our joys and sorrows, is likewise always a non-existence."

29. See WWR, I, 130 (§ 25), where Schopenhauer quotes, and apparently endorses, Diogenes Laërtius' statement of Plato's conception of Ideas: "Plato teaches that the Ideas exist in nature, so to speak, as patterns or prototypes, and that the remainder of things only resemble them, exist as their copies." The reference to and quotation from Diogenes Laërtius does not appear in the first edition of WWR.

30. WWR, I, 176 (§ 33).

31. WWR, I, 177.

32. WWR, I, 177.

33. WWR, I, 177.

34. WWR, I, 177–178.

35. WWR, I, 178.

36. See Malter, *Der eine Gedanke*, p. 67, where he says that "the severance of the knowing subject from the determination of the principle of sufficient reason" is

"synonymous with the severance of the subject of knowledge from the subject of willing," and that "the liberation of the human being" is "the theme of Schopenhauer's philosophy." For an elaboration of this notion and several related aspects of WWR, Book 3, see my paper, "Art as Liberation: A Central Theme of Schopenhauer's Philosophy," forthcoming in an anthology on Schopenhauer's aesthetics, *Schopenhauer, Philosophy and the Arts*, ed. Dale Jacquette (Cambridge: Cambridge University Press).

37. WWR, I, 169 (§ 30).

38. WWR, I, 176 (§ 33).

39. WWR, I, 178 (§ 34).

40. WWR, I, 178.

41. WWR, I, 178.

42. WWR, I, 179. It is at this point that Schopenhauer refers to Thomas Paine's saying, *du sublime au ridicule il n'y a qu'un pas* (from the sublime to the ridiculous is but a step), and to Spinoza's remark, *Mens aeterna est, quatenus res sub aeternitatis specie concipit* (The mind is eternal insofar as it conceives things from the standpoint of eternity).

43. See WWR, I, 178.

44. WWR, I, 179. See also WWR, I, 199 (§ 38): "We can withdraw from all suffering just as well through present as through distant objects, whenever we raise ourselves to a purely objective contemplation [*Betrachtung*, consideration] of them, and are thus able to produce the illusion [*Illusion*] that only those objects are present, not we ourselves. Then, as pure subject of knowing, delivered from the miserable self [*das leidige Selbst entledigen*], we become entirely one with those objects, and foreign as our want [*Noth*, need] is to them, it is at such moments just as foreign to us. Then the world as representation alone remains; the world as will has disappeared."

45. WWR, I, 179–180.

46. WWR, I, 180. On the correlativity issue, see HN, I, par. 593.

47. WWR, I, 180. Somewhat later, Schopenhauer sums up part of this by saying: "In the aesthetic method of consideration we found *two inseparable constituent parts*: knowledge of the object, not as an individual [particular] thing, but as Platonic *Idea*, i.e., as persisting form of this whole species of things; and then the self-consciousness of the knower, not as individual, but as *pure, will-less subject of knowledge*" (WWR, I, 195). Compare, however, the discussion in chapter 30, volume 2 of WWR, where Schopenhauer claims that "the more conscious we are of the object, the less conscious we are of the subject" (WWR, II, 367).

48. With regard to the theme of liberation, which (as cited in endnote 36, above) Malter emphasizes, Schopenhauer holds that once we are raised to the pure subject, we get a glimpse of the fact that the whole vast universe in an infinity of time exists "only in our representation," that "our dependence on it is now annulled by its dependence on us," and that (as only philosophy can clarify) "we are one with the world, and are therefore not oppressed but exalted by its immensity" (WWR, I, 205 [§ 39]). As a matter of fact, Schopenhauer holds, if we were not will, we could not know the world as will (i.e., we could not know Ideas, the various objectifications of will as objects); "for, as Empedocles said, like can be known only by like" (WWR, I, 222 [§ 45]).

49. WWR, I, 180 (§ 34).

50. WWR, I, 180.

51. The first edition of WWR did not include the final paragraph of WWR, I, 181 (§ 34).

52. Young, *Willing and Unwilling*, p. 92. See also Hamlyn, *Schopenhauer*, p. 107.

53. WWR, I, 182.

54. WWR, I, 181.

55. WWR, I, 182.

56. WWR, I, 182.

57. WWR, I, 182.

58. That many observations are necessary for discerning an Idea is suggested in the following statement: "To grasp completely the Ideas expressing themselves in water, it is not sufficient to see it in the quiet pond or in the evenly flowing stream, but those Ideas completely unfold themselves only when the water appears under all circumstances and obstacles" (WWR, I, 252 [§ 51]). Note that here at least Schopenhauer talks as if water displays several Ideas, not just one; in a note from 1817, he speaks of only one Idea of water: "In order to grasp the (*Platonic*) *Idea of water*, it is not sufficient to see it in a quiet pond or in an evenly flowing stream, but this Idea completely unfolds itself only when the water is subjected to all the circumstances and obstacles which can act upon it" (HN, I, par. 691).

59. WWR, I, 182 (§ 35). One will notice that the objects considered are very unusual; a moving cloud, a flowing stream of water, and ice crystals are very much unlike, say, the building across the street, the table in front of me, a boulder in the distance, and so on, none of which (unlike Schopenhauer's examples of objects) seem to be in motion. Actually, with Schopenhauer's example of a moving cloud, one might suppose three things may be distinguished: the Idea of cloud, this cloud, and the many different shapes that this cloud takes (before it "disappears" or "vanishes"). So far as I can tell, Schopenhauer does not address this issue.

60. WWR, I, 184. Note too: "If we have read Herodotus, we have already studied enough history from a philosophical point of view" (WWR, II, 444 [Ch. 38]).

61. WWR, I, 230 (§ 48).

62. WWR, I, 184 (§ 36).

63. WWR, I, 185.

64. WWR, I, 196 (§ 38).

65. Young, *Willing and Unwilling*, pp. 92–93.

66. Ibid., p. 93. It is hard to tell what "its" refers to. It would be strange to speak of the brook's inessential aspects, since it seems that the brook is the inessential aspects—but of what? of the Idea (water)? But can it be said that the Idea has inessential aspects? Perhaps Young holds that the brook has both inessential aspects (which involve time, space, and causality) and essential aspects (which make up the Idea of water). But then the question is again: *Is* the brook the inessential aspects of the Idea of water or *does* the brook *have* both inessential aspects of the Idea of water and essential aspects that make up the Idea of water? Neither alternative seems attractive; and, more to the point, neither seems to make the brook and the Idea of water "identical." (I omit the difficult problem of the identity of the brook over time, in a slightly different place, and a bit causally

different. It looks as if an appeal ought to be made to a Kantian concept of substance in order to handle this problem. Relevant is endnote 59, above.)

67. Ibid., Schopenhauer, WWR, I, 185 (§ 36).

68. Young, *Willing and Unwilling*, p. 93.

69. Ibid., pp. 93–94.

70. See ibid., p. ix, where Young says that Schopenhauer is to be read as a Kantian.

71. No woman, Schopenhauer holds, is a genius (WWR, II, 392 [Ch. 31]; and PP, II, 619). See my "Schopenhauer on Women, Men, and Sexual Love" (forthcoming in *The Midwest Quarterly*) for an attempt to disentangle Schopenhauer's very complex views on women.

72. WWR, I, 186 (§ 36).

73. WWR, I, 186. Imagination, however, is not sufficient for genius; see WWR, I, 187.

74. See WWR, I, 195 (§ 37).

75. See PP, II, 230: "Just as a botanist recognizes the whole plant from one leaf and Cuvier constructed the entire animal from one bone, so from one characteristic action of a man we can arrive at a correct knowledge of his character." On this last point, see also FW, 50.

76. See WWR, I, 393 (§ 68).

77. Regarding token and type, see WWR, II, 427 (Ch. 37), where Schopenhauer writes: "Now, although the poet, like every artist, always presents us only with the particular, the individual, yet what *he* knew and wants through his work to let us know is the (Platonic) Idea, the whole species."

78. See WWR, I, 152 (§ 27); but also WWR, I, 134–136 (§ 26).

79. Although Schopenhauer often talks as if the intellect and the will (in a person) are totally different from each other, and, in a way, totally opposed to each other, he should say—as I suggest here—that the intellect is a "form of will." Essentially, the same point has been urged by other commentators. See first: "Any bodily organ [including the brain, the 'objective' counterpart of the intellect] is phenomenal insofar as it is regarded as existing as one among other objects which can be seen, touched, measured, weighted, etc.; but every bodily organ also has its own inner activity, and this activity is an expression of a will which animates the organism as a whole. . . . This, of course, entails that we should not interpret the phenomenal world as merely representing the results of cerebral activity, but as being a product which, to some degree, expressed the underlying force of will which animates us" (Maurice Mandelbaum, "The Physiological Orientation of Schopenhauer's Epistemology," in *Schopenhauer: His Philosophical Achievement,* ed. Michael Fox, p. 56). The key claim is that the brain's activity, which is knowing, is "an expression of a will," in other words, I suggest, intellect is "an expression of will." See also: "As the intellect or brain developed to serve the will of the body in which it is lodged, to serve the will of the species possessing an intellect, the formal structure of this intellect, that is, the principle of sufficient reason, likewise functions essentially and for the most part in the service of willing. Thus thinking and willing are, for Schopenhauer, not characteristically different: Thinking generally is a form or kind of willing, just like eating, grasping, fleeing, etc. So too, what in terms of the

thinking intellect we call objects for a subject must be seen as, for the most part, also motives for the willing intellect" (James D. Chansky, "Schopenhauer and Platonic Ideas: A Groundwork for an Aesthetic Metaphysics," in *Schopenhauer: New Essays in Honor of His 200th Birthday*, ed. Eric von der Luft, p. 71, note 8).

80. See, e.g., Hamlyn, *Schopenhauer*, p. 110, where he writes that "It is impossible to see why the will should make it possible for [the intellect to master and abolish the will]."

CHAPTER 7: FROM THE WORLD TO SALVATION

1. It should be noted that the aesthetic contemplator is not identical with the genius (who, beyond contemplation, has the talent to reproduce what he knows); the morally virtuous individual is not exactly a moral saint (who, if beyond pity or compassion, reaching a state of resignation, hence indifference to suffering, should not even be called "moral"); and the ascetic is superseded by the mystic (who, surpassing all connection with the body, attains the truly mysterious state of, say, union with the All). The latter two differences are considered below; but for now no harm is done, I suggest, by running them together as indicated in the text.

2. Here denial of the will amounts to "forgetting" it. Schopenhauer says that "we forget our individuality, our will, etc." (WWR, I, 178 [§ 34]). I think that, for Schopenhauer, this "forgetting" is an active verb.

3. See my *Schopenhauer: The Human Character*, pp. 182–192, 209.

4. WWR, I, 378 (§ 68). It will have been noticed that I translate *der Wille zum Leben* sometimes by "the will to live" and sometimes by "the will to life." The latter expression seems especially appropriate when sexuality or propagation is involved, as in this chapter. Janaway always, I think, uses "the will to life."

5. This final claim, but in terms of malice, I contest in *Schopenhauer: The Human Character*, pp. 101–103.

6. WWR, I, 378.

7. WWR, I, 379.

8. WWR, I, 379.

9. WWR, I, 380.

10. WWR, I, 380. For "his action now gives the lie to his appearance," the German goes thus: *sein Thun straft jetzt seine Erscheinung Lügen*. Literally, *straft* means punishes.

11. WWR, I, 380. Here it is said that *er* (the ascetic) *straft den Leib Lügen*.

12. WWR, I, 380.

13. WWR, I, 381. But later, at WWR, I, 404 (§ 70), it is said that denial of the will is not done at will, or (I suggest) by deliberate intent; yet it is (somehow) free.

14. WWR, I, 382.

15. WWR, I, 392.

16. WWR, I, 392.

17. WWR, I, 392.

18. WWR, I, 393. The phrase in German is *die läuternde Flamme des Leidens*.

19. WWR, I, 393.

20. WWR, I, 394. The will to life contradicts itself in that it wills life (pleasure) yet life involves displeasure and suffering.

21. See WWR, I, 383: "A saint may be full of the most absurd superstition, or, on the other hand, may be a philosopher; it is all the same. His conduct alone is evidence that he is a saint; for, in a moral regard, it springs not from abstract knowledge, but from intuitively apprehended, immediate knowledge of the world and of its essence, and is expressed by him through some dogma only for the satisfaction of his faculty of reason. It is therefore just as little necessary for the saint to be a philosopher as for the philosopher to be a saint. . . ."

22. WWR, I, 395. Schopenhauer cites examples from Plato's *Phädo* and Shakespeare's *Henry VI*.

23. WWR, I, 389.

24. That Schopenhauer has to recognize the distinction between "subjective" and "objective" willing I have argued in *Schopenhauer: The Human Character*, pp. 182–192; that this recognition really has no place in his general scheme and that it allows an exception to the will-body identity thesis I have argued in the same book, pp. 208–209. Here I attempt a more sympathetic reading.

25. One could argue that the ascetic's denial of the will is motivated by egoism, since he or she withdraws from the world in order to escape from suffering and misery; see WWR, II, 638 (Ch. 49). Or one could argue that "the highest degree of asceticism," namely, "voluntarily chosen death by starvation," indicates madness—a notion that Schopenhauer entertains at WWR, I, 401 (§ 69).

26. Malter emphasizes that the turning of the will can be shown to be possible only by keeping firmly in mind the "identity" of the knowing with the willing subject; see *Der eine Gedanke*, p. 98.

27. Suicide, Schopenhauer claims, is not denial of the will; it is only the eradication of an appearance of the will, namely, the body. Actually, Schopenhauer holds, the suicide ceases to live rather than ceases to will; consequently, the taking of one's own life does not exemplify the denial of the will. Apparently, however, simply allowing one's body to die, through voluntary starvation, can amount to denial of the will; see WWR, I, 400–401.

28. WWR, I, 402.

29. See GB #201 (letter to Johann August Becker, 23 August 1844).

30. WWR, I, 402–403.

31. WWR, I, 403. Instead of "willed," Payne has "desired." The German reads: *es wird . . . keine Geschlechtsbefriedigung gewollt.*

32. See WWR, I, 402.

33. WWR, I, 403.

34. WWR, I, 403.

35. WWR, I, 403.

36. WWR, I, 403.

37. WWR, I, 404. In GB, Hübscher says that this sentence comes from Helvétius, not from Malebranche (see p. 681).

38. WWR, I, 404.

39. WWR, I, 404.

40. In his discussion of "eternal justice" (§ 63) Schopenhauer mentions an experience that may come to even the wickedest person: the experience of dread (*Grausen*). Until this individual's eyes are opened to the "better knowledge" (*bessere Erkenntniß*) that, as it were, all individuality is an illusion and, in reality, all is one,

the individual has only "the wholly obscure presentiment" that everything is not so alien to him. But: "From this presentiment arises that ineradicable *dread,* common to all human beings (and possibly even the more intelligent animals), which suddenly seizes them, when by any chance they become puzzled over the *principium individuationis,* in that the principle of sufficient reason in one or other of its forms seems to undergo an exception. For example, when it appears that some change has occurred without a cause, or a deceased person exists again; or when in any other way the past or the future is present, or the distant is near. The fearful terror at anything of this kind is based on the fact that they suddenly become puzzled over the forms of knowledge of appearances which alone hold their own individuality separate from the rest of the world. This separation, however, lies only in appearance and not in the thing in itself; and precisely on this rests eternal justice" (WWR, I, 353). I offer an account of eternal justice in *Schopenhauer: The Human Character,* pp. 192–201. Schopenhauer's discussion of dread is well developed by Mark Cyzyk, in his paper, "Conscience, Sympathy, and Love: Ethical Strategies Toward Confirmation of Metaphysical Assertions in Schopenhauer," pp. 24–31.

41. WWR, I, 408. Instead of "thought" for *Gedanke,* Payne has "idea." On the previous page, Payne has "from our principal idea" for *aus unserm Hauptgedanken,* which should be "from our principal thought."

42. WWR, I, 409.

43. WWR, I, 409. See also HN, I, par. 66 (written in 1813).

44. WWR, I, 409–410. Note that the world and the individual self vanish simultaneously.

45. WWR, I, 410.

46. WWR, I, 410.

47. WWR, I, 410.

48. WWR, I, 411.

49. GB, #280 (to Julius Frauenstädt, 21 August 1852). The two previous letters, GB, #279 (to Julius Frauenstädt, 6 August 1852) and GB, #278 (to Adam von Doß, 22 July 1852), take up the same issue. See also GB, #202 (to Johann August Becker, 21 September 1844); and WWR, II, 641 (Ch. 50).

50. GB, #503 (to Michael Sikic and Camillo Schramek, 1 September 1860). I quote from the version of the letter given by Hübscher, GB, pp. 640–641.

51. WWR, I, 410.

52. WWR, I, 411.

53. WWR, I, 411.

54. WWR, I, 411–412.

55. WWR, I, 391 (§ 68). See HN, I, par. 220, where Schopenhauer (in 1814) writes that "as long as the body lives, a total absence of willing is impossible. . . ." Also relevant, though dealing specifically with "pure contemplation," is the remark that "an absolutely objective and thus perfectly pure intellect is just as impossible as is an absolutely pure tone . . ." (PP, II, 65).

56. See WWR, I, 395, where Schopenhauer cites as an example Benvenuto Cellini.

57. See WWR, I, 390, where Schopenhauer says of resignation that "it frees its owner from all care and anxiety forever."

58. Gardiner speculates that Schopenhauer recognizes two concepts of mysti-

cism: "On one of these, mystical awareness, [it] involves simply a true insight into the inner nature of the phenomenal world considered as a whole, and into our own natures regarded as elements of and participants in that world. . . . On the other, while mystical awareness presupposes and springs from insight of the sort just described, it is itself to be understood as comprehending some 'deeper' apprehension, about which, however, nothing can be significantly thought or said . . ." (*Schopenhauer*, p. 299).

59. Young, *Willing and Unwilling*, p. 34.

60. Ibid., pp. 34-35. As noted above, Schopenhauer sometimes does regard suffering as "*absolutely* inescapable and salvation impossible"; see WWR, I, 391.

61. Ibid., p. 35; see also pp. 131-132.

CONCLUSION

1. WWR, I, 4 (§ 1); see also HN, I, par. 599 (1816).

2. WWR, I, 278 note (§ 54); see also HN, I, par. 570 (1816).

3. In HN, I, par. 158 Schopenhauer speaks of the "kind of world we have willed"; in HN, I, par. 222 he writes that "No law of nature rules over us, and we are nothing but what we have made ourselves into; an external power is as little able to save us as to annihilate us"; and in HN, I, par. 245 he says that "this intuitable world" is "only the mirror in which we ought to see what we are. . . ." All of these notes come from 1814.

4. WWR, I, 360 (§ 65). That good and bad are relative to the individual will is also emphasized in BM, 204.

5. WWR, I, 374 (§ 66).

6. Seldom does Schopenhauer suggest that *Mitfreude* is a genuine ethical trait; usually he reserves for this ascription nothing but *Mitleid*.

7. It may be that Schopenhauer's pronouncements about the world, life, and existence reflect his own egoistic will, or it may be, in his view, that in some non-subjective sense the world simply is bad. I suspect that Schopenhauer uses two criteria of good and bad—one subjective and relative, and the other objective and universal. Probably he holds that within the general context of an objectively determined bad world human beings largely determine, through their individual wills, whether the world is tolerable or not. It is the latter, not the former, determination that one's will makes. (Much more could be explored on these matters, but this is not the place.)

8. WWR, I, 275 (§ 54).

9. WWR, I, 275.

10. WWR, I, 276.

11. WWR, I, 277; see also 282.

12. WWR, I, 280.

13. WWR, I, 276, 281. In "Reference to Ethics," the final chapter of WN, Schopenhauer quotes Aristotle (*On the Heavens*, I.12) to the effect that whatever originates also perishes (141).

14. The following discussion is limited to volume 1 of WWR. Much more about death, fear of death, and so on occurs in volume 2 of WWR (see especially Ch. 41, "On Death and Its Relation to the Indestructibility of Our Inner Nature") and in

volume 2 of *Parerga and Paralipomena* (see especially Ch. 10, "On the Doctrine of the Indestructibility of our True Nature by Death"). In one late passage (PP, II, 274) Schopenhauer even suggests that death, as normally understood, precludes knowledge (with its subject and object division) but not necessarily consciousness!

15. WWR, I, 283–284 (§ 54); see also HN, I, par. 608 (written in 1816).

16. WWR, I, 284–285. The end of the first sentence here probably means "to become clear and distinct as to what they are."

17. WWR, I, 285.

18. See WWR, I, 278–281.

19. WWR, I, 285.

20. WWR, I, 281.

21. See PP, II, 276: ". . . all beings living at this moment contain the real kernel of all that will live in the future; and so to a certain extent these future beings already exist."

22. PP, I, 252.

23. PP, I, 264.

24. PP, I, 265.

25. PP, I, 301; see also WN (the chapter on "Animal Magnetism and Magic"). Concern with psychic phenomena occupied Schopenhauer from early in his life, from at least 1815 (see HN, I, par. 487 & 502) to the end of his life (see numerous late letters).

26. It is also captured in the judgment that "If an all-powerful being had to create this world or none, it ought to have created none." Consider the chapter called "Rebellion" in Dostoevsky's *The Brothers Karamazov*.

27. This final claim, along with an account of Schopenhauer's "philosophical pessimism," figures prominently in my *Schopenhauer: The Human Character*, Part 3.

28. Malter deals with many of the issues I have discussed, though (often) in much greater detail and (always) in a style very different from my own. His work takes into account a vast scope of recent literature on Schopenhauer, which is conveniently cited in his *Literaturverzeichnis*, a bibliography covering 20 pages in small print. Guenter Zoeller, in a session of the North American Division of the Schopenhauer Society (conference held in Chicago, April 1993), provided a fine critical summary of Malter's two books on Schopenhauer, called "Schopenhauer and the Problem of Metaphysics: Critical Reflections on Rudolf Malter's Interpretation."

29. For an evaluation of Schopenhauer's critique of Kant's ethics—which critique, incidentally, consists of several objections recently urged against Kant—see my *Schopenhauer: The Human Character*, Part 2, "Ethics and Virtue."

30. Husserl's accounts of perception (*Wahrnehmung*) and of "ideation" (this latter is the forerunner of the later *Wesensschau*), as presented in *Logical Investigations* (1900–1901), bear strong similarities to Schopenhauer's accounts of perception (*Anschauung*) and of aesthetic contemplation. And Sartre employs many ideas found in Schopenhauer, not the least of which is his characterization of free will as "existence precedes essence," which is virtually identical with the phrase Schopenhauer uses in FW, 59–60, "an existence without an essence," to designate the same notion.

31. Schopenhauer's moral saint resembles Buddhism's Bodhisattva, and his ascetic or, better, mystic resembles Buddhism's Tathagata.

INDEX

Designer:	U.C. Press Staff
Compositor:	Prestige Typography
Text:	10/12 Baskerville
Display:	Baskerville
Printer:	Braun-Brumfield, Inc.
Binder:	Braun-Brumfield, Inc.